THE PLACE OF MINDS
IN THE WORLD

MACMILLAN AND CO., Limited
LONDON · BOMBAY · CALCUTTA · MADRAS
MELBOURNE

THE MACMILLAN COMPANY
NEW YORK · BOSTON · CHICAGO
DALLAS · ATLANTA · SAN FRANCISCO

THE MACMILLAN COMPANY
OF CANADA, LIMITED
TORONTO

THE PLACE OF MINDS
IN THE WORLD

GIFFORD LECTURES AT THE
UNIVERSITY OF ABERDEEN
1924–1926

FIRST SERIES

BY

SIR WILLIAM MITCHELL
K.C.M.G.; VICE-CHANCELLOR OF THE UNIVERSITY OF ADELAIDE

MACMILLAN AND CO., LIMITED
ST. MARTIN'S STREET, LONDON
1933

COPYRIGHT

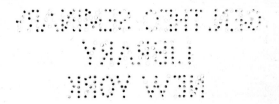

PRINTED IN GREAT BRITAIN
BY R. & R. CLARK, LIMITED, EDINBURGH

TO

JOANNA   HAWKER

PREFACE

DURING the war the question of the power of minds was prominent as well from their degrees of devotion to the cause, as from the drastic mental effects. The power of the cause, the strength of mind, and the stability of brain took so separate a prominence that they looked independent. When peace removed the cause, and required humbler causes to take its place and its power, their connexion was again a question, and the loss of prominence did not help. The three are as easy to distinguish as the qualities of a thing, but with the same disadvantage that the analysis looks thorough enough to ask how they are connected. Feeling and brain-change are so easily parted that the line between them looks the one across which work must be done in knowing and doing, or beneath which the real agent is working out of reach. No work is done there either across or beneath, but across and beneath the line between feeling and object. This is the living line, and so natural that we draw it in every thought, without thinking, as we draw our breath. The other pair, as easy to separate as mind and brain, and as hard to connect, are the real power of the object or cause, and its felt power.

The three factors in definite connexion constitute the mental causal system. It provides a programme for the problem of the power of minds, and it is none the less capable that it is general, holding for the meanest kind of mind as for the best.

Not only has mind a general causal system, as nature has, the discovery of mind follows the same route as the discovery of nature. The sensible world is the surface of nature; it consists of phenomena, and therefore answers all its own questions. The deep questions that seek a better grasp accept the surface, and their answers have to be verified by it. There is the same route for mind; the course of feeling, consciousness of every kind, is the mental surface; it is called the subject, being organised with reference to objects. Its first concern is always with the real character of the objects. That is also the concern which accounts for the coming of minds, and for their place in the world. The advance from physical to mental life advances nature from a world of stimuli as causes, to a world of objects as causes. Whether this world is nature proper is a question that soon includes the other worlds as well, in which we live and place ourselves. Nothing answers it but the objects themselves in their worlds. To make anything object is to make it declare itself. Whether the real world agrees to do that, and how far, is the first of the three problems to the mental surface. They begin by challenging the surface. The first one is that the feat is impossible, that the surface is really polarising itself, and that the object, as well as the subject, is therefore mental.

The other two problems challenge the surface knowledge of himself by the subject. One is that he gathers himself into a collection of qualities and faculties; the other is that the collection includes no knowledge of the brain. The two are like the under-surface questions to the sensible world. The mental surface, like the physical one, is kept from error by its ignorance, and prescribes the two under-surface tasks. There are just the two. One is to analyse the subject-structures and their course, in order to make them intelligible; the other is the endless empirical task of psychophysical correlation, which makes them calculable.

But they are subordinate to the first problem, because the structures and courses of consciousness, which they make intelligible and calculable, are organised; their power is all to know, appreciate, and make real. The objects to be known, appreciated, realised, are therefore the fundamental cause, to which the other two are means; it is none the less efficient cause for being final. The answer to the first problem answers for the place of minds, as the other two answer for their power.

The general mental causal system departs from that in common use, which, made general, is: There is the world, and here are our means of knowing and working in it. That simple way comes on troubles, which open it out; the general system generalises it. For the world is only offered; it has to be found, and from the whole in hand. From this the rest has to discover itself; and our means discover themselves with it. Lord Gifford, in his will, advises that even "the greatest of all possible sciences, indeed in one sense the only science, that of Infinite Being", be treated as "a strictly natural science, just as astronomy or chemistry is". It looks an error, as well as hopeless, but first on the same ground that puts real nature out of reach. The contrary way is that of isms. Instead of proceeding from the whole in hand, they separate the means, and forecast from them. That is why, while every ism has an opposite, neither forecasts any knowledge that can decide between them. Most of them hope that time will tell, but the hope grows less as the separation of the means increases, till there is none when the separation is thought to be complete, and our constitution on the one hand faces the world on the other. It is then that we complain of knowing only phenomena, and of using only conceptions.

The complaint grew precise, and then active, during the last third of last century, the main epoch of isms. They were still persistent, if rather exhausted, at the end, when James Ward gave his lectures at Aberdeen on *Naturalism and Agnosticism*. The complaint against the fundamental conceptions had grown so precise that physics, including astronomy and chemistry, was held to rest on a list of contradictions; it had merely taken the best ground available 'under the conditions of consciousness'. The thing looked so certain that it gave a world-view which was generally accepted. Though the real world, which wrought the known ones, could never be known, it gave them common laws, which could be found. The behaviour of their elements, at first chaotic, led to rhythms and harmonies, which led to structures. The elementary chaos was in nature, and had come to law in the kinetic theory of gases. Structures had evolved from lifeless to living, thence to minds and societies, all exhibiting the same laws, and results, in their internal and external interactions. Ward's lectures were directed against that way of seeing the world, the 'synthetic philosophy' of Spencer; the gas theory was too abstract as a model; against atomism itself there was the current doctrine of energetic; and the analogies among the worlds were too superficial to count. But then the lectures went on to say that physics must leave an opening for the work of minds, that the statistical character of the kinetic theory left room, and that the laws of motion, say the law of inertia, should be left liable to exception. The proposal was as unreasonable as the call was reasonable. One more contradiction went on the list against our plight from knowing only phenomena.

Twenty years later the situation was altered so entirely that Weyl could say, near the end of his book *Space-Time-Matter*: "Whoever looks back over the ground that has been traversed . . . must be over-whelmed by a feeling of freedom won: mind has cast off the fetters which have held it captive. He must be inspired by the conviction that reason is not only a human, a too human, makeshift in the struggle for existence, but that, in spite of all disappointments and errors, it is yet able to follow the intelligence which has planned the world, and that the consciousness of each one of us is the centre at which the one light and life of truth discovers itself in and from phenomena." The unexpected advance was all from the whole in hand; no reflection on the place of minds, and the unlikely character of their means, did anything to hinder or to help; there was nothing but the impossible feat by which every mind prevails on things to declare them-selves, unaffected by being felt. The route made its own revolutions, and found relations that no one expected between the surface and the depths of nature, and between nature for each of us and universal nature. They make the physical route a model for the route in all the worlds. When, soon after the war, I was invited to give these lectures, I decided to devote those of the first year to it, as the way of life, putting mind out of account, as it puts itself, and using only the two obvious, if striking, advances of mental on physical life: its find-ing nature to be a world of objects, and its being free to follow them unhampered by its brain or other past. But it was a mistake to postpone the general argument, as I found from my old friends in Aberdeen, who said that it needed the second series to make the first one tolerable. And so I have recast the whole. The delay has had the advantage of letting the route go farther;

and the portion that has been pushed into the second book, while it leaves this one self-contained, will introduce the two factors which have to answer for the power of minds.

SUMMARY

INTRODUCTION

I. THE THREE PLACES

§ 1. Mental is like physical life in not being an organ, and in not having a site; but the advance takes it beyond the analogy, for knowing is living as well as means of living. When restricted by the analogy, the reading of the principle is too narrow, or too abstract, and creates the two surface gulfs. Page 3

§ 2. The narrow reading makes mind crown us in the cortex like a halo. It sets a distance between seeing light and the light, and is due to the oversight in asking how a thing becomes known, which is not removed by distinguishing between stimulus and object. To have to treat knowing as duplicating is always to have failed. 11

§ 3. The abstract reading avoids duplication by leaving the gulf empty; but every phenomenon is to, as well as of. The reading fails to distinguish the living line between seeing and light from the correlation line between seeing the light and its neural correlates. But also the gulf is maintained from the deep or third one, which is inferred from the history of nature. 14

§ 4. The three gulfs have the value of the best failures of analogy, when they define the demand for a deeper analysis. 18

§ 5. Of all the tricks by which life has made nature support it, none is stranger than the trick of being conscious, which unites here to there, and past and future to the present. In this new environment, where it is objects that stimulate, nature no longer compels reaction to forces, but responses to values, letting conscious creatures do as they like, and rewarding or punishing them. 21

§ 6. The exclusion of minds from nature is by minds themselves across the living line. Theories, and other intellectual organs for analysing and grasping, articulate with nature like eye with light, or hand with tool, though there is no motion at the joint, since they are abstract. 23

PART I.   THE GULFS

II. THE SURFACE GULFS

§ 1. The sensible world consists of phenomena, and answers all the questions that it raises. They ask either what is the law, or what becomes of; and it is these that are taken deeper, till the second is absorbed in the first. Page 29

III. THE THIRD GULF

V. OUR RELUCTANCE TO LEAVE THE GULFS

PART II. A MIND'S OWN PLACE

VI. ORIGIN OF THE OBJECT

VII. SERVICE OF MINDS TO NATURE

VIII. THE MENTAL SURFACE

without being felt. It distinguishes our completions of every object from the accretions that are added by notions.   Page 172

§ 2. The distinction identifies the working knowledge of a thing, and also the working knowledge of a self; as the physical surface, the sensible world, is final for correcting the working beliefs about a thing, so the course of consciousness is final for the working beliefs about a self. The errors in the completions are merely failures to analyse; the animating of a thing, and the encasing of a mind, are completions. The mental surface, like the physical one, develops itself to answer questions about mind when the questions are good, and to correct them when they are bad.   175

§ 3. But why should consciousness presume a unity or mind for itself that excludes nature and other worlds? It presumes nothing; the notion that it must is due to sources that cause the separating and uniting to look trivial, and be overlooked. The actual unity was the one fact that science left behind with philosophy, because knowing makes no difference, when it departed from the world in order to occupy the parts.   177

§ 4. A mind's working knowledge of itself has grown in its life-history, and is in every way like its working knowledge of a thing. If a mind could remember all the events of its history, they would no more be itself than a thing is accumulated history. Both teach us our ignorance of them; their unknown powers prove themselves by means of those that are known; they prove themselves necessary. To discover this necessity, in mind, as in nature, is to open out a system from its appearances or surface, and to prove all discovery by returning to find the surface more intelligible or systematic.
                                                                              179

§ 5. The reputation of the working description of oneself has been as notorious as the common-sense description of a thing. But, as there, the attack is wrong if it supposes that the surface facts are not final, and may be corrected from some depth or other. It does not matter that the facts can be beliefs like the sense of freedom, and persistent self-deception. But three grounds of objection are clear of the error: First, the polarising of experience into subject-experience and object-experience does not coincide with the division into mind and object, for the object-experience remains with the mind. Secondly, when a self is left with body and mind, is it not left as two? And, thirdly, the description of a self by faculties and their connexions merely classifies.   183

§ 6. The surface is too superficial to answer, but it holds the data for all three, and the criteria for the answers. It removes a confusion from the first one; for the separation of subject-experience and object-experience is by psychology, and later than the living one where the subject keeps all the experience. The objection then becomes the problem whether the objects that he deposits can be the very things that exist without him, to which all knowing makes no difference. The answer, which comes entirely from the object, answers the question of the place of minds.   186

§ 7. The three objections, the three problems that the mental surface raises on reflection, and cannot answer, are answered by the three factors that constitute the mental causal system. Because the felt object is the fundamental cause, the other two its means, and because its weight depends on the whole which it is felt to carry, the problem of its reality is fundamental for the working of minds, as well as for their place. The other two problems will occupy the second series of lectures. They concern the power of minds; that about brain looks for depth to the correlation line, that for subject looks for depth to the living one.   188

PART III. THE FIRST OF THE THREE PROBLEMS FROM THE MENTAL SURFACE

IX. FROM SURFACE TO DEPTH IN NATURE

§ 8. Against Avogadro's law all the charges against physical laws of human creation can be made, but it was by way of exceptions to it that it proved itself the cornucopia of physical chemistry. Allied with the exceptions to the laws of Gay-Lussac and Dulong and Petit, it produced a deeper cycle that brought the cohesive, chemical, and electrical bonds together.   Page 220

§ 9. The failures of the gas theory to account for the distribution of new energy open the question of the obligations on a theory to go beyond its performance. They test the groping power of its grasp. The final failures were well-defined enough to join the arrest of the far finer distribution of energy by the theory of radiation. The ragged figures for specific heats, which had appeared to echo the final chaos of nature, and our final arrest, became fundamental for completing the cycle by carrying it through the atom.   223

X. THE CYCLE THROUGH STRUCTURE

§ 1. The theory of radiation also approached, until it was able to measure, its essential element, the quantum of action, which it had not only ignored but never suspected. The quanta were as capable of statistical treatment, but, behaving as if entirely particle, and as if entirely wave, they brought a new contradiction, which, however, reversed the old horizon. Instead of the gloom of increasing chaos, final theory is now failing before facts that are well-defined.   Page 230

§ 2. The approaches to their definition; if minuteness measures the mental power to penetrate, and the willingness of nature, it can be judged, apart from spectroscope, in the three pairs of quantities in the Einstein equation, and the means of reaching the six.   233

§ 3. In the equation three kinds of energy are not equated merely, but united; the old errors about energy correct themselves; and energetic finds itself removing the fear from which it was born.   235

§ 4. The development of photo-electric and electro-photic collisions brought the properties of solids at last into the cycle, and threw all structures and their energies on those of the atom. The structure of the atom also yielded; its exploration was directed by five pointers from radioactive atoms; and the result was the general analysis of every structure in nature.   238

§ 5. Reflection on the same.   242

§ 6. The three radioactive products, besides pointing to their origins, were instruments for exploration, and extended the gas theory to include them.
                                                                                                      244

§ 7. The discovery of isotopes came from the fourth pointer by the use of apparatus for separating them, as theoretical as practical.   250

§ 8. The fifth pointer, the group-displacement law, made the periodic table intelligible, brought the periods into the individual atoms, and set the problem of valency.   253

§ 9. The difficulty in passing from structure to its maintenance, and its action, developed into an arrest, identical for our problem with that through corresponding states. Knowledge less fundamental all remained valid, and gained by becoming more intelligible. But the new predictions of final arrest were able to affect the question of minds. The fact that proton and electron cannot be imagined makes the arrest at structure the more instructive.   255

XI. TO THE FAILURE OF THE FINAL ANALOGY

§ 1. The data and criteria have now all to be cultivated, but they have easily kept theory in control by their wealth and precision.   Page 259

§ 2. The planetary atom was introduced for hydrogen by means of two impossible postulates. It met the demands of the known constants, and worked like magic in mapping the atom's interior to account for the facts. But it did not succeed in correcting, nor in accounting for, the postulates.
262

§ 3. Nor did Bohr's magic wand, the correspondence principle, which might have been expected to find an opening by pressing on the resistance to it. Its failure had first to remove two presumptions that had never been in doubt, and that had made classical mechanics appear to be final.   268

§ 4. The translations by the principle continued to create, and to satisfy, the demands of the planetary picture, till its ambition was clearly arrested. 269

§ 5. The transcribing could still be made, stopping at the energy-changes, instead of carrying them to positions of the planet. This gave, in place of a picture, a table of numbers in two dimensions for which an algebra was already in hand. Taking over the classical forms of mechanics, it developed from itself a statistical one, which did not depend on the motion of a particle, and offered a new origin for h in its fundamental equation.
274

§ 6. The removal of the other undoubted presumption, viz. that particle is more final than wave, resulted in the deepening of the classical theory to wave-mechanics. The two products of the failure of the classical analogy came, after being rivals, to a unity which marks the present end of the material development.

The course provides a series of challenges that are critical for the first problem from the mental surface; the royal road proves itself to be the way of life all the way in nature, where it had looked unlikely; and, since physical conditions are explored as directly by abstract experiment on the body of knowledge as by concrete experiment on the body of nature, theories are organs related to understanding as eyes to seeing, and related to nature as eyes to light.   275

XII. THE PRODUCTS OF THE FAILURE

§ 1. The quarrel whether light is particle or wave, which had been settled, but had broken out again for the photon, reached the atomic interior, and was involved in equating the two new expressions for energy, that for the photon and that for any moving particle. Wave-mechanics came from the idea that the motion of a material point may always be accompanied by the propagation of a wave, whose length depends on the momentum of the point. The idea was verified by picturesque experiment. Page 277

§ 2. The theory predicted the new waves from their individual roots, but it had also to predict the presence of waves of which there could be no phenomenon, their speed being greater than that of light. These unwelcome waves open four fears whether phenomena can keep theory in control. And the theory raised these two questions: If wave is to displace particle, of what stuff can its body be? And can we grasp it without particles to help? They all reflect on the connexion between our grasp and existence, and their question is purely physical. The four fears are whether the

XIII. RIGID AND FLEXIBLE

XIV. CLOSE OF THE MATERIAL DEVELOPMENT

and, in general, the direction of energy require a further explanation. Its discovery in probability, or statistical mechanics, appeared merely to be making the best of a mental failure.

§ 2. This error was due to a perfecting of nature that closed it too soon. The element of action is a couple, like space-time, and provides the same advantage. It came to light in the final sense barrier, which is converted into a rational boundary.

§ 3. The advantage has been obscured by two confusions, one from dipping our bodies a second time into nature, forgetting that they are there already, the other from the notion that to rest on probability, including the principle of uncertainty, is to give up the real pursuit.

§ 4. The rivalry between matrix and wave mechanics was removed by experiment which, though entirely formal, succeeded in reaching their common ground by the same route that opened the way from level to level. The formal equivalence of the two left alternative readings, of which the statistical one is permanent. It completes the greatest of the cycles, which, by returning, has completed the kinetic theory of gases with which we began.

§ 5. The surprises to reason along the route have been completed by a threefold surprise on turning back. The projections from surface to depth, which had to begin as analogies, prevailed by leading to analyses, till the properties thought worthiest of being final gave way. The converse surprise is that three surface characters, which looked unworthy of depth, find themselves fundamental on the very ground that expelled them. The first objection was to superficial causes on the ground that events are caused only once, and therefore only at depth. The second objection was to probabilities on the ground that they are our substitute for nature's necessities.

§ 6. The direct reversal for those two is to be found also for the flexibilities of nature. They are the most important for understanding our articulation with nature, but find us most unwilling. The principle of general relativity completes the reversal.

XV. TRANSITION

§ 1. The first of the mental surface problems challenges the feat of consciousness that its objects are the same unfelt as felt, and that their reality, and their distance in time and in space, put nothing between minds and them. Since the number of physical objects that can be felt is few, and all have to be found from the few that are wholly felt, the challenge is very great. The answer to it has to come from the objects themselves, and is the same from all worlds. Nature answers by proving itself intelligible in the way that it is sensible, containing the abstract organs that reason creates out of it, as it contains the organs of sense. From containing, it has gone on to prove that it is nothing besides the system of phenomena, its insuperable difficulties possessing nothing unintelligible. The restriction put on system by substance,—that nature should be the nature of a substance,—is not supported, but removed, by the self-evolution of nature. The opening of the atom has removed the hope that the atom is the source of ignorance, and its nucleus the source of novelty.

§ 2. May we not move the secret deeper, and pool all nature in the aether? But no energy going there becomes its intrinsic energy, and none comes out that was not given it by matter. Aether names not a stuff that fills space, for space has no existence without it, but the physical as distinguished from the geometrical properties of open space. The physical properties are the functions that the aether performs for matter in conveying the energies and changes of electromagnetic systems, and gravitation. The conveyance is governed by distance only.   Page 340

§ 3. The notion of the aether as a stuff calculates what matter would require to have and be, if it had to do the conveying, and then transfers this power and structure to the aether; but it also hopes that proton and electron will reduce to aether strains. The notion therefore conflicts with its hope; but recent models for the carriage of radiation show the strength of our appetite.   345

§ 4. Our sense-equipment is blamed on two grounds that are errors; and the aether, though it originates nothing, has been made the origin of everything. The two possible ways of deriving nature as we know it have been tried; they betray the strength of our appetite better still than the models do. The aether had to inherit the 'intellectual necessity' which made Tyndall endow matter with the 'promise and potency of all terrestrial life'. The necessity has been lost with the universal time-stream, and the protean matter with unchanging space. But Maxwell's 'intellectual satisfaction' with space-filling can remain for gravitation, radiation, and origin, on account of the two discoveries regarding mass. These, besides bringing substance finally into system, introduced the two steps to relativity. In both discoveries the contrast and correspondence of the material and the formal explanation open our closer articulation with nature, and require the new depths to take up the old weight: 349

§ 5. The discovery that mass consists of energy, and that all energy has mass, was found first from the electron without thought of space-time, through which it was then found to be universal. The result for the void is that radiation has all the properties that a thing has when out of sight, and so far takes up the origin of matter. The space-time discovery developed the classical theatre by changing the seats from fixed to moving; time no longer ran in three courses; and a universal frame for space was found to be everywhere. Real nature holds phenomena in the way that space-time holds space and time, which are its phenomena.   354

§ 6. The discovery that mass and weight have an identity deeper than their con-trast opened the way to the principle of general relativity, which has brought the theatre itself to new foundations. The thought-experiments had been made, and it had been seen that the 'entire universe' would come in; but real experiment looked impossible, because the old theatre kept our eyes in the wrong direction. It came in through the new foundations, and the cultures were successful.   361

§ 7. The new theatre, instead of discounting individual points of view, makes law depend on meeting them all, and rests on an intrinsic frame that includes them all.   367

§ 8. Conclusion.   370

INTRODUCTION
THE THREE PLACES

I

INTRODUCTION : THE THREE PLACES

§ 1. THE topic that I have taken for these two courses of lectures is the function of minds in the world. The present course will be occupied with their place, the next with their power. Their place has really to be inferred from their power; but their power is thought merely apparent on account of their place. Nature excludes minds; yet its best effort is to provide them with seats; and the seats are so secluded that we ask how the things that we know can be the very things that exist, and how our power to alter the course of nature can be other than its own.

If a situation so awkward were within nature, it would be welcome. There conflicts have always been the occasion, and usually the means, of reaching the fuller system which accounts for their appearing. We are to find the same advantage when we add minds. They have three places which at first fit ill with one another. Two of them are in nature. One place is the world about us, where we feel at home; the other is the cavity of the skull, where we should feel in prison.

The third is a mind's own place, which is to feel, or be subject. The other two exclude it, because they are in nature, and nature excludes all feeling. It is a place like the place of life, which is not an organ, nor placed in any, but includes them all, and is their unity. When feeling came, life entered on a new kind of unity; and, wherever we say there is feeling, we may say that life is mind or subject. But it is in making object, or know-ing, that the new kind of unity is best seen, and most easily when the objects are the sensible qualities and things out there. They are never in the brain. Con-scious living does not find them in that place, but in the place where it feels and proves them to be. Out there it is at home with them. If you say they must be where they are felt, not where they are felt to be, we have the useful kind of conflict. For seeing and hearing cannot be in one place, and colour and sound in another at a distance from theirs.

To solve the conflict we begin to populate our heads with sensations and other images. When they fail to work as feeling works, we can remove them for being either metaphors or accretions. The last metaphor will-ing to go is light, the light of consciousness; and the last accretion willing to go is the space occupied by the brain-process to which a feeling is due. All the physical conditions then become organs and means, just as for organic life. Conscious living, like unconscious life, proves itself; it does not have to defend itself against its means. But the conflict breaks out again. The means challenge the reality of the things that they let us know, use, and prize. The conflict forces us to a deeper unity with nature than organic life has, one that we never suspect in our everyday living.

Such deeper unity bears on Lord Gifford's problem of the unity of the world; but that lies beyond our topic, as does also the problem of an immortal life; we shall have only the future of minds on the earth. Our limit needs protecting, for those two are more attractive. It is protected best by the contrast between unity and simplicity. If we ask what is most immortal in nature, and yet not abstract, we look for what is simple, because, being without parts, it is incorruptible. No such thing is known, and, if it were, a mind refuses to be immortal in that way. And, if we ask what becomes of things when they change, and when they disappear, we seek a simpler and simpler material, finally an aether, that may exist in different forms, visible and invisible, and so be immortal. Again the thing is unknown, and a mind refuses to unite in that way with the world. Unity is the reverse of simplicity; there is none without synthesis; and it is greater the more it really unites, or determines. Unity feels simple, but, if we take it apart from what it unites, if we take by itself the unity of a mind, soul, or self, and its feeling of being always the same, we have not found an unquenchable spark, but made an abstraction. And, in order to be concrete, a mind needs not a substance to maintain it, but the matters which it unites and may command. It is like nature in that respect.

This protection would fail against the other problem, the unity of the world, if the connexions between minds and nature did not form a bridge, but kept the dark, and let only the two ends come in sight. Thinking there is no bridge we ask: Why not borrow light from the world as a whole, which must in any case unite the two ends? And is there not something to say about the whole, seeing reason must be satisfied? No, the light from the whole is borrowed light already; and the last thing that reason wants is to be left to itself. We can argue to what there is from what there must be; it is the way of every argument; but what there must be, or logic, is only a mill, grinding and sifting what is fed to it. If we see a gulf instead of a bridge, it is because we do not proceed from conscious living, where the ends are subject and object, seeing the light and the light, seeking the food and the food. The living bridge is no darker than the ends. The sciences of the physical end ask their facts to prove themselves, and then use nothing but the mill or must-be, which is logic, to make them intelligible. The sciences of the mental end are in the same position. Though their facts are of heart and will, as well as head, they can prove their profession, or fail; and the problem is to make them intelligible. When we take the ends together, as in conscious living, the connexions are now the facts that prove themselves; and the only problem is to make them intelligible. We shall have to ask what it is to be intelligible. If, instead of going across the living bridge, we go from end round to end by way of a universal substance, of which they are aspects, we contract both it and them; and the injustice is even greater if we go round by way of a universal mind.

That might have been my reason for speaking not of mind, but of minds, in the world, though the difference is no more than between life and lives. There would be good reason, too, if it prevented the lifeless metaphors from being too attractive: the stream, the field, and the light of consciousness. But my reason is that minds in living prove themselves, and that knowing is living, and not only a means of living. We may call the fact our principle. It is required of all conscious creatures, even the lowest.

The principle may seem too narrow or too abstract. Either defect would make it ineffective. Its reach comes out best by contrast, first with the narrow reading, and then with the abstract one.

In the same conscious life there is a development of one and the same view of nature. There are as many of these views as there are minds; and the question is never whether, but how, they combine into as many views of one and the same physical world. Though living bodies vary, though they live in air or water, and though every creature makes its body central, all their views, moving and resting, are taken whole, without allowance, and completed in the universal one. That is how nature unites them; as they prove themselves for each, so they are pooled. They are not merely united, as languages are, by having a common meaning; they mean one another directly, because they are parts of a universal one; they are natural languages. Suppose them all in one mind, if it helps you. Different as they are for different organisms, and for different grades of science in mankind, they have nothing artificial; nature keeps and accounts for all their differences.

Can it be so catholic, and all-suffering? There has always been fear of losing the self-existing and self-acting systems, with which alone science is concerned. Physics need not undertake a heavier burden than the immediate objects of sense; and it takes only sensation for its final criterion. Can either physics or nature be loaded with more: with the common-sense objects and worlds for different creatures, and with those that man finds at different grades of understanding? Let nature be responsible for sense-organs and their union in brains; that will not answer the question. Does nature actually adopt those weird worlds for its own?

The question leads to a plausible error. The bodies of all creatures have grown in directions which they cannot retrace, and which prevent their better development; why should minds have escaped that fate? Are they not, as they have grown, each an *idea corporis* to suit the need and habit of its body? Surely we are set in our groove; and however far-branching we force our grooves into nature, can we ever call them the very ways of nature?

For answer we have the nature of thought. Its function is to devote itself to objects, taking them as they prove themselves. If it is deceived, they are there to put it right. Nothing else has the right, not its means of knowing them for instance, whether it knows the means or not. Can it be that seeing and other thoughts are a trick to which the beasts remain bound, but man only till his eyes are opened? The ignorant, and all creatures, use their eyes like windows, knowing neither the stimulus nor the structures that the stimulus excites; when we know better, is there no correction? There is none; but we then become liable to notions, and easily to the notion that what is felt occurs in the brain. Then, since all that we know has been felt, it would follow that the brain is the place of the mind. The notion is the narrow reading of our principle. We should be spending our conscious lives in that recess, fed through nerve and blood to seeing, knowing, fearing, and desiring the things that should be there, and are not. The notion is common to those who think that mind and brain are connected there as aspects, and to those who think them connected there by a silver cord. Both read conscious living from its means.

The reading remains narrow when the physical means are supported by mental. If a mind is not in a brain, where is it? We want everything to be in space, or in something, such as consciousness, which may borrow the properties of space. We carry a load of such wants from our past; for there are appetites in knowing, as in liking and doing. They are oldest and strongest in perceiving or common sense. They show themselves, too, in understanding; we want everything to explain its behaviour by push and pull. And, modern though it is, reason also has its appetites; it must, we say, be satisfied. And what is more reasonable than to assume that, if things are known, they defer to the structure of our minds and their organs? On the contrary, thought is free enough to empty itself of all demands that are not made by the object.

We should like to take consciousness, or feeling, as a field, rather than to take it as it is; everything is so much distincter in space, and a field has boundaries that keeps its contents together. But not as feeling does; it is always living; it is the seeing and believing something or other, loving and hating, yielding and seeking, pointing and grasping. There are no physical acts like those, none that is not borrowed from them. To place them in space, to place any conscious living, is to place a writer's thoughts in his lines. His meaning is theirs, but is not there; and the words would not have been there but for their meaning. *Paradise Lost* remains on the shelf day and night; when read and brought to life it has nothing independent of its words; and it would not survive their loss. That connexion of thought and words is a case of the connexion of mind and brain. It is therefore better than any physical case of end and means, better even than life and organ. Being part and no parallel, nor analogy, it makes no claim to stand for the whole, but it is ample against the analogies.

Means and end have no quarrel with cause and effect, being themselves cause and effect. The difference is the factor of value, and value does nothing but through a mind. When we say that mind is first of all alive, there is no reading from the physical living on which it depends. Rather, since life and health are ends, the question is whether that lower and earlier living is not being read from the higher and later.

To read conscious from unconscious life is also to omit the very relation to objects that constitutes knowing. Such omission is the abstract reading of our principle:

The abstraction severs thought from its object, letting their mutual dependence escape. Objects have the better of the cut, because thought is devoted to them; it sets them out, and keeps out of them, that they may reveal their very nature. The cut makes knowing suffer more the more it needs no effort, and we just look about. That error comes only on reflection; it never occurs in the seeing, hearing, and thinking themselves.

The correction is easy; and, again because the error is plausible, the reaction against it has to go farther. Thought stoops to conquer, and conquers most when its object 'fills the mind', and the mind forgets itself. To make object, to be obsessed or possessed by objects, is a thing so natural to man that we forget how singular it is, and unnatural. Of all the tricks which life took to make itself at home none could have been foreseen so little as this one. None compares with it in increase and independence, though it came so late, and not clearly before the cerebral cortex. Instead of being tied there, and complaining that it can know 'only phenomena', thought has found that nature contains nothing but the system of phenomena; and it extends the system to the ages before there were any phenomena.

The way from the surface of nature to its depths was pioneered by analogy and artifice. These disappeared as the deep levels became able to develop themselves for us. Though the entrance is from the surface, from phenomena, the depths offer no likeness to the surface; nor, though they control the surface, do the depths require the surface to be like them. We can transfer all that to the subject and his behaviour, for he feels and verifies his own behaviour as he does the behaviour of things.

When he goes deeper into his mind than he feels, it is as when he goes deeper into sensible phenomena than he feels them. The explanation of minds to make them intelligible is precisely as the explanation of nature.

§ 2. But the narrow and the abstract readings have to choose other ways of following nature than the living one. They come on the disconcerting gulfs, and that is their value.

The gulf of the narrow reading is the distance between a thought and its object; the gulf of the abstract reading is the absence of relations between mental and physical. Both should prevent our knowing nature, yet neither has ever done it, and for a simple reason. We ask what the means are by which a thing out there is known. If the answer were complete, no question would be left; neurology would satisfy and be satisfied. But the narrow reading puts quite another question. It asks how in the world a thing outside my head can come and be known inside. Our principle never meets a question like that, because, in living and learning, we begin with knowing, and make objects prove all their claims, including their place, and their kind of existence. When we go farther than animals do, we continue on their course; when we ask about the means of knowing, nothing is undone. Because that is the beginning, and the course, in practice and in science, the gulfs are never met on the way. They and their questions come from beginning after the cut, with the thing out there, for instance, not yet known.

And what, you say, can be wrong with that? Are things not already there waiting to be seen, or at least understood? And was not nature in the world long before minds? Yes, but nature is not responsible for the gulfs till we place our minds in our heads. It is only then that we ask how in the world things out there can enter, and be known as they are. The question prescribes the answer, and, for answer, a likeness. It requires the shape that I see out there, or that I handle, to be in duplicate, even in triplicate: as a sensation, as the immediate or cortical correlate of the sensation, and as the external quality, the shape itself. The middle one has to be dropped as a copy; for it should be like the sensation and like the quality, and it is like neither. But what follows when this middle shape is dropped from the cortex? Can the felt shape remain there? The instance is crucial; in other instances, when a feeling feels no shape, it can perhaps assume a brain shape without being found out.

Rather than give up the site, though there is never a likeness between its filling and what is felt, we add a new 'dimension' to the place. Or, with less care, feeling is made a flicker here and there in the brain; it was called a phosphorescence, when that was yet the gateway to a mystery, long after 'no phosphorus, no thought'. And, with all the care in the world against confusing feeling and any filling, till there is nothing but correlation without likeness, we try to keep the feeling to the site. Must not the two correlates occupy the same space at the same time? The brain space is never felt; but must not the feeling lie or hover there? And the time is always felt; must it not be the very time of the brain change?

In that way the light of consciousness could be enclosed in the skull, and called "a glow pervading the brain". Mind would crown us in the cortex like a halo. One might call it the firefly view, if anyone did keep it, when he saw it. And how can it be evaded if we carry our minds in our bodies? We come nearer the fact, if we carry them there as life is carried.

But we have to carry conscious life farther; it goes outside the body. Its light is a searchlight; it reaches things where they are. And it does not move to them; there is no distance between a thought and its object. The distance which puzzles the firefly view is nowhere but in the physical means, part therefore of the total object, and no gulf. There is no distance between my seeing the sun and the sun, any more than if I saw it in a dream. From which the firefly view takes courage again, and refuses the tempting way of a searchlight. It says that I never see the real sun, but a duplicate in my cortex and its glow.

To treat knowing as duplicating is always to fail. The particular error will appear when we ask what a thought needs in order to be true, and its object in order to be real. These questions are within our principle; and our present concern is that all the valid questions come within it; for, if they were answered, there would be no more to ask; no one would ask any more. The questions that come from the narrow reading and its gulf are not among them.

Our appetite for a place in which to put feeling is quite regular; for our first grasp of every new object is by analogy. But the real value of analogy is to abolish itself by bringing out the characters in the new that defy it. The light of consciousness, from being at first a glow through a small volume of cortex, becomes a searchlight, which, unfortunately, has to act at a distance. Then it has to be living, which no light is; and searching, which nature never does. If, therefore, we miss the real value of analogy, the course appears to be going from bad to worse. That is why we are glad of the dream-sun, and return to the glow which is pure physical. In it, and made by it, ideas could be images, and emotion an ebullition. The ancient interpretation

of dreams had the same idea, but in reverse; a mind
was then the image, which left its body, and went
abroad.

§ 3. The abstract reading is better than the narrow
one, because it evades duplication; its varieties are its
ways of escaping. It creates a gulf by severing the connexion between thought and object, but it leaves no
space nor time in the gulf, nor anything else that we
know. The gulf is now like that between the qualities
of a thing, or between a curve and its formula; it is the
absence of relations between two systems that may
vary with one another, and be correlated, but that exclude each the other, and show nothing between. Every
phenomenon, every sensible appearance, is in two
systems; it is to a subject and of an object. If 'to' be
read as 'of' we have this gulf. Phenomena would then
have two aspects, through one of which they are part
of a mind, and, through the other, part of nature. The
gulf holds the union of the two aspects, but, keeping
the secret, is 'impassable'.

It is really bridged by the relation 'to'. As there is
no concrete gulf with distance and time in it, so neither
is there this one between my thought and my hand,
when I see it, and between my will and my hand, when
I move it. Conscious living does not meet the abstract
gulf, because it does not come on the question that
creates it. The erring question is: Here are all the means
that produce a sensation, what is there in them that
becomes the sensation? Or: Here is nature before there
were phenomena, out of what did they come? And:
Here is my will to move my hand, at what point, and
how, do I interfere? This question, for they are one
question, thinks that it is asking about the relation of
mind and nature below the surface. It rests on the

correlation line between them. But the living line, the relation 'to', puts its own question beneath the surface, and the answer uses the correlation line without finding it mysterious, far less a gulf. Its own question is no doubt repellent: What is the deeper service of minds to nature than the one which they give and feel on the surface? We much prefer the other question, and its parts. The reasons for our preference are in us all, and it is useful to gather them. Our trust in them, our belief in the gulf, has two causes in the history of knowledge; it has also a reason in the history of the world; and it persists on physical principles:

One cause is the very virtue of thought in retiring when it makes object. It has succeeded so well in making nature display and speak for herself that it and mind seem names for nature's discards. Mind has been assigned all the rubbish; there is nothing unreal that has not been thought mental. Nature takes all that moves, and all that motion requires; nothing mental moves, it only changes; mind is left with all that can go nowhere, having nowhere else to go. Dreams lie there, our waking errors, and all the casual oddments. But much more: the very ways to truth, with all approximations, and why not truth itself, since ideas alone are true, not things and facts? The adventures that occur in books are there, their scenes and their storms, whether once they were real, or the writer is romancing. And we have to go farther, if we are serious that what is not physical is mental; we should fill mind with a stuff, the kind that dreams are made of, and the better kind, a mental aether with forms for all feelings when it lights up. If we take that way to our minds, and our mental furniture, we are ghosts of the things that banish us. That is a natural source of the gulf: knowing first what is physical, we take the rest for mental. Where to draw the line was always a question, and its answer as uncertain as the words mind and nature. Physics moved the line as it advanced, finding more and more to be mental, till everything had the two aspects, with nothing knowable between, but only the gulf.

The other natural source of the gulf begins also with what nature excludes. It excludes all feelings, but has correlates for them all in the brain, which now, instead of the world, becomes the thing with the two aspects. Psychology and neurology keep an eye on the parallel course, and, the clearer the correlation line keeps them apart, the better the course is understood. This line is now the gulf. But is it a gulf, if both sciences cross it every time that they correlate?

It becomes a gulf only when we stand by, and watch for some movement across it. For there is none, and we think there ought to be, if a thing existing on one side is made known on the other, and an appetite on one side makes a stir on the other. It is the line of correlation, and we mistake it for the line of conscious living. Not in practice; we never correlate a sensation, or other thought, with the object that it knows, nor a desire with the object that it desires; we correlate the thought or desire of this object or that with the physical conditions. These include the stimulus outside our bodies, and the states inside that it excites. But the object is never the stimulus nor the brain state.

It seems too gross a mistake to have made so much trouble; but it came by analogy, which is the natural course of knowledge. When man passed from asking about things to asking about thoughts, it seemed that truth must be a likeness between thought and thing. That error, like the mixing of object and stimulus, rests on the confusing of the two lines. Their confusion is nothing but failure to analyse, and is therefore the cause of the gulf, rather than a ground on which we rest it.

But the other two sources of the abstract gulf are grounds; we adopt them. One is in the history of the world. Minds and nature, the nature that physics knows, began with each other when phenomena came into the world. Should we not ground them on whatever substance or force begat them, and presumably still supports them? That is the ground of the third and final gulf. The abstract one, however, can ignore it, and proceed merely from the common birth of minds and nature in phenomena. At the start, if they were twins, they were surely identical; why not start with their birth, if mind is life, not with a late superstructure like subject and object, and its living line? For is the line not late, perhaps as late as vertebrates? No, it goes all the way down. Also the earth was here before phenomena were born. But, surely, looking back, do not the two lines converge, the living and the correlation one? Should we not begin where they are identical, and then see them diverge? No, however near we reach the simplest organic sensation, we are never nearer a likeness between the feeling and its physical correlates. Nothing neural will ever tell why it gives any feeling, let alone tell the kind.

The other ground of the gulf consists in the physical principles that appear to conflict with minds as lives. Does not nature decline all intervention, and require brain to do all that we do, or all but feel? The correlation line would establish the gulf by being the more fundamental, and able to criticise the living line. It would also have to criticise itself, because our intervening proves itself precisely as our knowing does. Each depends always on a vast number of nerve

c

elements of which it needs to know nothing. They have to prove themselves means.

How in the world the means of seeing can produce light and seeing, we no longer ask; the means remain means, and no longer prescribe. But we let our means of intervening prescribe, though their right is just the same. We presume that will, or emotion, or ideas, must impinge on brain somehow, if they alter the course of nature. Men who argue that they can, and men who argue that they cannot, make that their common ground. Our principle of conscious living says, on the contrary, that the means cannot prescribe. For doing, as for knowing, no depth of nature can conflict with the surface, where all is felt, and where all that is believed and done is able to prove or disprove itself. No discovery beneath the surface proves or disproves the physical existence of anything found on it. Physics confines itself to making the surface intelligible. The result has been to transform all views of nature copied from the surface, but still to question nothing there, nor prove it, for the surface proves itself.

§ 4. Nature insists on creatures learning very different worlds; but it is one and the same world that slays them when they fail. How it slays them they do not know, but it contains the one that they in particular should have known. Yet they are all so different. Think of the difference in the sense organs on which different species depend, the different instincts, the different outlook for birds, fish, and creeping things. The data are so various, and must combine in such variety. Are all those objects of sense part of nature, all of them severally and combined?

We do not like the idea, for we have two grounds against the variety, even in our own felt world. One ground soon gives way. The same thing has many visible appearances; we select some, call them real, and read the rest into them. But it is merely because they are most convenient. And we read them all into the tangible appearance, and call it the real one, because it is usually the one with which we have business. Still there is no more than convenience. If you doubt, you have only to ask, What is the real length of the standard yard? And so we give up this ground for thinking that some appearances are part of nature and some are not. But the other ground has just come in sight: Must not nature use one real length? What though other lengths make themselves good, each from a proper point of view at rest or in motion, can they singly come to nature's one and the only one? We thought not: the one real length was part of nature, and the phenomena were not. But we were mistaken. The one real length does not exist. With its departure the notion to which it belonged has gone too. The phenomena, each and all, are relative to observers, but, far from veiling real nature, this is the relativity that has opened up the absolute system of nature.

The discovery is of nature's foundations, but of them only. They do not of themselves take up the variety to man, let alone the variegated load from all kinds of conscious creature. To impose all that on the foundations we have to rely on the bare if remarkable fact that one and the same nature rewards and punishes us all.

But the fact has had a second reading that again we like better. Instead of letting phenomena be real parts of nature, why not read them as products, peculiar in being felt, and therefore feelings? They began as the vague, uneasy sensations of tiny organisms; they developed with a developing physical reaction to organic and external stimuli; when, at last, the mental life of the higher animals arrived, was it not spent in their heads, which contain all that they feel? By some happy chance they feel nothing to be there; a pain in the foot is felt to be in the foot, the best place for it; but is it not really in the head? The shapes, the sounds, the heat that we feel to be out there, and to grow greater as we approach, are they not really in sensations, and sensations in heads? Each is felt after a long chain of events, the last of which discharges a trifle of the energy stored in the brain; what is a sensation but the flash of the final explosion? And, when the past lives again, is it not there, old sensations glowing once more, or new ones glowing like them, and knowing it? We speak of the light of consciousness, and place it in the head.

No place could well be darker, but the happy accident persists: nothing feels itself to be there, but elsewhere or nowhere. It is the grass that looks green, as it is the foot that feels sore. Yet there is no green but to eyes that see it, and where is seeing but in heads? Is it not the glow in the head that is green? That is nonsense, you say; the light is a searchlight, and goes outside the head. So it did in ancient times, as I said, when men could believe that in dreams they left their heads and roamed abroad, and when they could account for seeing by light streaming from the eye to meet the other coming through the void. But consciousness will not stream outside.

For that matter to call it a light, whether glow or searchlight, is all metaphor, and the more misleading that it works better than any other, and we take it for literal. Sound and odour have the same sort of right, and so it is easy to be quit of all metaphor, because no one will accept the sound of consciousness nor its odour, nor even its flavour.

There seemed nothing for it but to charge the world of common sense with a useful error in always placing phenomena elsewhere than in heads, where they ought to be born. For a long time that was done by sober men like Locke, whose discussion made the inference familiar. He deprived things of all properties, except mechanical ones. These gave things power to act on our organs and receive back the product as all their other qualities. A bolder Englishman (Hobbes) was more ruthless: "Whatever qualities our senses make us think there are in the world, they be not there, but are seeming and apparitions only; the things that really are in the world without us are those motions by which these seemings are caused". The view grew popular, and the sciences were thought to support it. Was there not first nature unadorned, which became producer of life, then of sensitive animal surfaces, behind which phenomena came, which later found an organ to project them as landscape, and the other apparitions? But the sciences refuse the picture. Physics and geology know nature as it was before there were phenomena; they know it as part of the system of phenomena, and they need invent no observer, nor other 'as if'. Also physiology knows of nothing that becomes a feeling. In place, therefore, of nature as producer, there came a producer, or source, at once of nature and minds. Phenomena were no longer hybrid, and the doubling looked a merit; must not reason in nature and reason in mind coincide? The mystery could be piled on a common source, in a world beyond all knowing, across the third and final gulf. That refuge began to dissolve with the discovery that space and time are not independent of each other. Like the one perfect length of a yard the whole world to which it belonged is unknowable, because it does not exist.

§ 5. When we turn to a mind's own place in the

world we shall have to ask how and how far it can penetrate nature. The answer will gather the facts that define the place. But first we shall remain with the gulfs in order to gather the situation from their closing. And, as in these matters we presume so much without intending, I shall mention, to prevent confusion, two unexpected characters that are to establish themselves throughout, though they can only be convincing in the end. We come to the first if I continue what I have been saying about the plight of our minds in being devoted and rejected:

We distinguish grades of mind into high and low, and into mature and immature, according to the kinds of object to which they are devoted. And growing things are known from what they grow to. That was first said of nature as a thing itself; and there we begin the answer to our grudge; for the things in nature that induce us do not exist but for minds. They are not in heads; they constitute the common-sense world; and the depths of nature are nothing but their completing. Think of the physical objects that prevail with a farmer, a physicist, or the rest of us; they are not the small parts that we happen to be feeling; far their greater part need only be meant, and the meaning unfelt, being mainly taken for granted. The power of the object lies in its value. Felt or meant, particular or general, that makes it a new kind of cause in nature. Physical though it is, power and part of nature, nature can do nothing with it but through minds.

The way for this new kind of cause was prepared in the environment by which living bodies carry on their unconscious life. But only prepared; for it is only to our reading that their environment consists of objects. To the living bodies, plant or animal, it consists of nothing but the stimuli that they take, and either use or·resist; sense-organs themselves are in that position; they never have their objects for their stimuli. In the history of life on the earth an ever greater complexity of the organism makes more and more of the world into a fit environment; and individual bodies are able to modify themselves a little to make it more fit; but the world of stimuli to which they react remains much the same.

The conscious world, on the contrary, grows with the mind, racial and individual. Of the curious tricks to make nature maintain life, none, to repeat, has been so strange as the trick of being conscious, which unites here to there, and past and future to the present. In this environment, where it is objects that stimulate, nature no longer compels reaction to its forces, but response to its values, letting conscious creatures do as they like.

It was therefore with the greater grudge that we learnt from physics and physiology that the trick had never imposed on nature. Both had found a fact from which they concluded that nature lets feeling flatter itself in ignorance, letting so much else live and flourish before restoring it to the dust. Such origin had always been argued: what could there be in nature but new shapes of old material? There was also the ugly picture of ideas or wills impinging on nerve-cells. And now there was the conservation of energy. It forbade not only feelings to be active, but memories, and even sensations, to take anything out of nature for themselves. It let them be neither causes nor effects of anything physical; they were by the way. That was the return we got for our devotion.

But, in protesting against the humiliation, we overlooked the two advantages that it offered at the same time.

§ 6. One lies in its leaving empty the connexion

between mind and brain. They may be correlated, and completely, a specific brain-change for every feeling, and a specific structure for every mental power. But, before correlation and after, each must find its own relations, its internal relations, and keep them; each has its own system; neither may copy from the other. There are similar purely physical situations: the geometrical properties of a sphere occupy no energy, they were not produced in producing it, and they remain when it goes. Why not, as there, begin to fill the empty connexion? Feelings are events; why not make them occupy the same room as their brain-events? Because they feel no site that holds them; the only space that they feel is elsewhere. But a spatial connexion between mind and brain, and therefore mind and nature, had always been presumed. It was accepted by the theory of energetic, when it made mind or feelings a form of energy. The picture was only less ugly, because less definite, within a field of energy than with feelings impinging on particles; it kept the same line between feelings and nature, and placed it in the head; and it kept the question whether and how the line is crossed.

The question is at fault, as we see on turning to the other advantage from the exclusion of mind by nature. For mind excludes itself, and by quite another line. We draw it in every thought without thinking about it, as we draw our breath. For no one confounds his thought with its object, whether the object be physical or not. When the object is far too full to be felt, as by the farmer, the line is easily defined; but it is equally there when the whole is felt, as in a taste or other sensation. The fundamental error about the connexion between mind and nature is to confound the living line and the correlation line. The living line is not within the brain, but between seeing the light and the light, hearing the music and the music, counting and number, plotting and the plot. The correlation line within the brain is between seeing the light and the corresponding brain-events.

But we had better take an instance. The green of the grass out there can be correlated perfectly with the stimulus thence to my eye; also, though imperfectly, with the effects that it produces on my eye; finally, and quite imperfectly, with the brain-effects. Between the events in the four—green grass, stimulus, retina, brain —there is no likeness, though they correspond completely; in particular it is only the grass that is green. The grass is not green in the dark, because the stimulus is absent, nor green to the colour-blind, because a retinal structure is absent. But neither is it green, unless it is seen; it has to be a phenomenon. And so there remains a fifth connexion, that between the seeing and the colour. At first we add the seeing to the series as a fifth event, but that will not work. For the seeing does not come after the green; there is never one before the other. And, what is worse, there is no distance between them; you cannot have seeing in one place, and the colour in another.

The contrast between the two lines is as obvious as that. If it arrests the analogy with physical life, so much the better. Physical life includes all that is spread out in its body without itself being spread out, but the spatial drag is enough to make it seem a real question whether my foot or my head has the pain. Every good analogy that does not end in identity retires altogether after defining the new factors. Here they are the two advances in evolution. One is the service to nature in advancing it to be a world of objects. The other is as definite. The bodies of all species have grown in directions which they cannot retrace, and which prevent their better development; but the advance to and through mental life removes that restriction, as is obvious in the life of knowing. The living line frees its objects, and lets nothing mental nor neural, nothing but their difficulty, hamper their pursuit. However ancient, convincing, and successful a way of thinking has been, it offers no resistance but a grudge, when we see it mistaken. We discard it. That goes to the very character of the grasping organs that we create. They are, for nature, the theories, equations, devices, by which we penetrate it; and they constitute the theatre from which we seek to see the whole play. They are not mental, any more than number is, or an eye. They are related to nature as eye to light, and to understanding as eye to seeing. They look more like spectacles than eyes from their easy discarding, more like tool than hand; but their flexibility and their easy discarding are part of the living advance.

PART I
THE GULFS

II

THE SURFACE GULFS

§ 1. THE two developments in physics that are always proceeding have gone beyond the bounds that were set them. One passed them with the discovery of the quantum of action, the other with the discovery of the connexion between time and space. The discoveries closed the old outlook. One of the two developments we may call formal, the other material, to show that all nature comes into them. But they merely continue to answer our two early questions: What is the law, and What becomes of? What the law is, or rule, begins to be answered by every creature that can expect. What becomes of things and properties when they disappear is a later question; for life needs it less, and it has to be answered through the law. But both are already answered in every world of common sense. There an animal must learn the signs of prey or other food, of enemy or other danger; it has to measure times and distances, and unite shapes visible from all angles. The more signs the more qualities in the object, and the more qualities the more signs; an object becomes common to several senses, an object of common sense, a thing.

The variety in a thing, and its connexions with others, have all been felt. Together they form a world that is entirely sensible, even those things that cause fear or curiosity, because they hold unknown factors; a dog's beliefs are expectations that he can prove or disprove by his senses. To him the external world consists of phenomena. So does ours to us at first; but his is clearer, because he does not think about it. We keep as clear as he in practice, but our efforts to understand the course of things infect them with notions or prenotions of self, substance, and force. The infections are easy to remove, however, because they are not objects of sense, not phenomena. A common-sense world consists of phenomena.

Wide as it is, it is only the surface of nature; but always of nature. The depths, infinitely vaster, do not contain phenomena, far less consist of them. The surface is their phenomena. They did not appear before there were organs of sense. In those earlier days nature had no phenomena.

If we try to picture it in that black abyss, we see feeling come like a light; we speak of consciousness as a light, the light of consciousness. Far down the scale of life, where sensitive organs begin to give some flicker of a feeling, we see the feeble spot of light intensify and spread; at last it becomes the conscious field for higher creatures, and expands into the clear world of things that lies in front of us and the highest animals. Thinking of knowledge as a light, we think of omniscience as seeing everything. If we meant the picture, we should be giving science the task of bringing the depths of nature to the surface, and converting them into phenomena; it would be like the frog in the fable, that caught sight of an ox. But physics knows the length of the optical spectrum, and that there is no dark nor light without eyes; it never had the frog's ambition.

§ 2. It had more than a little of his discontent, but for the reason that our knowledge of nature is all through eyes and other senses. However perfect they are, their objects are phenomena. It became a familiar saying that 'science knows only phenomena'. Reason felt as if degraded. Having no sense-organ between it and its objects, it had thought itself in contact with things as they are. Senses had been indispensable, the primary producers; but their crude and broken material could only hint at nature proper, for they were not even mirrors. They could not dictate what is real, and reason thought that it could, and that they were its servants, and could be criticised. Now the old order was inverted: the slaves had become master, and reason their slave. Sensations refuse to be corrected, and they are the final critic of all that claims to be in nature. To satisfy reason had been to satisfy nature; now reason had to satisfy sense or phenomena. That was and remains the revolution.

But it was not complete in two respects: reason still dictated what real nature ought to be, and it prophesied that phenomena must fail to disclose their unity or system. They might not have such a thing, and it would not be real nature if they had. The dictate and the prophecy have now gone, or are going. The dictate has been lost by finding that real nature is no other than the system of phenomena, though a system so concrete that no one had dreamt of it. The formal development made the discovery; it found that the relativity of phenomena to their observers is no misfortune nor mere fact, but a principle so general that it is the test of a law being universal. Therefore the dictate went at once.

But prophecy is tougher, the prophecy that phenomena cannot let us go far. It was expressed in another gloomy saying which grew familiar, and was even repeated by an early pioneer of the new route: "all science

consists in pushing difficulties farther back" (Schuster).
To a later adventurer, twenty years later, the growing
difficulties have taken another colour: "the deeper knowledge from recent years has taken shape in the unity of
the physical picture of the world; far from reducing the
number of questions to be solved, it has multiplied them
a hundredfold; that is the mark of progress" (Gerlach).
But that had been a good ground for despair, and is the
only good ground: the outlook from physics. There
was another in the notion that phenomena are partly
mental, as well as physical. What unity or system
could be expected from a material so ambiguous? The
despair lay in this picture of the field of knowledge:

The field is bounded for animals by the reach of
their senses. Man extends his reach first by instruments
in aid of sense, and by the apparatus of experiment. It
remains for imagination and reason, having already
done well in the sensible field, to carry on alone. They
go on together till imagination is baffled by the growing
complexity and minuteness. Thence reason alone must
go on. It proceeds by developing the theories or systems
that have already established themselves. Provided
they keep contact with the surface, it can work them
some way into the growing chaos, whose bounds, however, are the two infinites, the great one and the small.

§ 3. If we look at the work of imagination and reason,
we can transform that hopeless picture of the field.

Objects of imagination are like sensible objects,
except that they need not be real, and that, as a rule,
they let us handle them as we choose. By their means
we forecast and recall; they give us an independence
of time and space; a historian may rehearse a hundred
years in an hour. Add fiction, poetry, plans, and
dreams. All that material, the material that we imagine,

we have known before; a man born blind has no visions
in his dreams. When we imagine the course of nature
beyond the range of sense, the interior of an atom for
instance, we have only what sense has given. But we
may seem to have more. When I divide an inch into
ten parts, then a part into ten, and so on, a time comes
when it is no longer possible for eye or instrument to
follow. But can I not proceed in imagination? Try and
see; we cannot picture a smaller part than can be seen.
The mistake may go farther. "We find ourselves totally
unable to form any mental image of unbounded space,
and yet totally unable to imagine bounds beyond which
there is no space. Similarly at the other extreme: it is
impossible to think of a limit to the divisibility of space,
and equally impossible to think of its infinite divisibility.
And we labour under like impotencies in respect of
time. . . . It results, therefore, that space and time are
wholly incomprehensible" (Spencer). The four impotencies need not have been given to imagination;
they belong already to sense. They mean that a phenomenon cannot be infinite nor infinitesimal; and they
mean no more. Infinite and infinitesimal are both un-
imaginable, but they are not incomprehensible, nor
even beyond proof. Nature does not consist of phenomena, real or imagined; they are the actual and the
imagined objects of sense; they are never but factors
in the physical fact, which is too concrete, we shall find,
for sense or picture. They are purely physical for all
that; there is nothing ambiguous about phenomena.
No object is made mental, nor altered, by being felt,
imagined, or known in any way. Physics has succeeded
in excluding all action at a distance; its laws are therefore of structures and motions that have to be raised and
reduced enormously, if one wants to imagine them; but
there is nothing distorted by that.

D

The hopeless picture of the field proceeds Past the bounds of sense, instruments, and imagination, reason carries on alone, relying only on logic, which knows no bounds. It would not know them if it met them. At one time it could expect them, and even seek them, believing phenomena to be more or less unreal. There were expeditions of the kind throughout last century, and they were useful in discovering contradictions all afterwards resolved. The picture of reason pursuing its own devices represents the work of theoretical and statistical physics. They make a purely logical attack on the unknown by elaborating systems that have already proved themselves in surface fact. To keep in touch with its base it looks to the devices of experimental physics, and suggests as well as helps to invent them. They bring their products within our native range of sense.

Like imagination, therefore, the theoretical and the physical devices of reason decline to play the part that makes the picture hopeless. Instead of lifting and advancing the bounds of the field of sense, reason cultivates the field within them. Nature flowers in phenomena; they lead us to their roots; and they do not ask the roots to be like them, but only to produce them and make them intelligible. That is the real and the useful picture of the material development of the field. It is not corrected, though superseded, by the formal development.

§ 4. The whole development has been independent of the notions of mind that were taken by the workmen. The deepest workmen, when they looked up from their work, believed that, working on phenomena, they were working on shadows, no matter how solid. They took opposite views of the substance that threw the shadows.

Thorough radicals took them for projections from the minds to which they are phenomena; thorough conservatives thought them projections from the world of which they are phenomena. Though conflicting so acutely when they were at leisure, at work they were at one; it was only when they remembered their minds that they quarrelled. "If either Helmholtz or Mach were right, not only common sense but exact science would have been at fault from the first; for surely the whole evolution of physical knowledge till now has aimed at the completest separation of the events of external nature from those of human perception." [1] That from Planck, who also summarised the history of physics as the gradual elimination of our human additions, in order to reach nature as it was before there were phenomena, and must remain. The conflict could be so acute, and yet never matter, because it was about the extra-physical relation 'to' or 'for'. The disputants would all have been glad to have done the work of one another. The work has ended the dispute by finding phenomena not to be shadows of anything, and to be parts of real nature instead. The division between the extremes has been dissolved without a thought. For the work never met it, having confined itself to phenomena and their system, ignoring the subject with his sensations and understanding, which exclude themselves.

For that reason the extremes were better than the middle and usual view that phenomena are products of the means of feeling them, and hybrids, neither pure nature nor pure mind. How to separate and assign the two strains in them and their system became a problem, and the problem became the controversy between the dignity of mind and the power of nature. That quarrel

[1] *Phil. Mag.* 28 (1914), p. 69.

too has gone, to the regret of no one; for those who favoured the prepotency of mind have discovered that they had been taking too mean a view of mind, and those who favoured the prepotency of nature have discovered that they had been taking too mean a view of nature.

It is a simple exercise to read the truth in the extreme conflicting statements. On the radical view "science is in reality a classification and analysis of the contents of the mind; . . . in truth the field of science is much more consciousness than an external world".[1] On the conservative view the very aim of physics has been "to emancipate nature from anthropomorphic factors, . . . to see it constant, independent of times and peoples, the same if our earth and its dwellers were consumed".[2] The middle view, besides the problem of the strains, could make a thing an emulsion from the means of knowing it: "I see a book . . . let us suppose that the full or adequate object perceived is equal to twelve, and that this amount is made up of three several parts,—of four contributed by the book, of four contributed by all that intervenes between the book and the sense-organ, and of four contributed by the living organ itself".[3] That analysis offers an indispensable exercise, if the source of the error is not clear. And it should be carried a stage farther to ask why a physical writer can say that we fail to grasp the aether because our brains are made of matter (xv. 4). All those restrictions on the sensible world, that it cannot be pure nature, have been removed by itself; for the system which makes it independent of being felt has been discovered from itself. The complaint that we know only phenomena has passed into their paean. "Whoever

[1] Pearson, *Grammar of Science*, p. 52.
[2] Planck, *Die Einheit des physikalischen Weltbildes*, p. 35.
[3] Hamilton, *Lectures on Metaphysics*, i. p. 147.

looks back over the ground that has been traversed, leading from the Euclidian metrical field, which depends on matter, and which includes the field phenomena of gravitation and electromagnetism, . . . must be overwhelmed with the feeling of freedom won; mind has cast off the fetters which have held it captive. The conviction must enthrall and inspire him that reason is not only a human, a too human makeshift in the struggle for existence, but that, in spite of all disappointments and errors, it is able to follow the intelligence which has planned the world, and that the consciousness of each one of us is the centre at which *the one light and life of truth* discovers itself in and from *phenomena.*"[1]

The discovery from the formal development was followed, in a few years, by a discovery from the material development that was only less upsetting. It is that statistical probabilities, which have to guide our lives, lie deeper in nature than their elements. Both revolutions bear heavily on our question of minds as lives, but all the more that they are incidental to the continuous course of discovery:

For inferior physical knowledge does not spend its life in error, but continues good beneath the surface as on it. On it the beliefs, or expectations, of all kinds of creature prove or disprove their truth completely, though one kind has more truth than another, and none ever has the whole. The passage thence to notions carries the same analyses deeper, seeking still the invariant factors and connexions. It is liable to the same correctible errors, the risk of error still increasing with the gain. It is the living line which continues to be followed; all the correlation lines keep their place; and there can be no quarrel between depth and surface.

[1] Weyl, *Space-Time-Matter*, p. 311.

Their quarrel came with the further ambition to combine the invariant factors and connexions, into the system or unity of nature. The ambition itself continued the living line, increasing the gain, and with it the risk of correctible error. But it could rise to a divided loyalty, now to surface, now to depth or system, and so make room for incorrectibles. In the actual advance of physics the continuity from the surface remained without a break. Cultivation kept requiring, or suggesting, farther analyses. They have gone so far that not one surface factor, however solid, uniform, independent, has been left to be copied, instead of analysed. The depths of nature that have been reached are now like nothing sensible, nothing imaginable, though the surface remains their sole critic. To prove themselves nature's they had to find ways, and also means, of cultivating phenomena; and the approving cultures, by also correcting or suggesting, sent them deeper. The one thing that at present concerns us is there: the levels beneath the surface belong to nature for the same reason as the grades of truth on the surface.

That gives another shock to our loyalty to nature proper. We resent the new load even more than the surface one, for, though we do not like phenomena to be parts of real nature, we are willing that they be its products, whereas notions are surely ours. But whatever we assign to nature proper we infer; we infer it from the level that we have reached; all therefore can remain continuous, correctible, devoted to developing the sensible world. Whence then the divided allegiance?

It came when early sceptics divided the sensible world into sensible and world. To-day it still comes only after sensible is extracted from its world. There is nothing of error in that, and there is nothing to be

qualified later; a theory is none the less fundamental
that it renounces all duty to levels, and all further duty
to the surface than to calculate certain cultures of the
spectroscope. That relation, if carried through for the
whole surface, would remove the error which creates
the divided allegiance, and the abstract or spaceless
gulf. The error, again, is that the purpose of going beneath can ever be to prove the existence of anything on
the surface of the sensible world. No depth can do that;
the surface does not need it; the situation that nature
sets for us is never reversed. The surface laws are all
empirical, and liable to exceptions, but the exceptions
too are on the surface, both alike nature's, and a task
for the depths. To the power of proving real existence
in the sensible world the error easily adds the power
of criticising and prescribing. The source of the abstract gulf between minds and nature, and between
minds and their brains, is as familiar as that. The
source of the spatial gulf between phenomena and
sensations of them is even simpler; and I shall begin
with it.

§ 5. What is the difference between the blue sky and
my sensation of it? And how are the two related so
that my sensation can be true or correct? The natural
answer, on passing to so new and unpractical a question, is that my sensation is an impression, and thereby
like the blue, or at least like the shape of it. Which is
easily seen to be impossible, but the reasons are important on their own account, and for searching ourselves. They are three:

(a) An impression has to be made on something with
a surface. If a mind has a spatial one, I suppose it has
not to match the sky; but the prodigy would only be
greater if we reduced the mental size to the small

cortical volume on which the retina 'projects' itself. And we do worse if, in place of mind, we say that consciousness takes the impression; for there is none before the 'states' of it, nor after, nor apart from them. A sensation is not an impression made on consciousness, for there is no consciousness waiting to take it. An impressible consciousness is a myth, and a hint that we search our behaviour. It is an instance of the myth to which we resort when we are at an end of understanding; we turn a property into a field having a substance, or separate existence. When it comes to be generalised by further analysis, it proves refractory. Time and space are such fields and substances. The field of consciousness yields more easily than they have done, because there is clearly none before it is filled. If neither mind nor consciousness will take the impression, perhaps the brain? But there is no blue there, and it presents the second reason:

(*b*) For an impression should be like the stamp, and a sensation is not. If it is like anything physical, it is like the object; and the object is never the stamp. Between the sky and the part of brain by which we see, there are successive courses of events, radiant, chemical, then neural; each prior one is the stimulus to the next; it does whatever stamping there is; in each course there is a corresponding order, so that they may be correlated; but no likeness is impressed from one course on the next; there is only correspondence. And there is nothing singular about colour being the object; even the shape of the blue is not outlined in the brain. The same holds for every sense. The shapes and sizes impressed on the skin, and projected inwards, not even they are repeated in the brain; when a man dives into cold water, no little image of him shivers in his skull. Take space itself, or any sensible quality whatsoever, always it is quite unlike the means that are said to convey and impress it. Between the external object and the brain-change there is only correlation. Between the brain-change and the sensation we have still only that, but it has been the habit to put more; you can still see diagrams of the cortex to fit the mind, and of the mind to fit the cortex. And it is here that the sources of the two gulfs unite, and control the controversy about the mind's place and power. They put the immediate correlation line in place of the living one, ask how ideas can jostle nerve-cells, or be secreted or qualified by them, and whether energy crosses either up or down. None ever crosses; it is across the living line that we know and do everything; the correlation lines, immediate as well as remote, discover the means.

But we had better again observe our own guilt, for we are too sure to take notice. We do not think of leaving in mere correlation the most important sensations and the corresponding brain-changes. We keep a likeness for them, a self-mirroring. Is not the correlate of the sense of space a little space in the cortex, of the sense of movement a motion there, of direction a direction there? No, for the three are everywhere in the brain, and in action all the time. We presume self-mirrorings also for important feelings like the sense of difference, the sense of likeness, the sense of order, and even of number; but again the brain has them everywhere without giving sensation of them. Most of all we are sure of a likeness or identity between the sense of time and its correlate. And now the argument against the others does not hold; for we are always feeling the lapse of time. But the unsettling of our guilt is the greater; for we feel a second or two all the time, and at no time in the brain is there ever any length of time.

(*c*) A sensation is not an impression, for there is no surface to take it, and it is not like the stamp; what, thirdly, of its likeness to its object in order to be true? The answer is so important that we may take it in two:

If a sensation is an impression, we cannot say it is like its object, for we cannot compare them. That is one answer. To compare them we should be able to lay a sensation of the blue sky beside the blue sky; but we should only be setting one sensation of the blue sky against another one. This was the reason, the only reason, for the scepticism of Hume. He saw no way out, because he had no doubt that a sensation is an impression; he always used the word. If we give up the theory we have no trouble with truth. When the members of a club speak of its rules, it lies with their thoughts to conform with the rules; and the rules do not care whether the thoughts are true or false, full or meagre. There we have the two conditions required of a thought that it may be true. One is that its object can be compared with the real or other object that it takes for standard. The second is that the standard one is unaffected by the thought of it; we must be able to use the standard whatever its real character, and however distant in time or space. To use it we have to grasp it, and our grasp has to let it speak for itself. We know its character from experience of it, and not merely when we know it well enough to predict, but when we decide that it cannot be known. As known and as unknown, the standard has come into our life. In no other way is it possible to compare the object as we think it with the object that it claims to be. The instance of the rules of a club covers every case.

But, in securing truth have we not lost reality? This asks for the other part of the answer. If a real or other standard object is felt, must it not be of the same stuff

as feeling? Would not the blue and the shape be sensations of a sort, and things but ideas? The question is
a remnant from the analogy that truth is a likeness
between thought and object. And the answer is that
truth, so far from asking for their likeness, never even
asks them to be compared. When a thought questions
whether it is true, it compares itself with nothing; it
compares the object in its grasp with the object that
it wants to grasp, and has made standard. The very
function of every grasp, whether by sense or by intellect, is to make the object prove its character. The
grasp alone is mental; nothing becomes mental by
being known, or known about; the grasp sees to that.

This time the reflection on ourselves is that the guilt
has always the same cause, has never the excuse of
original sin, and can itself reach the remedy. It comes
from always knowing by means of what we have
known, and therefore by means of objects. We live
long before asking what the connexion is between an
idea and its object whereby the idea can be true; and
we need the instance to be simple, and its question to
be as clear as the one whose confident answer we have
seen to fall to pieces. The remedy is reached by pressing
home the analogy, in order to define the resisting
factors; and the value of pressing it on the simple instance is that the outcome is the same for every kind
of thought.

§ 6. The simple instance ought to close the space
gulf, but, at the first remove from bare seeing, there is
the question of memory; and other questions of site and
substitutes follow soon. Since my thought is here and
now, how can the past be my present object? Are not
the things that I feel really images? What else are they
in dreams, where they feel quite the same as when I am

awake? Is not the living line merely a polarising of experience, the object as mental as the subject? And the simple case is not so simple; looking back from seeing and seen, through tasting and bitterness, to feeling and pain, do we not see the line disappear, the object become a quality, and the line imaginary like the equator? Then, looking forward from sense to science, where does nature begin to free itself? Is it not rather being absorbed, assimilated, made knowledge, the more it is made known? How can it be real things that we ponder, turning them over in our minds? Can things remain the same and real after going through the means of knowing to become ideas? And do ideas really act, their ghostly fingers pressing on the motor roots that guide my pen?

The answer will be as I have indicated. The living line is not a polarising; for every thought keeps all the feeling to itself, leaving none for the object that is felt. If I knew an object completely, none of it would be my knowledge of it, nor everybody's knowledge. Even if an error, a joke, or anything else that has no existence but for minds, it would not be their knowledge of it; the knowledge would be as many as the minds, and it one and the same known, mistaken, or forgotten. The question about real things may look the heavier for that. Let all feeling be on the knowing side of the living line, and none on the known; and let the line be the relation 'to'; if thought requires things to be independent of itself, how can they be real things and other minds that it analyses, and dead things like yesterday that it laments? Is not its work done on mental substitutes, on ideas, views, memories, judgments? No, ideas and views are names for things in the relation 'to'. The relation is not physical, nor therefore the turning over, but the things are the very things, and not substitutes;

the very function of thought is not to alter their physical or other character in handling them. When your ideas quarrel with mine, and when they agree, it is because they claim to grasp the same object as mine, and to find it independent of our grasp. And the things that we handle in knowing are the things that nature handles in changing or preserving them. The water that I see, desire, or dream of, is the water that I drink. A distinction used to be made between the physical and what was called the metaphysical division of a thing, the one analysing it into pieces, the other into properties. That extra-physical division is by knowing, and it analyses not something mental, but the very thing that can be broken as well.

The closing of the gulf waits neither on those questions nor on any explanation. To account for ideas, or knowing, by doubling is to account; we readily mistake it for bare fact, partly because the analogy is unwitting, mainly because minds are constantly constructing plans and unreal objects, which we think must therefore be mental. Like all imperfect knowledge, and in agreement with mind as life, the analogy works well. It works so well that we want the sensation of shape or blue to remain like the actual one, though no longer its impression, being quite unlike the stamp. That is already to slip the ghosts of things into the mind, spiritual bodies that copy their objects in everything but the power to play a real part. They are marionettes for our private rehearsal, before we take the real stage of life. But they are no better than the *lapis philosophicus* of *The Alchemist*: "'Tis a stone, and not a stone; a spirit, a soul, a body, . . . if you make it fly, it flieth". And when it was seen that there is no duplication, one blue in sensation and another in the sky, one sun in the mind and another up there, it seemed that things as they appear are not things as they are. "Ideas seem to have something in their nature unfriendly to other existences. They were first introduced into philosophy in the humble character of images or representatives of things: and in this character they seemed not only to be inoffensive, but to serve admirably well for explaining the operations of the human understanding. But, since men began to reason clearly and distinctly about them, they have by degrees supplanted their constituents, and undermined the existence of everything but themselves. First, they discarded all secondary qualities of bodies; and it was found out by their means that fire is not hot, nor snow cold, nor honey sweet; and, in a word, that heat and cold, sound, colour, taste, and smell are nothing but ideas or impressions. Bishop Berkeley advanced them a step higher, and found out by just reasoning from the same principles, that extension, solidity, space, figure and body are ideas, and that there is nothing in nature but ideas and spirits. But the triumph of ideas was completed by the *Treatise on Human Nature*, which discards spirits also and leaves ideas and impressions as the sole existence of the universe." [1]

§ 7. The facts that close the space gulf next close the spaceless one, as the success of any function closes doubt about its means. Here the doubt is due to ignoring the living line, or identifying it with the central end of the correlation one. Across the living one, the relation 'to', there is the world of objects; across the correlation line there are all the physical means, extending from the cortical processes to glands and all viscera, to the sensory organs, and thence to every kind of external stimulus. Correlations can be made at any point on the

[1] Reid, *Works*, i. p. 109.

route without knowing or imagining either the intervening or the cortical events. It is a wonderful advantage, the very advantage that the 'energetic' reform
pressed on physics, and a notable addition to the other
living values of imperfect knowledge. And physics is
the best example, for it is able to confine itself to the
remotest part of the route, the external stimulus, careless of the neural correlates. The same holds for the
correlates of our emotions and actions. All are means
incorporated in the organs of the conscious functions,
just as for the organs and functions of physical life.

There is no likeness between any mental factor and
any portion of its correlates immediate or remote. We
may well assume that there is always a brain-change
for every change in experience, with a difference for
every difference in the experience; but, if we knew the
change completely, and the whole physical condition, we
should be no nearer a likeness than between language
and its meaning. This instance is an instance, however
artificial the language; but it is more familiar in the
natural language of emotions. They express themselves
at the surface of the body as attitude, glance, blush,
tone of voice, many a way. If we could track these back
to their organic correlates and thence to their nerve-
centres, we should see and read them in the original.
Every other experience has likewise its original expression in the brain. To say so is to impose no more
restriction than to say that every thought can be expressed. But we may as well go farther, in order that
the question may be clear. The structure of a sentence
expresses the structure of a thought, though the parts
of the thought have no spatial, nor even a serial connexion with one another. In that sense we can say that
the structure of a brain expresses the structure of a
mind, and is the mind made visible and tangible. The

inference is never from what brain can do to what mind can do, but always, first, the opposite. To restrict the mind by what we think the brain can do is quite like restricting the literature of the world by the letters of the alphabet, because it cannot but consist of them.

In the order of discovery, mind accounts for brain as meaning accounts for language. There is also their order of existence, which is another question; but to ask whether the conscious brain may have grown without the help of consciousness is to ask if speech may have come and grown without a meaning. No future knowledge of mind will give man more power over it than to know its correlates, a knowledge always growing. There we have a real gulf to fill. If its filling were at last fully known, the difference and the connexion between thought and its object, or will and its object, would be no other than we know them now. This real gulf of ignorance does not prevent the knowledge that invades it from being sure and exact. Psychology does not have to imagine a filling in order to pursue the psycho-physical knowledge, all of it correlation, which is its daily pursuit. Physiology alone is concerned, and the situation for it is no worse than physics and chemistry knew before the opening of the atom and the molecule.

§ 8. If the gulfs have no place even in our ignorance, we have to look to their origin for their hold. They go back to placing mind or feelings in the head. To learn their hold, and realise the strength of it, we have only to try to unseat feelings. For where are they, if not there? It sounds the voice of reason, but is just the tyranny of space; we are as free to be rid of it as to lose every other belief that fails in its profession; and the best way is to look without analogy at a mind's own place. The first gulf requires that the space which we

see and know is in some space in our heads wherewith we see it, or has its image there. But there is no
distance between seeing one part of a landscape and
seeing another, but only between one part and another.
Seeing unites the parts not by spreading itself over
them, nor by bringing them to a focus. It unites them
as hearing unites music, and as thinking unites the field
of an argument. We rightly speak of a felt expanse,
but the notion of an expanded feeling wrongs both
feeling and expanse. It blots out the unity which is the
service of the feeling; and the expanse, instead of being
one space, is a substitute. The spaces in dreams and
errors are rejected by actual space, but they are not
expanded feelings. To call them mental, because they
are not physical, is an instance of two common sources
of confusion, as we shall find. One is making our mind
a receptacle for all rubbish, the other is our not analysing till we know the need. The living line, the relation
'to', is no part of the object, whether the object be real
or unreal.

It is the bridge, in the first place, between minds and
nature, and then between minds and their other fields
of knowledge and action. A field of action is the more
critical case, and will best introduce the final physical
gulf, and its closing.

E

III

THE THIRD GULF

§ 1. THE physical course of a purpose runs in cycles, the action passing through a nervous system and the external situation which is being altered or maintained. Purpose does not enter the course at any point, nor is it spread over the whole; it is again a uniting, such as that of hearing and understanding, though now practical. They, too, take a purpose, when they do not like their grasp; and their purpose commands the physical means no otherwise than the purpose of a juggler. But consider his interference, because it is more explicit.

The cycle in his performance is all physical; yet it would fail if he did not feel it, and again if he were distracted. His purpose makes him subject of the whole cycle, the part that goes beyond his body as well as the part within, unifying it in two ways. For he apprehends the whole, all the time, from the little that he feels; and, through the same little, he gives it the practical unity of his purpose all the time. As he improves, the little can grow less. He can also learn to practise without balls, and with the poorest images of them, or none; he can substitute inchoate movements for his actual ones; and, finally, he may go through the performance in his head, or dream it passively, whether he likes or not. Let us say that nothing is then left but the brain part of the cycle. The juggling does not occur there any more than at first; what occurs is much the same unfelt part of the cycle as before. The unreal balls are not there, nor anywhere; we may call them ghostly, if ghosts can feel heavy; like everything else they are ideal, since they are felt; but they are not mental, unless the real balls are called mental because they are felt; which would be a pity.

In the real cycle, when he is timing himself to the fraction of a second, it is because he is not confined to it, nor even to the current second. He uses the time of the whole, and better the more he can take it for granted, and concentrate on its intervals one by one. They are felt as parts of it; he does not contract it into one of them. The physical times, like the spaces, that he feels, are accepted and absorbed by the whole. The whole is the space-and-time system, which is also physical, for neither space nor time can be empty. Let us put him into it, and ask how it absorbs his performance:

The cycle needs physical forces at every point; and they are as adequate within him as without. But if the physical course becomes all, does not his purpose yield up its power? The question comes from the classical aim for physics. "An intelligence which knew for a given moment all the forces with which nature is animated, and the relative positions of the things which compose it, and were vast enough to submit these data to analysis, would embrace in one formula the motions of the largest bodies of the universe, and those of the lightest atom; nothing would be uncertain to it, and future and past would be alike before its eyes. The human spirit presents a feeble copy of this intelligence in the perfection to which it has brought astronomy. . . . Every effort in the pursuit of truth beings it nearer, though the distance to go must remain infinite" (Laplace). There we have nature offering to absorb the careful timing of the juggler into its own far finer analysis of the time-stream; for the cycle cannot be in two

moments at once. That 'at once' is the unity served by
his consciousness; the actual stream of events requires
it; and we see where and how a purpose interferes:

The immediate correlate of a present feeling is presumably a sequence of events, never the point-present
of the brain-stream, but a process. The present that
we feel is always long enough to give a sense of change;
it is therefore as infinite, compared with nature's instant, as the shortest line compared with a point. But,
if the brain correlate is a process, it never exists as the
classical stream counts existence. And there is more.
The classical stream allows no co-operation between
one event and a following one. Its advancing front
carries the whole energy, actual and potential, at a
point of time. Each point-event, once it occurs, passes;
it has done all that it ever will do; if ever again it makes
a difference to anything, it is through a mind. The past
of the stream, however near the present instant, is
frozen; there is no co-operation along the length of
time. But every experience is a length and alive.

That all-embracing present instant of the classical
stream is only a boundary, and holds no time at all.
But, when we give the boundary a little breadth,
letting an event have some length of time, we find
ourselves dividing into instants again, all past but the
present; and can we help it? No, but that is not the
question. It is not that we cannot help dividing, nor
that reason requires us, but that time does. And so does
number. Having abstracted and begun to divide them,
we meet nothing that allows us to stop. Not only is
there no error in the abstracting, dividing, and combining, there is none when we replace time or number
in nature, and charge them with every necessity that
has been found in them apart. That is why the pure
stream can take the very times that we feel. It can

divide them to suit a speed like that of light, and yet have no quarrel with the juggler's timing. For he keeps the temporal order of the events that he times, though he times them at once, and all the time. When I walk across the fields, the acres that I see all the time are as real as the yard that I stride. And so it is with the seconds that I feel all the time, with the times which they include, and with the hour and the week which include them. And, as a felt expanse is not an expanded feeling, so my feeling of change is ill described as a changing feeling, and worse as lasting for two seconds, though it does. The unity is omitted, which is the service to nature, and to the classical stream. My changing feeling is a feeling of change, and it unites the two seconds not by making them simultaneous, nor by squeezing them into the time that it takes to feel them, nor by having their image there and the real time that they mean elsewhere. These devices are due to the notion that without them our grasp is impossible. And so it would be if it had to copy.

The length of time which I hear or see in a process is the very time that exists; it is present to me, two seconds or so at once, like any other object with its properties. But does the length let a late event act on an early one, an effect on its cause? No, when an end determines means, as the juggler's does, there is no such liberty. His end or purpose is the unity existing all the time, and the physical fixity of the order is indispensable to the means by which his end becomes an effect, the physical end. How he came by his desire is another matter, but the means came with it, as when a child reaches towards a light without knowing how. Every desire commands its means, if they exist, and forthwith proceeds to interfere by using them, unless it is thwarted by a conflicting desire.

There is no conflict between minds and nature. There is plenty between understanding and a difficulty, and between the spirit and the flesh; but it is all as between a plant and the weather, only now on the higher level of life. The mutual service of minds and nature leaves no claim and counter-claim, as if we had to divide the world between them. Minds claim none of the physical burden, and, like the juggler, they throw on the surface of nature no burden that its depths can decline.

§ 2. Though we do not have to draw the living line between mind and nature, we make no mistake about it. Look at the blue or the shape of the sky, and there are a hundred sensations of it; but it is one. They have to conform with it, and it is unaffected; if some of us have green spectacles, it is blue nevertheless. Whereas it is common property, the hundred are private property; it is the common object that we each make ours by feeling it. Whereas it is an object of sense, our feelings are no such objects even to ourselves; we see blue, we do not see our sensation of blue. A cloud in the sky moves about, but our sensations do not, nor even rest; they are in change, but not in motion. The sensation of an explosion does not explode; our sight of the blue vault is neither blue nor hollow. Though you may never have thought about the line between seeing the blue and the blue seen, which marks these differences, you recognise them at once, because you have always used it.

But is it good? Does the line between thought and physical object hold against our later knowledge of nature? Yes, and yet, at so early a check, Locke thought not; and he used our principle—it was his discovery— that knowing is living, and grows by living. His 'new way of ideas' was new because it left them free to prove themselves and grow. He came on it as the one way to exclude prerogative and presumption, and let us know what there is in the world that we are fitted to know. But it led him to curious perplexities, which Hume developed into a conflict between reason, which condemns the living line, and life, which finds it indispensable:

The 'new way' was to follow the life of ideas from their birth as sensation, in order to see through what real things they can take us, and how far. But Locke would have said: there is not one real blue, there are only the hundred, each in a mind; and, in addition to the hundred felt vaults there, which are blue, there is one vault above, not blue nor even black. All four statements are foreign to the sensible grasp, which we call common sense. They do not continue its way of life; they condemn it, and would put it right, if they had not come to knowledge too late. Berkeley, who followed on the new way, could keep the blue with the vault, but by abolishing the one sky in addition. That broke with the sensible world more than ever, though he thought not; and Hume, who agreed that Berkeley was right in reason, thought that life could never agree. There, in the conflict between reason and life, the new way lost its hope. Its abandoning gave, and still gives, the friends of life a livelier hope; for, if the way of life and the way of reason diverge, and at a point so early, dry, and clear, perhaps there are two authorities; may not the best of life be irrational, or alogical at least?

It was quite in accordance with reason that ideas should be free to prove the existence of their objects. But they had to be born; that was the misfortune. They are born as sensations, and are then free to grow as ideas. But sensations are events, and every event has a cause. Ideas were given their freedom, but their birth was against them.

One might think that, if their birth were made honourable, they would feel no restriction. That was done; Locke placed the causes of sensations in nature, Berkeley placed them in mind, the mind of God, and Hume let them be anything, seeing they made themselves unknown. It did not really matter what they were, since they kept out of the way. On the way there are only ideas, or phenomena, as ideas came to be called. The way wanders through a world where all things and minds remain products of something else than themselves, with which they can never compare themselves. By faith they might be shadows; that was all.

This gulf is the secret source of the two gulfs on the surface; but it can persist when they are closed. They challenge our means of knowing nature; it challenges the nature that we know. The three have it in common that knowing is a product; they place us in a groove and say that the freedom which we and the higher animals feel is the freedom of ignorance. The surface two are closed, if the new way, which is our principle, does not come to an end. But the final gulf is deeper. It would feel the shock if all nature were knowable, and merely little known; but it would not close. Must not all still be product, shadow at best, alive as parasite, not the real thing. That was and is the proper source of the gulf. But it has found others:

§ 3. One is the appeal of reason to itself. "Deep down somewhere in the processes of thought the ultimate test of reality appears to be the Law of Conservation. . . . Only what is conserved has the right to be considered a physical existence. . . . Does the soul exist? If so, it must be immortal." [1] But it is the very

---

[1] Soddy, *Matter and Energy*, pp. 41, 108.

aim of thought, the more it is reason, to disclaim responsibility and to follow instead. If it says that only the permanent exists and is real, it claims to have found, beyond itself, that those conceptions coincide, namely, permanence, existence, reality. Reason, like the rest of thought, is devoted to the object; it intends to be devoted even when it strays. No reason boasts of its origin or its history. When reason appears to be relying on its past, and on the strength of conviction, it pleads ignorance. It can grow proud, or merely obstinate, but both are familiar effects of ignorance. Being challenged, it then passes from pleading to claiming ignorance, and the right to act on principles; but it never finally appeals to principles on the ground that it cannot get away from them, but always because they are in things. Even the principles of logic, which are called the laws of thought, are also laws of nature. Nature has the better claim to the title, for thought can be illogical, and nature never.

There is a more insidious appeal to reason on behalf of the gulf. If nature were logical not in itself, but by conforming with reason in us, it would follow that there are forms of thought which we inherit, and that they develop, and differentiate, in the life-history of each of us, fixing themselves, for instance, in the forms of the sentence. That notion has been so attractive because of the analogy; it fits mental to physical life; the things that we know would be the work of a stimulus on a growing structure. But they would be hybrids as freakish as the book of twelve elements from three sources.

When reason wants the real to conserve itself, it has not yet observed that we know nothing of the kind which is not abstract. When it discovers this, how does its appetite behave? It submits, the better we understand; and it has no structure that prevents our understanding. When it discovers that to be concrete is to change, it may insist on a final unchanging particle, but not, or not for long, because of the strength of its own appetite. When it hears that time would stop, were it not for events, it offers more resistance, and may say: events or no events, who can think of an end of time? Yet it will not listen to itself even there; its ear is all for the object.

But since any invariant that we know is abstract, must there not be a permanent substance to support it? A law of nature does not change, and laws are abstract; is that possible without a permanent support? As possible as a law of the Medes and Persians. The supporting pedestal would be useless; for a law of nature tells of a behaviour, and there is no behaviour where there is no change. But the appetite for substance persists; why is that? Partly because no appetite dies by condemning it, here because we may not notice its origin. It begins in the other of our two exhaustive questions. Besides wanting to know the law we want to know what becomes of; and the only answer that we want is that the disappearing thing or property persists unseen in other form. Finally we seek substance because nature itself, and even things, appear to offer it:

Knowing nature first as a community of things, our first notions account for their independence and behaviour by a substance and its force, like the subject and will that we feel in ourselves. When, on looking for them in things, we cannot find them, may they not be merely out of reach? So it was answered. Substance and force were allowed to remain, because the way of thinking was so old; and logic, when it came, assumed that the old way is the only way.

§ 4. There might seem, here at last, an inborn bias

in our minds. But that is not the case; the demands are from the object. One of them is from that individuality in things which art of every kind cultivates and science ignores. But, that quite aside, and taking things only as for knowledge, we find them speak with two voices, whose common source keeps out of sight, and lets them quarrel. A thing analyses into qualities, and into particles. Neither analysis, if completed, would exhaust the thing; and for two thousand years they appeared to be incompatible.

That is the kind of situation which, if it could be final, would call for a better world, from which ours would be parted as by a gulf. Other dilemmas have been whether, taken as a whole, nature is finite or infinite; and whether, taken in its parts, the last word is with discreteness or with continuity. They have been employed many times as a challenge to the competence of our kind of mind. But the mind's concern is that the dilemmas are physical, and that nature cannot give contradictory answers. On the surface they seem contradictory; therefore they challenge minds to reach the facts which prove that the dilemmas are due to abstractions. By creating the number-system reason took up the challenge, and exonerated our minds, as we shall have to see.

But can nature take it up, and control the abstractions, nature as we know it? That is the real challenge, and to our minds. The answers have carried far, and into physical conditions that were quite unexpected.

§ 5. There are opposite views of the conflict and the issues, according as we see them from the waiting gulf, or from the way of life. Seen from the gulf the surface conflicts grow worse as their questions go down. Seen from the way of life they are never met by meagre minds that keep to the surface, or sensible world; they come only when we seek a better hold than the surface affords. Then, the more they give trouble, the more they prove nature to be not piecemeal, which is one essential to its being intelligible.

Our choice between gulf and life has been thought to be between humility and arrogance. And it is true that the way of life is arrogant, knowing so little. But it presumes only that nature is logical; whether also intelligible, it goes to find. And the gulf, the humble reading, has no humility in its ground, and very little in its consequence. Its ground is that nature is illogical, the nature which we know. Its consequence, if the gulf is made absolute, gave to analogy the final word in the 'synthetic philosophy' of the known world. That is humble only in this that analogy need never be wrong; but it is more than bold if it remembers the history of analogies that have been taken for final, and not in alchemy alone.

The humble reading does not go the length of Hume, and say that life is illogical, but only that nature is; it has created philosophies to keep our life logical. Those which began with Kant find, in the failure of nature to meet logic, the superiority of mind in man. Those which ended with Spencer embroil our minds as well, and make the gulf complete. He concludes that the last combining word will be found in the laws which are common to nature, to minds, and to all their works. It is the very ecstasy of analogy; and the conclusion can be no better, given the gulf.

We may distinguish the view of nature from the gulf as of two kinds; one makes the nature that we know artificial, the other makes it superficial:

The artificial view is natural enough; it presumes an observer for everything. We always presume him in describing absent things, and without error, for they are not altered by observing them. But, if we ask what things are when they are not being observed, the answer would be wrong; it would amount to saying that the object of sense is also the stimulus. When we assume the depths of nature to be like the surface, we carry that blunder down. If they were alike, then all should be imaginable, and questions at the surface could be repeated at the depths, where there are never phenomena. The proofs that science has to rest on contradictions rest on so simple an error. An easier instance than the three conflicting pairs which I have mentioned is attraction and repulsion: "We cannot truly represent to ourselves one ultimate unit of matter as drawing another while resisting it". Yet physics never seeks to evade nor to square such a conflict, but to use it (ix. 7). That view of nature which makes the system of phenomena consist of phenomena, or be imaginable, may be called, then, the artificial view.

The superficial view is quite as definite. It detaches the surface of nature from the depths, and has to go the length now of saying with Hume that life is illogical. Reason, he said, puts all things that we ever know into our minds, for they must all have been felt; when felt they are feelings, and, when remembered, they are no better. Yet life puts them outside our heads. His successors made it a clever trick of the growing brain. The trick seemed less of a miracle by detecting its early stealth. For, before putting things outside the body, the brain had had practice in putting the body outside. If it is my hand that feels cold some feet away from my brain, it can be the sun that feels hot at no matter the distance. Next, the means can be found without which the localising trick does not happen. And, finally, physics has detected the later stages of the trick. Did not the brain of vertebrates carry things too far, once it got them beyond the glow or halo? It clothed them in qualities like hot and blue, that should have remained in the head; it made qualities from different senses fill one and the same space; and it gave the group of qualities a self, as well as a space, to keep them together. When man came to notions and speech, the model was so fixed in his inheritance, and working so well, that he made everything conform. He still makes a thing of everything, even of the world itself. When he thinks of his mind he makes a thing of it. And that lets nature have revenge. For he gives his mind a shape when he thinks about it; or he adds his mental qualities to the physical qualities of his head, and makes a thing of himself in that way; if he is not a thing, he thinks he is nothing. Is that the story, and its exposure?

If it were, the bad ending is no challenge to the way of life, where things prove all their claims. The superficial view, therefore, has to find them at fault; it has to find error in beliefs without which life would fail. And it does not hesitate. It knows that other errors have lived long, and says: let short life, which needs cunning, speak for nature as known; real nature is with long death, which needs none. The view could claim the history of physics, whose aim had always been to discard the gloss that man gives, and to ask what nature would be if he were dead (ii. 4). Sense would thus be our first and worst approach to real nature; that remained the conservative view. But the radical and opposite view of the cleansing of nature was that sensation is also last, and the essential thing, and that the whole duty of physics is to calculate the course of sensation. The two cleansings gave themselves each a difficulty: the conservative had to keep the deeps from growing abstract, the radical had to find pure sensations. Physics welcomes both cleansings, and yet it does not come across either difficulty. It is because both parties are partial, and have lost sight of the whole. The whole is the way of life, where nature is first of all the sensible world, not a world that is not sensible, nor a sensible that is not a world. The insensible depths complete it, and are discovered by making it calculable. The one blue vault that we see is one, because it completes each of the hundred views of it; and the blind can claim it for theirs too, though not in that quality.

The important thing is not that the artificial and the superficial views of nature are mistaken, and that the way of life makes nature free from deferring to our constitution. The important thing is that the point from which the views are taken seems inevitable, and then that the freeing of nature frees also our minds. Let us take the two in that order.

§ 6. The point of view that seems inevitable is that sensations are products, because they are events, and every event has a cause. But, besides being products, they are true. The two characters were combined in the error that sensations are true because they are like the qualities which are their objects, and like them because they are impressions made by the objects. What happens when we press the error home, and find that a sensation is like neither its cause nor its object? At first we think the fact a pity. We insist on a proper cause, though beyond our knowing. The older ways to the gulf, in particular the veil of sense, were also in search of a cause.

But the 'new way' intended to be new, and was not hampered by the notion of a veil. It lay on the fact that things in being known, the very things, come within our

experience, are part of our life. That is why beliefs can
be no better than their proofs. That is also why we do
not need to know the course of conscious living in race
or individual; it is irrelevant. Our conscious living soon
takes the clear subject-object form, which knows and
proves the objects to form a world; it knows nothing of
them but as it has lived them. It is still in a conscious
living that man comes to reflect on himself as subject,
and forms notions of mind and nature. The whole way
is the way of life. But one piece of knowledge was taken
out of the way, because it appeared to be prior: the fact
that sensation is a product. Brought into the way the
product is followed up in the correlations of mind with
brain and the rest of relevant nature. That leaves the
way open; the correlation line is within it. But the
pioneers did not leave it open, as they intended; they
enclosed it by making sensation, and therefore all conscious life, a product. The conflict between life and
reason which they found and bequeathed is due to that.

The source has been overlooked, because they had no
other purpose than to keep open and follow the way of
life as itself the way of reason. On the old way, which
they meant to abandon, the sensible world was a
manifestation, from which reason had hints of the real
forces and substances. The old way had often been
cleansed to secure devotion to the manifesting facts of
experience and experiment; Bacon's cleansing was of
that kind. And the new way had nothing against
that cleansing at the start. It merely brought a more
thorough cleansing by following the life-history of
ideas. To the pioneers the new way might even open on
the old, until Hume found that impossible. For, assuming with them that ideas, the known world, must be
product of another one, he found that all books about
the other one must be futile, and should be burnt. It

was this that was challenged, never the assumption that impressions are products.

Nor was it questioned by the glad followers of the new freedom, even when the way became genetic, and the way of evolution. Spencer, in fact, went farther, and undertook to prove the assumption. His *First Principles* has for its argument that the new way is built on quite a number of contradictions, and can only be a trick, though the race has made it, and thriven. And so the controversial questions have been about the world beyond the enclosed way, whether any of it can be known; and about the world within the enclosure, how much of the other it can manifest. But the question really is whether our lives within the enclosure are preserved. And the enclosure need not be the skull, which is the popular version; there would be prison enough, if our conscious living did not make its own way, but were a product. We look prisoners of nature still after merely being expelled; but our actual release is through the living analysis, which exposes and follows the bond:

If we cannot say of nature that it is a product of the means of knowing it, we cannot say it of the sensible world, which consists of phenomena, nor therefore of any phenomenon in it. Though a phenomenon has no existence except it is felt, its existence is determined by physical conditions, as completely as if it were unfelt. That holds for the whole phenomenon except its being felt. Nature expels the being felt, not to some other place, but to be subject. It excludes seeing from the surface, as it does science from the depths; they exclude and free themselves.

This mutual freeing I mentioned as the other important thing about the living way. If knowing and nature were always as intimate as seeing and light, or

F

counting and number, there would be small temptation to sever the living relation, and then wonder how the two meet, as across the first gulf. Nor would there be any question that the things we live, and thereby learn to know and use, are the very things that exist; which the second gulf prevents. But it is the easier to mix the knowing and what is known, a thing which knowing never does, and so to create the third gulf. Locke, who saw the danger of losing things in ideas, had a way of saving them. He employed the later forms of conscious living to throw light on the earlier, from which they grow. That was consistent with the continuity of the new way, and with the claim of ideas that the existence, of which they are true or false, is other than theirs. But because he assumed that the first ideas are products, it was easy for his successors to compound every later idea from them, and find that ideas can report nothing but themselves, and the remnants of their predecessors. That was the origin of the fear of knowing 'only phenomena'. The growth of the mind, or subject-factor, was also made a compounding, and now without fear. Part was by association, as if a cohesion; part yielded new properties, as if it were chemical; part grew as if living; and the living ideas differentiated into subject-experience and object-experience. What better could come from a product?

The freeing of mind and nature together from the groove of being products is throughout like the freeing of light and seeing. The whole conquest of nature is like the conquest of light. Light is not a product behind my eyes, but all in front; and seeing is not behind, and the light in front, for they are never apart. All the causes that produce light and seeing, or number and counting, come within the conquest.

The freedom won is not only from gulf-producing

causes, but from the actual causes in our conscious living, which may appear to prevent its freedom. Its freedom is to make objects its causes. Let us collect its kinds of cause by means of an instance, where their functions are clear:

§ 7. What are the causes of my belief that twice two makes four? Four answers have been given, of which three are good.

The physical cause has to be imagined. We have to suppose that portions of brain-tissue have already taken a disposition or pattern whose reaction gives my belief. The pattern has to be copied from what I feel, and is therefore diagrammatic at best. Room for it is found by following the growth of my sense of number from its beginning in perceptions, whose cortical areas are known. But there is no temptation to press the pattern on the room, any more than to press a colour, or a second, or anger, on their places. Two is a small number, but the sense of it is no easier to place than the sense of twenty; twice two is difficult, for there is no observer. Worst of all, the calculating machine has to substitute causes for reasons, which alone command my belief. What I feel would therefore be very hard to copy. Next, is the pattern to be histological, chemical, or electrical? And, in all, the same piece of tissue has to serve two masters; there is the belief which is its product, and there is its own cause from outside. Suppose we knew the physical means by which number makes itself known, why do they give knowledge at all, and why not of themselves but of number? These questions are too hopeless not to be in error. But rather than surrender a likeness we may think there is a secret one, the cortical cause being merely phenomenon. That calls for cause number two.

Since there is nothing in nature out of which feeling can come, and yet feeling comes by physical causes, is there not a secret cause of which the physical are phenomena? It would be the real cause by which number makes itself known through cause number one. Such causes were first introduced for the ordinary work of nature, but there, having been left with nothing to do, the concurrent causer of causes has become superfluous. Physical causes are no longer completed by such a means. They are completed by their system, or by a more general system, never by a cause from which nothing can be calculated. There is no reason for dealing otherwise with the cause of knowing number, and we strike this one from the list.

By the third cause my belief that twice two makes four is product of my past experience; and the force of the belief is product of an association of ideas, or their more intimate welding, that has grown from strength to strength, and made the belief inevitable. By the fourth cause, on the contrary, my belief is due to my knowing arithmetic, and its force to nothing but arithmetic. So far the two are quite separate causes, and conflict. They cannot be reconciled by saying that the third is a cause of which my belief is effect, while the fourth is only a ground, of which my belief is a consequence. For the ground is cause when it is known.

It does not enter like an autocrat, tyrannising over the power of old associations and empirical beliefs, as reason was thought to do; it rules by persuading. But so do they. The fourth cause enters as early as the factors of the third, when the factors persuade. It is their unity, their function, their final cause, the end to their means. An idea is born knowing; its function is born with it, and it develops into a body of knowledge at the object's behest.

This language about a final cause, and about an object as cause, to say nothing of its behest, makes the fourth cause appear metaphorical, and ask to be dissolved into means. But it is the very character of minds, which makes them higher forms of life, that their reaction is to objects. Their degrading consists in reducing them to organised energies, mental or physical, which a stimulus discharges. Their actual decadence is a falling to that. My belief may answer from the theory of numbers, or from instances, or from the 'indissoluble association' of the multiplication table. These mean three grades of mind, and, though the higher among them grow from the lower, the lower do not become the higher, but become tools. If the three came to blows, it is the meanest that would prove universal; I might babble the table though unconscious. But the strength of my belief is not from the strong association either in instances or in words. They are both superseded, without any effort, when I happen to know better. There is nothing indeterminate about the final cause, which is the object. I am still bound to believe; but it is arithmetic, not habit, that has cost me my liberty to think that twice two makes five.

Far from conflicting, all the causes are always present, accounting for beliefs of every sort, and therefore for all knowledge. First, an object always directs me, and my accepting it, to rely on it, is a virtual purpose, or final cause. Next there are the mental means, the third of our causes. They constitute my power to grasp the object, a power that has been learnt, grown from my inherited power to learn. Finally, there is cause number one, the physical means. It receives its entire task from the other two. The task is unending, occupied with the correlation line, where its work enjoys the freedom of nature instead of the hopeless slavery of modelling twice two.

The situation being always the same, why do we dislike it, and how can we distort it? We dislike the word cause for three such different applications; but words are tools, and perhaps we are none the worse for having a few that are known not to work as counters. But we also dislike there being three; we want the cause to be of one kind. That is easily arranged: their mutual dependence makes them factors of one system.

And at that our real grudge discovers itself: there is one kind of cause that we presume to be universal, and the system refuses to go into it. It controls the course of events in the universal time-stream. But the stream no longer claims nature; and while it still remains good for our individual worlds, where space-time remains space and time, the stream cannot dissolve them without losing itself. The presumption had been that, but for minds, nature would go down the stream; and how could our worlds then really exist? It seemed the very light of reason, but there has come the light instead, from each great physical advance, that reason had been closing down nature too soon. And I am afraid that our real grudge is not against the loss of classical mechanics, which has lost only its outlook, but at losing the easy picture of nature as a course of events.

It is more, however, than our desire for a picture that makes us distort a causal situation which is always the same. It is our failure to maintain the living analysis. As we have doubtless all been guilty, it is always well to ask whether some difficulty that we feel is not due to dipping our bodies into nature a second time. When ideas came into the new way, they were called objects, and 'whatever it is which the mind can be employed about', but they soon seemed to be hampered by being felt, and therefore products of the means of feeling them. How could they be products at once of our organs, and of one another? The answer needs no more than to let the object develop, till it is seen to incorporate its means of being known. That was the course which physics left open by ignoring all feeling. But, when conflicts brought confusion, it was usual to think the human world ambiguous, and the solution possibly in the real world beyond the gulf. There seemed a fiction in describing nature before living bodies came, and their senses were dipped into it. The living analysis, with its causal system, goes through these troubles, discovers the reversal in our outlook which has brought quantum and relativity mechanics, and finds and fills the gulf between nature for each of us and absolute nature.

The route is equally open for other objects, including a subject's own mind, the sole condition being that they prove their pretensions. The origin of the new way was an essay to find the reach of human understanding. The results were not promising till Hume saw that the enclosure puts life into conflict with reason; he turned the essay therefore from the object to the means, and what they could reach. This 'mitigated scepticism' did so well that, in the third or fourth generation, it took the name agnosticism. To remove the enclosure is to restore the question of reach from means to object, whose development alone can tell the power of the means.

It may seem that an abstract artificial object like twice two cannot stand for actual existence like things, or the light on them. And, in fact, numbers, and the other 'ideas of reason', were never enclosed. Our instance is against that separation, for number is actual, though we count things as we choose. But nature goes farther: it accepts nothing but in connexion. When I draw a circle, I am not creating its properties, and

I could not draw it but for its properties. Nature, and my knowledge and ignorance of it are as there. The course of phenomena that I feel is like the drawing of the circle, and their system is like its properties. The drawn circle is a phenomenon of its properties; there is a mutual determining between it and them, as when I move and it becomes elliptical. Whether it is a phenomenon to any one, and whether the properties are known to any one, is immaterial to nature. But there is no trouble from the organs which are means. The organ of seeing the one, and the organ of understanding the other, are in the same position. And neither is an addition; both are analysed out of the physical situation, as are the circle and its properties themselves.

IV

THE PRACTICAL GULF

§ 1. It is a far way from simple things like the circle or twice two, and from light being outside instead of inside our heads, to the stir of economic and social worlds, and to theology and religion. We are reluctant to leave the gulfs without seeing whether the same disposal of life and reason holds as far. "The theory that man saves himself has prevailed in decadent periods, in which there has been least evidence that he was accomplishing the task."[1] Had that been said only of theology, it would have meant that the field is unaffected by our ideas of it; but Professor Paterson was also writing of religion, and he says that devotion must feel its own power to be due to the power of the object. Hard saying though that seems, people here in Scotland receive it at once, knowing that nothing but zeal for the ground which united their fathers made it the ground which divided them. Schism came from asking how the power, or grace, of God must work; the conflicting answers conflicted because they took each other for derogatory. Far as that is from twice two, you can see that the causal question is the same. Ethics and morality do the like, their imperatives commanding obedience without a bribe.

Like the sensible world, the worlds of religion and morals are much upset by reason, when it starts to make sciences of them. The likeness was welcome, for

[1] Paterson, *The Nature of Religion*, p. 51.

it is a pleasure to have life thrive against reason, no matter where. But reason has ceased to upset anything in the sensible world, except to cultivate it, and give it more value. Why now is the likeness not so welcome? In Scotland because you knew your heritage too well to see John Knox walk with Hume, even if Kant had an arm in each. You wanted an authority as able to control reason as nature controls it. Where were the corresponding matters of fact for mitigating the havoc of ideas in the other worlds: economic, social, moral, and religious? Each has countless matters of fact, both practices and beliefs, but they vary with times and peoples, and have always been conflicting. It is not so long since the sensible world was torn in that way too, and part was always rejected as not nature's, but ours. Now that has ended; and, though there never was such a time for physical theories, they were never so readily surrendered. Nature controls our inventions, but do the other worlds?

Before nature came to such control, there were the two simple restraints, and they continue. One keeps reason busy collating facts for 'induction'. It is a familiar way of handling also the practices and the beliefs of those other worlds; and it has the value of all comparative study. But it mistakes its reach, if it then says what is good or true in them, let alone what we ought to do and believe. It is given to saying both, but here you had early warning from the futility reached by Hume, when, collating what mankind has approved, and what forbidden, he found the universal moral law to enjoin "whatever is useful or agreeable to ourselves or others". The most effective course of induction follows the evolution of beliefs and practices, and seeks their origin. That was thought a ground for judging their present value, and their origin was actually thought to answer the question of their authority. With you the answer was different, and so distinctive that abroad it is still called Scottish philosophy. It set up, for origin and authority, the other simple restraint on the vagaries of reason. Our physical senses control them in nature, were there not higher senses to control them in the other worlds? Reason itself was made a higher sense, when not a name for them all; and all were high for having no physical organ between them and their objects. But the analogy fails just where it was wanted: the authority of sensation is due to its organs, and for no other reason than that they are nature's.

Lord Gifford, on the other hand, looked not to our frame, but to the object, for the development of the heritage. The same control of our beliefs was to be reached for the moral and the religious worlds as for the physical one; and he pointed to astronomy and chemistry by way of model. It was at a time, fifty years ago, when the classical system of mechanics controlled the model, and when as yet there was no hint that the system was closing down nature too soon. But the discovery came by continuing to cultivate and systematise the phenomena, till there came the mechanical systems of quantum and relativity, which define the place of the classical one. To endow our frame with authoritative senses, with conscience for instance, is to close it down, as well as to close the worlds. Its distinctive power is to be open, following and discovering the power of the object; and the object needs no other authority than its own power. Its power in every sphere in which a mind finds itself has the same causal system as that by which light, number, and the circle produce beliefs. That is to say, the objects are themselves the fundamental or final cause, and the other two, mental and physical, are its means.

§ 2. But beliefs are not our main interest in any world. Do our other interests go into that account? They need knowledge of their objects, but are never due to it; they frequently defy it, and they are far from following the order of merit which we have approved. But, first, there is no confusion with knowledge. It is easily prevented on their common ground; for knowledge, too, is a good, and needs an appetite, and the object that satisfies one appetite does not satisfy another. Appetites are not loose, or not looser than our senses. The connexions of our senses are seen on the surface of our bodies; they are better seen in the brain, better still in the connexions of their objects to form the sensible world; but they are found at their best when they are joined by the other organs of knowing, and the sensible world becomes intelligible as the surface of nature. The same holds for all desires, their organs, and objects. Their objects deepen into spheres of interest that are systematic, whose forces work in us without excitement, and even without requiring to be felt. A man whose life is absorbed in some cause is more intelligible to himself and others than one who lives from hand to mouth; and he is the surer of himself, and the more calculable to others, if his cause is quite unselfish. He knows that it is nothing to him unless he loves and pursues it, and that its worth depends no more on his devotion to it than truth does.

There is no cause, therefore, in human nature why spirit should be less confident than its intellect, when it looks to its power and its future, nor why civilisation must crack and only science be sound. But, though rarely now for knowing, we still distrust the other high forms of conscious living, because of their origin and history. And it is not reform enough to start from the resulting power as from bone or steel; the power depends, as in them, on their elements. We have to do for appreciating, and behaving, what is now done for knowing. Even for knowing we retain an echo of the old distrust; the objects of sense having proved their purity and power, we no longer call them 'only phenomena'; but we call intelligible objects 'only concepts', though they are, or they grasp, the very laws of nature. The power of a concept is independent of its origin, and of its user. Its history as hypothesis, definition, equation, is the story of its effort to grasp some necessity in a world which remains unaffected by the grasp. There are necessities in the objects that we appreciate, and about which we behave, just as there are for grasping and believing; but we are apt to think that the necessities are ours, or shared between us and the world. Then, instead of the object being the fundamental cause, as it always is, we make it a product, and its two instrumental causes, left to themselves, become rivals of each other. That is what happens when, ignoring the object, we turn to our frame, its instincts, and other gifts, and their 'sublimation'.

If we oppose to that the man devoted to a cause, because of the cause, who is heedless how he came by it, he is met by two charges, that bring together all mental responding. The first is that his devotion is a product, and that the cause which he adopted was adapted to him, as other causes to other men. The charge is good in making all mental situations the same, whether the causes that they offer are noble or selfish, hard or easy, standing or fleeting, good or bad. Their adapting themselves to him is also always of the same sort, but the same sort as the adapting of light to eye and eye to light. The word is therefore misleading, for the parts adapted were never apart.

The other charge is the one that is now to occupy us

for the rest of the lecture. It accounts for the rise in quality of a man's devotion, in particular for the rise of his devotion to causes that call for sacrifice, and offer no reward.

§ 3. There we have the same conflict between reason and life, though, now being practical, it is not so easily set aside. About the sensible world it was set aside by two doublings, first of nature into apparent and real, and then of each into fact in nature and fact in mind. The practical quarrel appears to be different, but only because no doubling conceals it; for both its origin and the answer are the same. However uncompromising the worth of a cause, it causes nothing but through desire. The man who delights to further the welfare of others, or other causes, can sacrifice his own, as far as his life. But he has to keep his delight. Is it a return? Reason wants a common cause for all desires, and the return would do this; it would bring the high among the trafficking desires. But life will not have it, and even less for lowly living than for heroic. In the other conflict, sense and science give all to the object; they are satisfied, but the satisfaction is no return. The two quarrels keep together, till the practical one is offered terms that would never do for knowledge. For knowledge will have nothing to do with compromise. Their parallel before the break is important, because all mental life comes into it, and because this lets the break define itself.

Living for causes without thought of reward is like knowing in two respects: it meets no check till reason attacks it, and, if it yields, it loses its world and dies away. Contrast the heightening of one who receives a good that he knows to come from another's love, or delight, with his humiliation when he knows that it comes from a sense of duty, or a source more self-regarding. And when the doer, being less than lover, weighs his delight, he finds that it and his doing die away. But the full parallel can be seen best from the point where reason did actually try to be radical for the fields of knowledge, and the fields of conduct. Reason made the course of sensation fundamental for the fields of knowledge; all other knowledge of nature was to calculate the course. For the field of conduct the fundamental thing was to secure a course of 'desirable consciousness', calculated from birth to death; what could be more final? But the failure is the same. No step could be taken except on the way of life: as sensation has to give a sensory object, so desire has to rest on an object. Every desire for pleasure fails, unless it provides itself with an appetite for this or that; in the words of Bishop Butler, "a man may have all the self-love in the world and be miserable". That is the rule common to desires; it makes them one in the mental causal system, not in the way of traffic. Knowing and seeking are so far parallel.

Where does the parallel break in their working? Nowhere, if we are clear about the causal system which takes up all mental working. Whence then the break between free thought and free will, the one asserted, the other denied? It was because we put a portion of the system in control. By putting another portion in control there came the opposite result; it kept thought and will together by refusing freedom to thought as well. A simple kind of psychology did this by using past associations to cause the responses. There is a still simpler way of picking the portion. It says that thinking and willing are courses of events, and an event is never free, but completely caused or determined.

Determine, cause, and free, the three words have two

meanings apiece, the second one always being to accommodate mind. They bring out the mental causal system, and why it keeps thinking and willing together, and from what alike free. Let us connect each pair. Nature determines the same events by causes, or their physical necessity, which mind determines by grounds, or their logical necessity. But the aim of mind is to impose nothing, and only to find. It finds causes in nature because of the grounds that it has found there; and there are not two necessities but one, for the physical one is logical without remainder. Take next the two meanings of cause, efficient and final. They go farther into the system, for the fundamental cause takes both at once. It needs both for each effect, as we saw for a belief at any moment. Similarly, food is related to hunger in both characters; and the sight of poverty moves to pity. Finally, the two meanings of free go still farther into the system, by taking up the relation to the subject whereby he is free. The relation frees him from causes that do not persuade; and it goes down to every creature which does what it likes, fleeing or seeking.

But the freeing goes farther in man, and reaches the seeming break in the systematic parallel between believing and behaving. The word always means 'free from'. There is nothing more essential to the discovery of causes than that they form systems which can be freed or abstracted. But our concern is with concrete systems, of which the mental system is one, and in them with the meaning of being free. All structures, lifeless and living, are free to select; they select from what they are offered, and living structures go to seek what suits them. As free to select, and to seek, they are also bound; there is no freedom from necessity. Nor is there when we pass to the other positive meaning of the word: a mind's freedom to select and promote a cause by making it object. The cause has to satisfy. The kinds of thing that different creatures can make object mark their mental development, including that of man; but the characteristic of his mind is that he makes object of anything, and can pursue it, if he wants and has power enough. He can make his mind object, for instance, and approve or improve it. Whatever the difficulty, it lies in the object; the subject is free to deal with it if he can, provided he desires. If he can, there is nothing in his equipment, nor in his past, that prevents him, nothing but his lack of desire. He can make an object of the lack itself, and take measures, provided he desires. That is where the break in the parallel has been thought to come.

The question of desiring did not disturb the causal system that accounts for knowing and believing. The disturbance begins when knowledge, or anything else, has to be desired, and sacrifice has to begin. We seek to end one freedom by being bound to believe, but can or ought the freedom of our desires look for a binding so desirable? We used to try and harmonise our faculties to make them fit for knowing nature proper. Nature, speaking for herself, has taken over their work without any question of harmonising them, or of deferring to them. But can or ought our desires, far more chaotic, find their ordering from a corresponding authority?

It used to be argued that they could not, now only whether they should. The old mistake is important. Since we never but do the thing that pleases us most, all things considered, it was argued that we always act for our pleasure. But the thing that pleases us need not be our own, nor anybody's pleasure. The mistake is important, if we suppose that the thing's value, which

G

is its power, depends on the pleasure that we feel, or hope to feel, from it. We never make the mistake when the thing is a truth; it satisfies us only because we believe that it satisfies fact. There we are saved because we set the truth in a world. When a man makes an object of his pleasure, to which other objects can be means, he sets himself a little world that its values may control him. If there is a break in the parallel, therefore, it is not from can but from should.

§ 4. There the break does not come at once when we ask: Should our spheres of action look for worlds to control them, as nature controls our beliefs and inventions? The very standards that have been set look inventions. Think of the social orders, the economic systems, the number of religions, to say nothing of the aims and styles in the history of art and letters. The inventions look conventions, convenient for our equipment of desires. They seem to defer to our equipment, instead of it and them deferring to independent worlds. The peoples who lived under them accepted them, suffering them, and suffering for them. But there is the question of their power: ought we to submit to them, as our beliefs and inventions willingly do to nature and the number system?

The difference and the difficulty concern the 'willingly'; otherwise the situation is the same. When nature was little known, the number system little invented, and beliefs and inventions in them were imperfect, there was no miraculous way of using nature as a standard; the beliefs and inventions had to discover it by the trials and errors which developed them. It is the situation common to all our spheres of action. When we say 'to my mind', or 'everyone to his taste and opinion', we do not ask the standard to agree. But we tend that way the more we find ourselves unwilling. Let us take the trying case, the moral world. It tries the truth of our mental causal system, because it is a world whose rough places require not softening, but a sense of duty, and because its laws are not followed if they are merely obeyed; they have to commend themselves to the doer.

If we break from the parallel, it is not because we do not want a moral standard as clear as nature is, when it grades our inventions and beliefs; it is because we also want it to defer to our equipment of likes and dislikes. The frankest break would make prudence the all-comprehending law and virtue. No one likes to do that, because it borders on selfishness. Butler's way looks better, because he was preaching to prove moral law unbending: "when we sit down in a cool hour," we cannot see our duty "till we are convinced that it will be for our happiness, or, at least, not contrary to it". Like nature the moral world requires inferior grades of work, but it would degrade itself by compromising. Compromise, however, the 'conciliation of egoism and altruism', came to be thought the problem for every member. The conciliation was, first, by a better counting of pleasures, next by grading them for happiness into higher and lower, seeing that men, who know both, will not exchange a high quality for any quantity of a lower, and, finally, by subjecting them all to the inevitable course of civilisation, and its inevitable rhythms. There followed the notion that civilisation is a veneer, and must crack under stress. What bond of loyalty, and finally the herd instinct itself, did not melt into primitive appetites with the pressure of distress?

That was the gulf to be negotiated, and first by moralising the natural man without letting him know.

The picture does not hold even for the brutes, and a selfish world would be about as weird as the sensible one which reason wanted to put in our heads. But why should it be reason again that insists on a gulf? Because it confounds the living and the correlation lines, but also more simply. It thinks that our complex causal system, being complex, is superficial to a simple one. Two grounds look so good that we all but take them for granted. A system consists of factors, and a factor of elements; are not the elements causes on their own account? Are they not the foundations of the system, even the material of which the system is built? Besides, when objects cause responses, they do it by persuading, not compelling; but responses are events; are they not compelled by a necessity of which they are unaware? We shall see in the next lecture why both grounds are bad. For the rest of the present one we shall continue the parallel with knowing and believing, in order to follow the course of the practical gulf that reason did set against the way of life. As the knowledge gulf was said to be between reason and sense, this one was said to be between reason and passion, the word passion denoting desires, as well as emotions of every sort.

The living solution was the same: reason became 'servant of the passions'. There life appeared to degrade reason, as it was degraded in being servant of the sensible world, which it had criticised, and even condemned. Again there was no real degradation, for reason is never a competitor with the passions, any more than with sense. It helps to settle their conflicts by nothing but by serving those passions that can command it; the strongest passion always wins. That is no more than the tautology about our always doing what pleases us best. But there comes the check. The sensible world is enforced by the whole of nature, whose foundations have been discovered through the very conflicts of sense. But a world of rights and duties has to be armed with sanctions to inspire a wise prudence by fear, and a wiser prudence by reward; for sloth can evade them, as well as passion defy them. And a moral world asks for more than the wisest prudence.

Reason has therefore to do more than explore the desirable world. It has the far harder question of convincing minds to make it theirs. The 'age of reason' which put the question, and began the answers, did both in revolt from the view of Hobbes that, when a man seeks the good of others, it is for his own, in particular for the pleasant sense of eminence and power. But that was merely the extreme answer to a question that seemed good: whether the desirable world has to conform with our equipment of desires by being broken to them, as the pure light of nature was thought broken to our senses. Beginning once more with world and minds apart, the answers followed the analogy which made sensations impressions. All disputes divided themselves into two isms according as one agent or the other was given control in the mutual transaction. Minds were wax to the social world, their sources of passion being, like sense, the receivers and moulders. The sources united themselves by a conscience, as our senses by common sense; conscience was "an imitation within us of the government without us". Though putty at first, the wax became adamant with age; a stronger civilisation could break but not recast it, though a genial one might soften it in time, and reform it. The analogy could go on indefinitely, and come to nothing that would answer the simplest question. As the simplest question for knowing is how a sensation has truth, the simplest for doing is how a liking has right.

The answer again is to take the actual beginning: here a restless little being differentiating the offered world, social as well as physical, exploring its values, and making himself at home. As when a thought doubts its truth it compares itself with nothing, but one object with another, so, when a passion hesitates, it compares itself with nothing, but the worth of one object with the worth of another.

When at any age a man seeks to know himself, he finds that he has to infer himself; he has to ask what he would feel or do in this event or that adventure. The conscious working of his mind is the active outcome of a very complex equipment that he does not feel; it is like the felt part of a physical thing. Tracing his mind back he finds that, instead of ever collecting itself, it has differentiated and expanded itself by differentiating and expanding its world. Its primitive appetites and impulses, and its very senses, differentiate themselves in that way, and no other. If it seems that there at last we come on our native gifts, and see the world playing on them, and them seeking the world, we are mistaken; we have lost minds and their worlds, and are left with organs and their stimuli. The working and the developing of a mind are to be understood only from its working with objects, and in spheres for whose values it is organised into love, pride, ambition, understanding, all its equipment. Plenty of truths, as well as analogies, can be found when the fact is disregarded; they are familiar in the language of the education, or other handling, of minds. But such truths have to admit among them the one which Law of the *Serious Call* satirised in the means by which man was "wheedled into the dignity and honour of standing upright". There was a time when man went on all-fours. The first law-makers saw how useful he would be to them, if they might have the use of his hands for their drudgery. "The difficulty was how to raise him up. But some philosophers found that, though he crept on the ground, yet he was made up of pride, and that, if flattery took hold of it, he might easily be set on his legs. Making use of this bewitching engine, they extolled the excellence of his shape above other animals, and told him what a grovelling thing it was to creep on all-fours."

§ 5. The philosophers of the age of reason went farther. They would enlighten every man about himself, and yet expect him to serve the best. He would come to anchor on two harmonies, one in human nature, the other in the nature of the world. To be upright, and to be kindly, are 'original joy', whereas guilt lives in fear, and malice in bitterness. That harmony in human nature made a man who cares for others care thereby for himself. And the harmony in the world was greater still; for there a man, by caring well for himself, cared well for others. On that comfort political economy began, and politics came to be founded. In the words of Adam Smith, "every individual necessarily labours to render the annual revenue of society as great as he can. He generally indeed neither intends to promote the public interest, nor knows how much he is promoting it. He intends only his own gain, and he is in this, as in many other cases, led by an invisible hand to promote an end which was no part of his intention." But the hand of God has not been so flattering to the old Adam in us, and requires the other harmony at least. You may have noticed how often the phrase 'men of good will' is being brought into international negotiations where every country is to gain. The old reliance on reason or harmony saw the same within a spirit, where the good will was called benevolence, and was persuading self-love not to be narrow. But the ground, instead of raising or creating the spirit, was in danger of lowering it; a high spirit could only debase itself by dwelling on the harmony. And epicures, reaching after the pleasures of a devoted spirit, used to find themselves stoics instead. But the fatal gulf is the failure and refusal of reason to occupy a ground of pure sacrifice; for a spirit knows and proves itself by nothing else. The question how it is created had to pass from seeking grounds that would be good enough, to seeking causes that would be strong enough.

The answers were still from our parts and the forces playing on them. The best head can be as callous as the best heart can be unwise. In the spirit, head and heart are at one, not less confident in themselves than sure of each other; the heart has no doubt of the head, nor the head of the heart. But the spirit can be wanting while the two are at one. Then, when the day of trial searches the heart, and finds it to fail, the head will find excuses for the heart, and the heart will believe them. They will seem reasons, and the small voice of con-science, which comes when they quarrel, will be stilled. Our fathers gave the voice great power among the ingredients; but it is only the protesting of the spirit, which when high makes no sound, as also none when absent, but only when it finds itself to fail. Finally, let handiwork be added to the communion of head and heart; we are then in the communities in which we work out our lives; have we now got the spirit? Family, factory, profession, village, nation, they all create a common spirit, and also make themselves causes.

There is devotion as pure without such machinery; and, if we take an instance of the two kinds under stress, it will be seen why the causal system has always to supersede co-operation, and alone makes it intelligible.

Families offer the best instance of a community spirit, but, on account of the late stress, let us use the national one. The national spirit is love, not pride, of country. As in families, it is eager to see beauty and every other value, and so begets pride; but, far from its offspring being always a support, it is always a danger. In father, lover, patriot, love falls only to sorrow when it is disappointed, and love thrives in sorrow; but pride, when disappointed, is angry and betrays the inversion. The force of a spirit, like every force, is measured only by its fruit. The fruits of the national spirit are belief, emotion, and conduct, but the force of the spirit can be measured from conduct alone, and in proportion to the resistance that it has met and overcome; it is measured by the sacrifice. When the war invited a man to enlist for a good that he would never see, he had to feel the opposing forces in him at their height, and rise above them without looking for their downfall. There was nothing in him that the call did not rouse. In some men sacrifice could win with little effort, in others lose with less, but consider the mind where the rousing was of forces that gathered in conflict: hopes and fears, pride and shame. Their conflict required a single object, and a single subject to settle it. When two conflicting opinions contend in you, it is you who ponder them on a common measure that you adopt. When your right hand and your left pull against each other, you pull both, and your left, though the weaker, can win as you choose. The single object, the call to serve, took this deliberate freedom past a man's equipment of likes and dislikes, and forced him to face his power to surrender. His vacillating responses went into the causal system equally with the steadiest. When he felt bound, it was never by a cause that he did not make a ground. The value which made it a ground had to satisfy him, as has the validity of any ground of belief. Consent is like assent, though consent can involve so great a sacrifice, and assent needs none as a rule.

Finally, from the instance, have we any support for the error that ideas are substitutes? It was always clear that only our behaviour in stressful times could prove the strength of our love of country. But that did not lessen our confidence before the times came. We could even take an increasing pleasure in contemplating ourselves in ugly conditions of increasing severity. Were these not substitutes for the actual ones, to be in which is only a horror? But, when the call to serve made a man contemplate himself in them once more, there was no difference except in the selection of horrors, which was no longer aesthetic. Nor was there much difference when he went, and they selected themselves; his images in pondering were of them as they became to his senses, not imitations that prevented him with a horror still too feeble. The question is not there.

It is no concealing of the real thing and its horror that gives concern to philosophers, but a concealing of the subject from himself. When a cool hour wakes him to the enmeshing of his mind by the communities in which he has grown up, what can he do in reason but adjust the nets to his advantage? In life he does not; and we may pass to the other instance of devotion; let the net now be thrown by one of the communities in which he has grown up. He behaves like a lover on whom propinquity has played the trick of making a maiden unique, who at first was no more adorable than the rest. If he remembers, it will make no difference; his eye will stay with his heart. But let his love measure itself against fears or losses, and suppose first that he grudges. Then his eye will pierce the glamour that his heart threw over his head, and he will see her, as he saw her at first, no better than she appears to others. Some who declined the call to fight could feel that they had risen to clearer air, where they could love the whole world. But let him refuse to measure his love, then, the more he has lost, the more he will seek to give; the men who served are keen to raise the country itself to the clearer air. And, finally, let a candid friend convince him that there is nothing better in this Blumine than many another, he will end by saying that he had rather be devoted to whom or whatsoever than live for himself. There we have the fundamental fact. The fact is that we love wherever we can; we begin with the spirit. When selfish we are not as we were born, but debased. The circuiting, the centring on oneself, does not come from arrested development, but from a twist, which reverses the outward look natural to a subject, wresting the pleasure from the value of his objects and actions, in order that he may savour it better. It would defeat itself, as in the tedious minds of the psychological novel; but selfish minds are not so paralysed.

The philosophers of the nineteenth century had no need to argue against the self-seeking harmony in human nature and politics; its own expounding had been enough. But, especially in Germany, it had been succeeded by the universal harmony, called idealism, where even a criminal, by infinite reflexion into his proper being, might make himself willing to mount the scaffold (Hegel). That sent other philosophers to the other extreme, where reason saw life to be all a trick. Worse than the work of heart on head there was the work of nature in blinding minds, converting pains into wants, and their mere removal into gladness. At first they thought the trick too old and deep to be countered, because nature had begun to play it so long ago on the minds of the lowest creatures; in fact, had invented minds for its own end. And it is true that every sort of creature is passionate for a good that it will never enjoy; it sacrifices with a reckless and ridiculous zeal for its offspring and its kind. Their successors turned the gloom into the reason for leaving it. Let man "drain to the dregs the cup of disillusionment, the cup of knowledge. . . . Humanity, mankind, sympathy, pity, all these things in the long run do nothing but bring man to mediocrity. Europeans, by virtue of their growing morality, believe in all innocence and vanity that they are rising higher and higher, whereas the truth is that they are sinking lower and lower, through cultivating the virtues that are useful to a herd, and repressing the other and contrary virtues which give rise to a new, higher, stronger, masterful race of men" (Nietzsche).

Our English writers have been more pleasant about it. They take it like the lover, who is glad that he is no longer capable of pure reason. If nature makes it pleasant for the heart, why should the head refuse the snare? Had we not better follow nature, and learn the simple trick of forgetting, which we learn in the family. There we are caught when our heads are soft, and we have no memories; parents being the fountain of pleasure and pain, we learn to please them, till, instead of pleasing them for a reward, it is a reward to please them; we grow anxious for their good, instead of keeping them anxious for ours. The doctrine did not come from perverse heads, but from the men who directed social beliefs in England for several generations. Mill and Spencer were not men to base sacrifice on a trick, if they had not found the same deceit in the simplest mental life. They found it everywhere, and they saw that there could be no compromise between the high view of life and the low view of reason. It was no matter that the high view is the practical one. They knew how good it is for the world that every man takes a high view of his own will. He feels free to choose, and can therefore feel remorse, believing that he should have chosen otherwise; but they believed that he could not; they thought that logic was against him, and that the value of his error could not make it true; nature had only to let him be ignorant of his brain, and therefore of the causes of his action. The deception was easy to believe, because they saw nature play us a trick more amazing. Did she not make us forget the structure of our eyes, look through them as through windows, and see the light to be in front instead of behind them? It was the same trick for conduct as for knowledge; nature made mental life flatter itself in ignorance.

The present century, which has removed the more amazing deception, as it seemed, by the advance of physics, has challenged the other one through the war. The very unselfishness, that the call demanded, inspired many men like a release. Wundt, whose long life had been spent in every field of philosophy, saw in the mind of his people "a fact of more value than all philosophy", because Kant and Nietzsche were being reconciled in an instant spirit, and not in a far and doubtful future after many measures. In France it was biology that took the shame, confessing that its notion of human nature had been depressing and debasing. The evolution of energy and life was rewritten to a climax, where it would be quite in the course of nature if the spirit of France were to carry its devotion and endurance from war to peace. Among ourselves there was no such belief in ideas that we blamed them for anything; but the new spirit was so simple and confident, it seemed the natural thing, and our writers fell with one accord on the social system for assuming we are selfish, and making us unnatural. They had no such accord, indeed, when they faced the mind to come. In one book that became popular, man might be weaned in a single generation; we had only to alter the social basis from force to power: from the force of reason, which is natural to men, and selfish, to the power of emotion for distant ideals, which is natural to women.[1] At the same time a deeper optimist gave natural human nature ten thousand years before the improvement may be considerable. "There is no law of progress, but there is no law which forbids progress. If there has been perceptible progress in the last two thousand years, the improvement may be considerable in the next ten thousand, a small fraction, probably, of the whole life of the species."[2] Now the future of minds is more questionable than ever; I mean their future on the earth. If the war was won to save democracy, it did less than nothing to save democracy from itself; and itself has always been the cause of its downfall. The sanguine prophets forgot that the war was a cause involving so many causes, and had the strength of so many social forces at their height. The nation was living to keep alive: there was a return to the simple values and virtues of a people at one. But the civil wars for comfort and luxury are more flagrant than ever, and from causes that the old harmony cannot extinguish. And the personal revolt from tradition knows itself for a new age of reason. Though mainly negative it has the

---

[1] B. Kidd, *The Science of Power.*
[2] Inge, *The Philosophy of Plotinus*, ii. p. 223.

advantage of feeling enlightened, and is willing, instead of afraid, to ask what we are living for. We know the answer for the life of knowledge. It is the same for the rest of life.

But at first we are struck by the contrast. We agree about the scale of real values in the world very well. And we know that the highest among them are without limit; they call for no economy; the more one man has, the better for all; what is gotten is nowhere lost. But when we look at their force, the scale is reversed, as if the force of a value must be the inverse of its excellence. We know no such weakness among beliefs; inferior knowledge, however vivid, yields to any better that is understood. But we assign our appreciating, striving, and enduring, not to the worth of their object, but to gifts of mind or body. The desires and values, which are felt, would be joint products of a stimulus and a structure, both unfelt. The explanation would go back to birth, because the structure of the gift grows by the exercise to which it is excited. And so we have the dispute whether the gift needs a mind to carry it, or whether glands, blood, and brain are carriage enough. It is as if the physical and mental means, the first and third causes, were wrangling for command of my belief in arithmetic.

For the situation is in fact identical with that in knowing. Truth does not command belief until it is understood; it does not compel the effort of understanding. The highest values have the same hold. I mentioned the kind of man who is most calculable. In times of peace, and common affairs, we know lives as heroic as from the war, and they are as clear and confident as from science. The thing to which they are devoted has a worth which compels them, because it is what it is, because it is independent of them, not because they appreciate or desire it; just as a thing which they believe is true in itself, and not because they are convinced. As in active life, so in art and letters; good work is best when the author loses himself, and the object has possession; and that is also best for himself.

V

OUR RELUCTANCE TO LEAVE THE GULFS

§ 1. WE are loth to leave the solid harbour of the head to launch ourselves on a mind's own place. The place looks abstract, because it is nowhere; and it carries its brain instead of spreading to be carried. Since, like blue, no feelings are qualities of the brain, we had rather put them in an actual or metaphorical dimension there, and see mind working with marionettes. "What exactly was passing in his head? If he acquiesced, could I trust him? The soul of man is well screened by barriers of bone; only through the eyes can its light be seen, and one of Ghaib's was sightless. Never before or since have I been so eager a thought-reader." No one would alter that. The description is a completion, with neither analysis nor accretion to speak of. It therefore conveys the mental condition of the two men better to everyone than the best analysis to any one. It is wrong only if mistaken for an explanation; it is not an imperfect, nor even a didactic explanation; it is just the best conveyance.

Some years after the electrical structure of the atom had been opened, a physical chemist wondered why so many had believed that, because matter resolves into dust, a dust particle should consist of dust (G. N. Lewis). There had been plenty of ground for presuming the kinetic theory of gases to be final; there was the raggedness of atomic weights and specific heats, and what were temperatures but measures of chaos?

The ideal explanation of nature became its reduction to matter and motion. Why was it so convincing, the completion by push and pull, and sought where it could not be found? Because it satisfies reason? But it is nature that we want to satisfy. We forgot that reason has grown in mankind, like every other appetite. We hanker after the explanation; the nearer we reach it the better we think our grasp, no matter of what; we impose it on the conflict of ideas in a mind, of impulses there, and of social forces. When the explanation fails, we seem to have a mystery on our hands? There is no mystery about the origin of the appetite. The only work we ever do in nature is push and pull; we turn a switch, the rest is nature's. Must not nature continue our work by working as we? That is the origin. What happens when we discover our arrogance?

An appetite tends to remain, and we find it a reason. To explain is to simplify; what can be simpler than push and pull? But only to us; in nature both are far from simple; they are the problem. They are the appearance of countless electrical contacts, which, in the perceptible sense, make no contact at all. Old as it is, the appetite then surrenders; reason will not satisfy itself unless nature is satisfied. All other kinds of thought are as devoted to the object, and are as free to follow it against their past.

Not all, one might think; explanation may yield at once to explanation, but sense-perception will not yield. An astronomer sees the stars as he saw them when a boy, for all his better knowledge; if you convince a man that they twinkle only in his head, his eyes will not believe you. Is it because reason, though old, remains free as yet, while perception, far older, is bound? On the contrary, it is the object that the astronomer and all men follow; it expands into the situation that absorbs the stimulus and the other means of knowing it; the means come into the object, they never correct it.

There is another useful instance in the grasp of other minds, which nature asks of many creatures. They can watch the purpose and the stealth of one another, and know themselves for rivals after the same thing, in a total scene that includes their several distances. The distances, like the spoil, are in the scene for each, which guides them all. The 'for' is neither a distance, nor a contact, nor the diffusion of their seeing over the scene; it marks off the place of each mind as having neither space, nor any other common medium, nor any likeness, between it and the world. That is only the surface fact, which therefore explains nothing about itself. But to dwell on it is enough against our inertial reluctance. We are reluctant to cross by this 'for' to a mind's own place, without carrying a spatial or other physical setting to hold together thought and its objects.

Our reluctance is less from habit when it resists the mental causal system on two grounds that I mentioned. The system consists of factors, the factors of elements, and the elements have a system of their own. Is not the object-system superficial to theirs? And the object produces by persuading, not compelling; but its products, the beliefs and behaviour, are events; are they not therefore compelled by forces beyond the knowledge of the subject? On these two grounds does not the object-system analyse into a simpler, from which it came? No, the elements and the forces are extracted from the world that we set before us. When they protest that they existed before every setting, and are independent of it, the setting not only agrees, but gives that for its intention; it is the one physical reason for mind coming to life.   To lower creatures, as to man, objects are so free to show their power that their being ideas, or known, need never come into account. When brought in, their being known is resented as an addition that must involve some conforming with our means of knowing. But that never happens; the only conforming is between organs and stimuli, and no one calls it conforming.

If that is clear, we can see the cause of our reluctance; we are confining everything real to a place in time, dating the system of phenomena from their beginning, as we confined everything real to space. If our reason was unwilling to make space a factor, instead of leaving it master, till we remembered that the reason is ours, it is more unwilling still to reduce the rank of time: let space go into nature, instead of nature into space, but surely nature goes into time, not time into nature. And so the arrival of phenomena, and then of the sensible world, which analyses for us into all nature, known and unknown, appears an eddy on the infinite stream. To that reason the intention in all knowing looks a trick: the freeing of phenomena from being felt, and of nature from being known. But the reason, remembering that it is ours, and therefore part of the trick, easily loses its arrogance, and returns to the reason displayed by the object. There the truth and the error of the infinite stream, which were always on offer, have been noticed at last.

Our correction by reason in nature extends to the other worlds, theoretical and practical. When nature looked alien and equivocal, as well as chaotic, the best of it used to be extracted for rational; was nature not the equal in reason to geometry, and the other orderly worlds of reason's own creation? Now the order can be reversed; we can compare them with nature. As nature is easily distinguished from our grasp of it, so those

created worlds are standing critics of the institutions
and the sciences by which we grasp them. It is each
world that determines its variety and history, and the
value of our efforts in it. The advances and the failures
of civilisation are graded, like physical inventions.
Between nature and those other worlds which control our creations, that is the likeness.

The contrast between them is more striking: they
depend on man for their working, and nature does not.
But the contrast is not negative, as we shall see from
our articulation with nature, which is not merely by
our organs of sense, but by our organs of understanding.
Nature is mathematical, and the organ by which we
grasp it is one of those very worlds that need man
for their working.

The contrast with nature does not prevent the likeness from bringing them all into the single causal
system for mental responses and pursuits. The theories
which restrict our conduct by the character and complexity of the means, and by the meanness of its beginnings, have all had their like in the theories of
knowledge. There is no more ignorance nor arrogance
in resolving and acting than in thinking and believing.
Yet it has been the advocates of free thought who
especially argue a bound will. They see phenomena to
be the very flowering of nature, but they see the lilies
to be idle, because they do nothing but through their
values, and values are only for minds. The high place
on which nature has placed our minds would be that
of the constitutional governor who called himself a
rubber-stamp. We should consider the lilies to better
purpose than that. The distrust of our power to do has
no other ground than the former distrust of our power
to know; it was because the power is a product. So far

as knowing is concerned, the quarrel between flesh and spirit has been settled. Nature has settled it by flattering both sense and understanding beyond their expectation.

And our practical power has grown with our grasp. But, the more deeply mind was proving its hold, the more it was finding itself dependent, and nature deaf and indifferent. The advance of our power to know was putting our power to do in retreat; for to know is to know law, and law is inexorable. It was a curious result, even contradictory, due to taking nature as our rival, and not as part of our lives. Was there not worse than a fall in prestige if "nature is only governed by obeying her"? It was a bitter fruit about itself that mind was bringing back from nature. But with its ripening, the bitterness was lost. For nature, by sweeping itself clear of mental elements, finally made its escape from producing them, which had been its old obligation. It has no elements of which minds, nor any sensations, might be compounded.

As knowing finds in nature means and object, and meets nothing at any depth that protests, so it is with appreciating, desiring, and seeking. Their organic means are distinguished from their objects, as our means of seeing are from light. Light exists only for a mind, and for a mind that has eyes; it is neither in my mind nor in my body, but what and where it proves itself to be. So it is with the objects of other mental acts than knowing: with beauty, for instance, food, and fishing. The kind of object does not matter; its force depends on our sense of its value. The force of tears is like the force of an argument; and, like that of meat and drink, its power is all in its appeal. It is by nothing but such individual persuasion that a whole people reflects its environment, physical and social, in taste, belief, and behaviour, as if it were moulded and herded.

When we look with suspicion on the organic sources of desire, emotion, and energy, it is as once we looked on the organs of sense in ourselves and other creatures. A recent enthusiast writes that "the rise and fall of Napoleon followed the rise and fall of his pituitary gland". Let it be true, and say more than that a nut, working loose, can wreck the whole machine; what then? There would be no correction to make on Napoleon's autobiography, had he written one. If his pituitary, from being means, had also become known to him, his knowledge would very likely have made a difference, but the difference would still have been determined by the objects to which he was devoted. Whether he sought them steadily or not, keenly or not, and selfishly or not, he was driven by nothing that he did not value. Value and truth rest entirely on their objects; if there is no value but for desire, there is also no appearance but for sense, and no truth but for thought. If the physical means of desire are mainly unknown, so are those of sense and thought; and their discovery comes into the object, and qualifies no truth nor value but through it.

§ 2. If it is disappointing that the better we know nature for itself, the more we find it as for minds, the disappointment would be greatest for omniscience. But, if the nature that we know is as for minds, and ours hardly count, does it not require us to find their substitute in omniscience?

Not even to find that kind of duplicate. It was natural to begin by copying a supreme mind from ours, and idealising it, and then to take ours for copies of it, or products, or reproductions. The same was taken as between universal nature and nature as each knows it, until the relations within the nature that we know

were developed. Their unity or system has expanded
as far as universal nature. The discovery was made by
following the everyday world which proves itself. Our
everyday minds have just the same ground; and it is
just as wrong, as it was there, to keep the opposite
course, which depreciates them, and supposes a supreme
one to which ours may approximate, or cannot.

When we turn from nature to our own minds, it
is from object to subject, not as to a residue, but to
seeing and knowing their objects, liking and dis-
liking them, doing and yielding. They are felt as
functions, not merely as so many varieties of feeling.
They therefore include their unfelt means. Doing and
knowing are never confounded in practice, for doing
changes the course of things, and knowing keeps them
as they are, changing only its grasp. But we as good
as confound the two if we make them varieties of a
common stuff, called, say, consciousness. Mental power
of every kind would lie in the stuff, and the difference
would lie in its kinds; our power to change things would
be one kind of feeling, and our power to know them just
another. Yet, in knowing and in doing, work that is at
first laboured and felt becomes easy and unfelt. We
live consciously, or in the light, only the disturbing and
the directive parts. The rest goes into the dark, and
works better there than if we still had to spell or feel, and
were able to take nothing for granted. Many generations went to produce a child's physical inheritance,
and its mental inheritance cannot be less complex.
Consider how easily a child's voice follows its ear, and
follows better, and how complex the mechanism is
that has grown to be the tool of so barely felt a control. Ages have gone to produce the rapidity with
which an infant reaches, in a year, the thought and
conduct of common sense, yet the rapid growth is

conscious, and is continuous with the slowing growth that follows.

It is more important to include the unfelt means than to say whether they are mental or physical. The two have no quarrel; they are always like the two subordinate causes, or means, that we had for a belief. When the means have the properties of therefore, or twice two, their work is not physical; when the 'cerebration' is discovered, nothing will be corrected in the mental description. But the difference between them can appear to aggravate the quarrel at the parting of nature and minds; for, when a mind loses consciousness, what has it kept? It carries nothing out of nature, when it goes, as do ghosts and other impostors. Nature keeps the colours and sounds, as well as the shapes of things; it keeps the changes that we make in them, as well as their own; it keeps all except their being seen, heard, sought, created. In the absence of mind it does not claim to keep them any more than to keep living organs in the absence of life. It excludes mind as it excludes life.

But nature excludes life as a cause over and above the organs. Even a vitalist has said that life is always effect, and never cause. Should not mind go with life, and leave all real business to the physical means?

The question forces us from the analogy with bodily life to a mind's own life, which is to be subject. The ground that a mind can be unconscious is the same as that nature is more than phenomena. The ground is not that we can put out the light of consciousness, and still put two and two together in the dark; the unfelt constitution of the subject is discovered from its felt work, just as unfelt nature is discovered from its work in phenomena, and from nothing else. A mind grasps itself as if a thing, we shall see, without having to import anything unfelt. The grasp admits three questions that it cannot answer. One is the deep structure of the felt collection of qualities and faculties in a self. The second is the correlative physical system. These two have to answer for the power of mind. The third question is the mind's procedure in making object. A number of questions develop from it that define our place in the world. They will appear in the course of answering the question how and how far mind can penetrate nature and make it intelligible. We shall now consider what it is to make intelligible, or explain, as well as how the mental causal system is entrenched.

§ 3. Reason makes things intelligible in the sense that the eye makes them visible, and the hand makes them hard. And, though eye and ear grasp their object with ease, and need no learning, while understanding is laborious, the difference is one of degree. There is a complexity in music and design which it needs pains from ear and eye to comprehend. Sense comprehends one kind of object, understanding another, but they both comprehend, as well as apprehend. An object of sense is felt as one, though it is many, because the factors are felt in connexion with one another. We begin to understand both it and them, when we analyse it into them and their connexions.

The mass of object that nature pours on us becomes less chaotic as the chance connexions in it fall away. It begins to be intelligible, for, as the word means, the factors can now be read or gathered from one another; they therefore determine one another, and can be inferred from one another. All knowledge is of such a determining. No question is good that does not seek it. But, so far, we do not call it an explanation, unless we call a sign-post an explanation.

The chaos clears into a community of things, till there comes nothing in the world that will not name and classify, and nothing that cannot raise an expectation and give rise to a rule. Under those three notions every one of us can comprehend without any limit; they are thing, class, and law. In the same empirical way a mind learns to comprehend itself under the three heads. For, like a thing, it has properties, powers, and adventures; the properties and powers can all be arranged into genera and species; and the adventures exhibit regularities which can be analysed for experiment and made exact enough to be called the laws of the mind.

But still we are said not to explain, and for several reasons. One of them is clear and good. A thing groups its properties, a class groups its members, and a law its instances, so that they become signs, and determine one another. But the factors are only coincident in the group; they merely happen together; they still determine one another as signs only, and not because they are necessary to one another. In an explanation we look for necessity. The several reasons reduce to this one, if they are good reasons.

But they have been so confusing, even to physics, that it has given up the word, and says that it never explains but only describes. Explaining, however, does two things which describing does not profess to do. It analyses not in any way but in a way that discovers and measures dependence. And, when it employs hypotheses, it is for this purpose; they are not, as in description, analogies or metaphors. These two professions are too important to lose; but, if we speak of explaining, we have to remove the confusions that never infect the notion of describing. One is due to the use of the same word for a didactic and a real explanation. A didactic explanation is by means of any kind, and especially by analogies, its purpose being to bring new knowledge within the knowledge of this or that mind. A real explanation is not concerned with the minds either that get or that give it. Things explain themselves; and, to keep that clear, we may assume that the question always is: How do things explain themselves to a man who knows them perfectly? This is the explanation that we seek. What are the confusions about it which are avoided in describing? We are liable to three.

One is the confusion of unity with simplicity and of generality with abstractness. To explain is "to derive a variety from a single principle" (Kant); but the principle has to keep the differences; it unites the variety by uniting them. "The soundest kind of explanation consists in the resolution of the complex into the simple" (Venn); that is also true, for so every theorem is demonstrated; but in a theorem none of the complexity is lost. Then there were the notions that, if nature is one, it consists of one stuff, that it is more perfect the simpler it is, and more regular the less the variety; the simplest of all things was the soul. From all such we are kept free by the term description, for describing dwells on variety and complexity.

We are more liable to a second error; it is that, in order to explain, we have to translate. From this comes the notion about the final terms of explanation that they are themselves unexplained; knowledge would deposit them like a dead wall round itself. Sometimes the only reason given for saying that we do not know things as they are in themselves, or in reality, is that we cannot translate them any farther. But, so far as a thing explains, it is explained. If there is a remnant which explains nothing it is not explained, but it has to prove that it exists; and it cannot do that and remain idle.

What is the cause of this presuming that to explain is
to translate? We explain all physical change and state
by translating them into motions; that might well be
cause enough without reflection. But the serious cause
lies wherever we leave obscurity between ideas and
their objects. We saw that it hides how an idea can
be true; now it hides how an object can be real. When
the real object appears to escape all pursuit, leaving its
ghost, or outline, in our grasp, it is because we look at
our hands and say: they can hold the forms of things
but not their matter, their essence but not their existence, their truth but not their reality, what is common
to each with others, but never each by itself.

Nature would have one way of determining, knowledge another. That is the third confusion, and we are
so liable that it is often made the sole reason for saying
that science describes and does not explain. But are
there not the two kinds of determining and the two
kinds of necessity? The question is from failing to connect thought and thing. And the answer is that science
pursues law, and, having found a law, does not then ask
for some force to which the law is due. The forces which
it finds, if it calls them forces, are part of the fact that
is caught in the law. It looks always behind law, but
always for another law more general. And there is only
the logical kind of necessity. That is why we can speak
of physical necessity; it is because nature is regular.
We can therefore mean the same thing by determine,
when we say that nature determines the facts, and again
that thought determines them. Everything in nature is
determined by other things; it means that all there is
regular; it means nothing more. And we merely add
that the regularity has been found, when we ascribe to
thought any part of their determining. It is always
there to be found, imperfectly as well as perfectly.

§ 4. Therefore, it is not derogatory to say of minds, as of nature, that everything in them is determined and necessary. If it sounds disparaging, we probably betray our mechanical prejudice. But, giving that up, seeing that nothing is rational that is not regular, we may still hesitate to follow the example of physics. Does not the utter difference between mind and matter deserve a difference in the kind of explanation? And so we leave mind to the old way of explaining its actions; we still equip the notions of thing, class, and law with force, when we apply them to a mind. As a thing it is said to manifest the indwelling force of a self with a store of energy. It has its laws, but it can disobey them, and prove its freedom. Or, instead of storing the energy in a self, we distribute it among the classes of mental action, to each class a faculty: hope contends with fear, conscience with desire, thoughts co-operate with emotions, every kind can unite or fight with every other. This is no other than the old physical kind of explanation.

It would be better to say of oneself, and every faculty, that they are forces, than that they are endowed with force. For it would then be clear that force explains nothing, merely naming whatever makes a difference; and they all do that. But they are said to be endowed, because they appear now with more force, now with less, being sometimes energetic and sometimes not. And they are said to be charged or imbued with it, as if it were a fluid. Such, at one time, were not only spiritual force, but vital force, heat, gravity, levity, metallic and other qualities or 'principles'; they quickened a body, but they entered and left it much the same, as if it were a vessel; there could only be more or less of them. They did nothing to turn the classification into an explanation. The failure confesses itself when the quality or principle is given the power to produce the instances of it. We do no other with the mind when we account for the variety of mental action by so many faculties and their co-operation.

Not observing that we merely classify, we come to the dead wall. We ask what each force is in itself: what the will really is, what its energy, what conscience, reason, and all the other forces with which we are endowed. There is no answer, because there is no question. They are not the matter to explain with the assistance of manifesting fact. The facts are the matter; they explain themselves by their connexions. The connexions may be superficial, or they may be deep; and so are the explanations of the fact.

§ 5. But when we pass from properties to concrete things, whether to ultimate particles, or to wholes, like nature, mind, or the world, have we not to ask what they really are? In the words of Lotze, have we not to leave the way of science for the way of philosophy, and try "not merely to calculate the course of the world, but to understand it"? But to understand is still to determine; and every science takes the route of understanding, instead of counting, whenever it can. It brings the facts with all their relations under thing, class, and law; but it seeks a better unity than theirs, the unity of a system. There, in the limit, nothing is irrelevant, and all is necessary. It absorbs all that is contained under thing, class, and law; for, though a system is one, it is not simple, but as complex as the facts that it makes intelligible. It is therefore an opposite completing to the one which was given to thing, class, and law, by substance, essence, and force.

It may, however, seem a flimsy alternative to their solid. When science purified itself from the dross of

cause, took to law and system, and its deepest laws
became differential equations, it could not meet a wall
to keep it humble, but was not that because it had
left the earth, and gone into the air? The suspicion
rests on several grounds. One of them is hardly articulate, and others are mistaken, but one is good. It goes
as far back as our primary impulse to find a footing in
the flux of things. Our first footing is secured by the
signs or associations that become empirical laws. Their
ideal is doubtless to be systematic. But there has always
been another way; and it seems more solid, for it rests
on the persistence not of laws, but of things. We ask
what has become of something that has disappeared;
we are glad to find that it has become something else,
and that the two are the same thing in different forms.
Physics, as well as chemistry, has pursued this same
thing, no less than they have sought law or system. The
theories of the atom include a long history of the search;
when energy was found to be indestructible, it was
welcomed as the substance; and, at worst or best, there
was the aether. Nature has always been open to both
routes; it has brought the solid or substance one to
an end for not being solid enough. So we shall see,
but we see at once the manner in which the two routes
become one; they unite in the notion of a concrete
system.

The reason to the contrary that is barely articulate
looks at the infinite extent of our ignorance, and sees, in
particular, that we can never exhaust a single concrete
thing. That is good ground for despairing, if we think
it despair, that we shall ever know completely any
systems that are not abstract, more or less. But, though
abstract, they are actual. For, whatever we find refractory must be regular, if we know it for actual; it
must establish relations with the facts that we know;

and the relations must be necessary. Therefore, when we contrast things as we know them with things as they are, it is with things as we know them to be.

But the contrast, because barely articulate, has been confounded with another: the contrast between thought and thing. When we first think about a thought, we look on it as a thing, and, for want of analysing, make it a duplicate. But the two contrasts are easily separated. Between a thought and its object, between thinking and what is thought, there is all the contrast that there is between drinking a pint of water and the pint of water that is drunk. The other contrast is between the water so far as we know it, and the same water so far as we do not know it. The water that we see, taste, and understand, is no other than the water that is drunk; the water said to be in our minds is the water that goes into our bodies. The property of being intelligible belongs to the water itself, and not merely to 'any water', if that is a flimsy, but to this pint and its history. To be intelligible is only one of the properties of the water. Each property is intelligible, but none consists in being intelligible. There are not two explanations, an intelligible one for the intelligible character, a real one for the real, one by means of the forces or laws whose ideal is system, the other by means of a stuff.

To take laws apart from things, and relations apart from their terms, is not merely to be abstract, they are meaningless. A system, however abstract, consists of terms in relation. And, when things open out so well that their elements are at last of one kind, the treasure is found in the shaft of their mine, and remains there. Atomic structure is treasure for no reason but this, that the elemental terms and relations admit of compoundings equal to the variety of thing and event at the surface, and all the way down. We like to picture the world as an ocean of energy, the surface rising in waves and ripples, whose laws we can learn. But the picture explains nothing; it merely puts the question. And the question is misleading if the ocean is taken for an indestructible fluid or other substance, which manifests itself now in this form of energy, now that. Energy has no such existence; all of it is in this form or in that; there is no neutral stock from which the kinds emerge, and into which they return. The energy that does all the work does it by changing, and not by remaining identical with itself. It is only the quantity that remains identical; and, there being nothing to threaten it, it needs no support. The very theory which found nothing in the world but energy, and called it 'substance in the strictest sense' (Ostwald), could also say (xiii. 7) that energy means 'no absolute', but just 'the tissue of quantitative relations' (Helm).

There has come the same reform in the notion of a self. The identity of oneself is indispensable, for to lose it is to lose one's reason, and go to pieces. But to abstract it or consciousness, and make either a changeless being, is again to throw it idle. It is the unity of its factors, not one more unit among them. They would go to pieces, and be nothing, without it; and it would be nothing without them. That is what is meant by saying that it is, and has, the unity of a system.

How far minds, nature, and the world are intelligible is another matter. We are considering only the aim, and, in particular, that there is always, and only, one. The failure of thing, class, and law to go farther is because they do not become systematic, not because a substance or force must always elude them. The community of qualities in a thing, of species in a class, and of specific laws in a common one, is not organic. The members can ignore one another; if any were lost, they would not be missed; the whole that unites them leaves their differences incidental. In a system, on the other hand, the differences are necessary to the whole, and thereby to one another. It involves and so determines them; and through it they involve and determine one another. Observe the result of its absence from class, law, and thing, when these give us grasp of a mind.

There are, first, the disputes that turn out to be a matter of words, that is to say of classes. The cure is to pass from them to the mind, of which they are sections. The sections of a mind which we naturally make and use are not the analysis that can set the problems for explanation. Presuming that they are, as we did for physical things, we have alchemy, and the notion of a treasure hunt. When like sections increase in number, we seize on their difference, being on the outlook for surface indications that may lead to the recesses of the spirit. We dwell on pairs like force and power, soul and spirit, genius and talent, wit and humour, fancy and imagination, passion and sentiment, reason and understanding, tempers and temperaments. As a rule the members of a pair mean much the same, but each has also a field of its own. This is usual with synonyms, but, hoping that the difference betrays a secret, we follow the two till there is no connexion, and we have both sections pure. Observe too the names for neighbouring emotions, and for compounds. Seeing that each has an endless number of different instances, there can be endless disputes. But, suppose all fields clear, and all disputes ended, what have we on hand? Nothing but classes and cross-classes, sections and cross-sections; or, as was said about the corresponding analysis of things, we have nothing but an increasing arsenal of weapons, as many as we choose, with a super-weapon

in self or his will. A novelist may play with the difference
of weapons to some purpose, but an explanation pursues
a difference for the sake of the connexion that accounts
for it.

As with the arsenal of classes, qualities, or faculties,
so next with laws, mental and physical. They have
limits and exceptions, and it is not so long ago since
laws of nature were said to conflict. Within a system
the limits of laws become intelligible and part of them;
and there are no exceptions. But we still see laws of
mind to be in conflict, and itself inconsistent. The law
of habit, for instance, is universal; but challenge a man,
and, if he likes, he will defy it.

And most of all with the knowledge that we gather
under the notion of a thing, or individual. Does not the
last word lie with it, seeing a cause is always concrete,
never abstract. Yet the characters that we collect in
the notion seem incoherent. A thing is one and many,
changing and the same, living and dying. It was
thought that a material particle cannot be real, because while attracting others, it repels them at the
last. And, if inconsistency was possible in a particle,
what more obvious in a self? The better we know a
man, the better we predict his behaviour; but the spirit
bloweth where it listeth; we know that he has only to
choose to put us wrong. So we rescue his will from the
machinery of character, and make inconsistency prove
his power. And, of course, we rightly resent our reduction to any other system than that of a self. But
there are many kinds of system.

§ 6. Consider, first, the kind that we create. The
purpose of every institution has formed it, and determines the working of it. Every part of the structure of
a bank, and every fact of its working, has its first and

proper explanation in the whole; every factor is an
organ. When we ask about the existence of anything
in it, persons or papers, we ask their function; it is their
necessity. There are two outside conditions. First, the
men who work the bank are more than bankers; once
they were not bankers at all. And, secondly, the bank
does not live on itself, but is fed from without. By those
two outside conditions every transaction is determined
as well as by the constitution of the bank. We have to
go beyond the constitution, but into what? Into other
systems. Let us look at them, for a mind is quite in the
position of the bank. It, too, has a system of its own,
and the system depends for its healthy working on
two outside conditions: on material that is not mental,
and on the environment with which we transact our
business.

A bank is one of the organs of trade, which is one
organ of the general social system, whose end is welfare. The division of this comprehensive system into
constituent systems, of which all the facts are factors,
can alone let the facts be understood. We grasp their
purpose, through it their coherence and their existence,
and all incoherence. Without it we know endless de-
bates about the causes and the justice of social facts.
With it the disputes divide into those in the course of
progress and those that come to nothing. Of the first
there is the present pull between 'safety first' and
'banks and bankers were born blind'. Of the second
there is the bone that a bank lends many times the
money that it owns, and at several times the rate of
interest at which it borrows. The fact can be appraised
from many points of view, all relevant, but conflicting.
Their quarrel is not settled by principles, nor by rank-
ing one moral principle above another, and all of them
above the principles of business. Nor is it ended by

forgetting principles, and observing the naked fac
that here, as in every market, the result is due to a
conflict of forces. The one final way is to divide the
whole structure, to which the banking fact belongs
into its constituent systems, and their mutual depend
ence. This opens out the bearings of the fact, and
thereby its explanation; for then the end, which is it
unity, can be brought to bear. It determines and
appreciates not as a principle, like justice or welfare
of which the fact is an instance, nor even as a system
abstracted, but as the concrete system, of which the fac
is a factor. This is always the explanation that we wan
for facts whose system has an end: for everything in a
machine, for instance, or in a farming system, or in a
system of education. We look to the internal structure
of the system, and to the external structure by which i
works. They make the events intelligible, their how no
less than their why.

There is also the infinite variety of material. It i
the other of the two conditions, always essential, bu
extending, never disturbing, the explanation. It need
not be brought in, but, wherever it can, it makes more
intelligible. Mix the two and there is confusion. Tha
can happen in the practice of institutions; and, when
the facts have an end which we have no voice in
inventing, it can happen in theory. Such are the facts
and theories of life and of mind:

"Life is a whole which determines its parts; . . . the
whole is in the parts, including the environment; . .
the elements cannot be isolated without changing them
. . . all living structure is actively maintained com
position, the atoms and molecules entering into which
are never the same from moment to moment."
Disease is not a foreign invasion, but "life itself in

[1] J. S. Haldane, *The New Physiology*, pp. 67-122.

conflict with the invader, trying to return to its normal type", though often, as in every struggle, its measures of defence leave evils behind.[1] I have quoted from two physiologists of whom one declines to call this vitalism, while the other claims the name and yet insists that life is always effect, never cause or vital force. So far there is nothing to dispute, there is only analysis. Like a social body, a living body analyses into systems; and its muscular, vascular, nervous and other systems are divided and combined into organs with their functions, up to the last elements of tissue. Every vital action is physico-chemical. Life is the unity, wholeness, health, *consensus unus* of the action, neither one of the units that are united, nor a force that comes in to unite them. It is their form, as the bank is of its units; it remains while they change and go, but it is nothing apart.

Like a bank and a life, a mind is a system whose factors depend on one another, and on a certain environment. The environment is now the world that one happens to know or know about. Through intercourse with it every mind discovers itself and is revealed. And again, there is always the second, or material, condition: there is no mental event, so we may assume, that is not also physical. Since every event in the body affects the nervous system, every mental event has no less to affect it than such endless complexity.

Yet psychology cannot err from ignorance of the complexity. The force of this will fail to strike us, if we confound it with something of another sort that may be said of everything. Every event has depended on the whole history of the world, and is, in turn, a cause of as many. To meet this we divide the world into systems, in order to discard what is irrelevant. But our fact remains after that. It is that even the simplest

[1] Grasset, *La Biologie Humaine*, pp. 155, 159.

event in the mental system depends on exceedingly complex physical conditions, and yet that psychology need not err because it is in ignorance of them.

It may seem amazing, and it ought to strike us, though the situation is no other than we have in explaining a bank or a life. But one may ask: Is not the course of our conscious life, determined by all that unseen physical complexity, too casual for an adequate explanation? Is not the mental explanation merely descriptive and provisional? And may it not be qualified, here and there at least, by the physical explanation as it comes in? To all three the answer is negative, just as for the bank. The issue of a certain credit to a client depends on the confidence of the banker, which depends not only on his knowledge of the client and the market, but on his own heart and stomach, and all the worries of his life. A book on banking puts these things out of the question, but it is not therefore provisional nor inadequate; its truth is not qualified when they enter; and they enter differently, and better for the banker, when he comes to know them, and so brings them into the environment that he knows and has to meet.

§ 7. Though the fact of bank, health, or mind, is itself undivided, we find the division, not merely make it; for the fact makes itself intelligible. The same extends to the order among systems. One is called higher than another because it implies the other, resting upon it, whereas the higher is not implied by the lower. On the contrary, it reveals the power of the lower: a molecule shows what its atoms can do and make, a living cell reveals the capacity of its molecules, a growing body the capacity of its cells, a mind the capacity of its brain.

Therefore the facts of a higher system cannot be inferred from those of a lower. This is fairly clear even in systems of human manufacture: every institution and invention seems necessary enough, but only after it has come. For life it has been enforced by repeated failure to forecast how organs ought to work. But it needs no enforcing with regard to mind for the simplest reason: the physical causes of a sensation can never tell why this one, and not another, nor why they give feeling at all.

The converse error is to infer lower system from higher. It introduces higher factors among those of the lower, as when life is brought in to supplement lifeless forces, and emotion to stir the brain. The properties that distinguish a system as higher present a lower with problems. When it solves them, it takes the higher system out of isolation. Music, which is mental, and has a mental explanation, is also a demand on the theory of sound. The mental explanation of fear now knows the organic causes which produce the feeling, and give it effect. Formerly the feeling was used in the lower system as a substitute. There was no confusion, but no progress. That is why the mental explanation appears to retire everywhere as knowledge advances. On the contrary, the mental explanation is being advanced. There is the same thing everywhere, back to the other extreme. Though all geometry can be turned into algebra, becoming far more powerful, and space more intelligible, number is not space, and is no substitute for it in still higher systems where space is a factor. "The science of numbers corresponds perfectly to things, but it does not explain them; it explains only itself. . . . The arithmetical ideal of the science of the external world offers at least one advantage: it is difficult to be its dupe. No one will think that the world is nothing but a set of arithmetical operations" (J. Tannery).

At this other extreme, among the mathematical sciences, we have the simplest notion of a system, and higher and lower systems easily related. A mathematical structure and its properties are analysable into simpler ones, and ultimately into terms and relations that are quite simple, having no secret, since their properties are assigned. They are assigned as postulates, and include the elemental laws of operation. From these elements the properties of the structures are demonstrated as theorems, and the theorems together constitute a theory, which is the system so far as yet seen. The number twelve, a cone, a rolling ship, each is a unity whose factors imply and determine one another within it. And each is only one of innumerable structures that together constitute a system where they are all intelligible. To 'reduce' them to their general system is always the aim. The reason is not merely that our grasp of each may be more convenient and economical. It is also that their properties are the more calculable and intelligible, because they now imply so much more, and are implied by so much more.

But between the two extremes it may well seem that things are too empirical for the systematic aim. The difference is in degree. For even structures of lines and of numbers have properties that are incidental to begin with; their properties are found as empirical laws; induction, which is their analysis, precedes deduction or synthesis in the early instances. Their difference from things is that the elements of a formal system hold no secrets, and in things they do. Though the powers of atoms in a molecule, or of living cells in a body, are not theirs in isolation, but like the power of a severed hand, they have each an adequate complexity, where every discovery promises to be of service in the higher system of the compound.

There are two stages. The secret of the atom yielded the ground for the valencies, which the higher system held only for facts. Then the ground was able to unite the facts far better; the atomic numbers took up the periodic table; the lower and the higher systems could coalesce. These two stages present themselves in developing the needs of every higher system. The first one is on the pedestrian course of the sciences; the second one is the arrival.

§ 8. But a mind may seem an exception. The first route is quite open; it is the way of all psycho-physical explanation, as when the variety of sensation is correlated and measured by the variety of the stimulus. But what of the arrival? Physical elements will never be seen to compound themselves into a sensation, nor physical structure into mental. Yet sensation is a product of physical conditions. If it will not analyse, as they do, into elements, must we prolong the mental line of the parallel, and equip the elements of nervous action with a subconscious secret? No, if we are right about the task of explanation, there is no necessity, and therefore no right. Subconscious mental units of that origin explain nothing, because they determine nothing. They remain shadows of the physical factors, indistinguishable from one another, shadows in the dark. Still to urge the parallel, as Spinoza did, and many since, is to force the world into our early notion of a thing.

But is that not better than to be left with a miracle? We are thought to face the dilemma when we analyse the neural correlate of consciousness, and again when we consider the coming of mind on the earth. The neural condition that gives consciousness consists of elements that give none. It is in the position of a molecule whose properties are not found in its atoms. But they come from atoms; they are not a gift; should we not suppose the same for the brain elements which are the correlate of consciousness? They need not contribute each an atom of feeling, but should they not contain, and contribute, a mental factor of some sort? For their physical energy is fully accounted for in that of the physical compound; none loses itself to become a feeling.

The question is even more confident when we look at the coming of consciousness, for it came like the dawn. Can two lights not be thrown on its dark age? Our experience has all degrees of intensity and clearness; may we not carry them back indefinitely to a dimness beyond the wavering margin that we always feel? Or, if this comes near the notion of an unconscious consciousness, there is unconscious mind. Far the greater part of mental work is unfelt. It is selective, resourceful, synthetic; and so is life; may we not carry mind back, and endow all life with something of the kind? If we do, what then? For the dawn must have no beginning, if it would evade the miracle.

Neither the dilemma nor the miracle is met in the course of life and its explanation. They are once more due to a reason which looks inevitable. But, first, the two arguments to solve them are bad:

The chemical analogy does not compel us to distribute mentality among the nervous elements. When a new property appears with a new structure, even a triangle or a spade, let alone a chemical compound or an organism, we do not divide the property, and say, for instance, that there is something triangular in a straight line. An element is not loaded with qualities in so simple a way. We may load it with potentialities, if we care to say that a bucket carries water potentially when it is empty. The proper course is to leave the elements in the structure; what properties they have apart they have to prove. That is the offset against the argument from the chemical analogy. And the chemical case is typical of the relation between higher and lower systems.

The other argument may still seem good. Suppose we take the whole world at any time, did it not beget from itself everything new, consciousness with the rest? But there we are still abstracting: we are assuming that the world at a moment is the whole world. Therefore we fill with potentiality again, and have now left ourselves nothing to fill with. There is nothing to fill the bucket but itself, and itself all at the instant. Every moment would be literally big with the whole future of the world. It is an impossible picture, though its logic was good enough to induce Leibniz to make it the picture of everything real.

What hold on us has a way of thinking that could force us to a view never welcome, and now demonstrably wrong? There is the reason that would squeeze the world into an instant, because only the present instant exists. But squeeze it into a period; what induces us to fill the period with potentiality, and believe that the present ordered hour, and our feelings here and now, were scattered somehow in the flaming blaze of gas? We are driven by the question what becomes of, and by its answer, which also answers whence. We expected that a more and more universal stuff, and its laws, would account for all change. Nothing was lost when it was found that none could be concrete enough, owing to space-time. The defect was in narrowing nature by neglecting the relation between space and time. But there is now the need for a still further concreteness, owing to nature being the system of phenomena. The defect has been the narrowing of nature by neglecting the relation of minds to nature. We proceed to it in the living relation of thought to things.

PART II
A MIND'S OWN PLACE

VI

ORIGIN OF THE OBJECT

§ 1. WHAT virtue is there in knowing, that nature should have been at such pains to cherish and develop it? When we look from its present power at its long slow growth, its beginning like a first hint of light, what virtue had it then and there? The light fell on nothing that produced it. It fell on something as new to the earth as pain was, or the precursors of pain, for we hope that small creatures feel small pain. Phenomena were as new as their organs. So was knowing, when it came, and made them literally phenomena and objects; it was not an old process in a new light. The mere uniqueness would be a misfortune, but for the virtue in it. Knowing serves its objects by separating and uniting them, and by finding the unity theirs. Let us now examine that more generally than we have been doing.

The act of thought is easy to distinguish from other conscious acts, because they require it. Liking and loathing, seeking and avoiding, are lost if they lose consciousness of their object. Thought is defined as the consciousness of an object. It does not exist before the object has been found, nor after the object is let go. This is secured in the definition by restricting the two words to their literal meaning. There is no difficulty with 'object', and then 'to be conscious of' means to know. Their literal meaning is relative, each referring to the other. In common use they have become

absolute, losing their origin. That is proper and convenient, but it opens the way to two errors. One is that
all consciousness is a kind of thought; the other is that
the object of thought is a kind of consciousness. They
are avoided if we observe that the act is no part of the
object, and that the object is no part of the act.

Can this be true? The object is what I see, dream,
think; and surely what I think is in my thought. Yes,
but the phrase 'in my thought' has two meanings. There
are the properties of the thought; they are in it. And
there are the properties of the object; they are not.
The act can be analysed into all that is felt in it. These
properties we may, if we must, call its content or contents; they constitute and exhaust it. They are given
a common name, and called an act, because they have
a common function. Their function is to present an
object, not any one, but just the one present to me;
and, of course, it is present always to me, the subject,
here and now. As present to me it can be in the past
or the future, here or there, real or unreal, mental or
physical, concrete or abstract. If we say that the object
is in view, or is in my dream, in my opinion, memory,
mind, we should mean simply I see it, dream it, remember it, think it. The feat is fully expressed by verbs,
by each in its own way, and therefore by none more
simply than by think or know.

It is useful, however, to observe the physical
analogies, because they are copied from it, not it from
them. A thought refers to an object, points to it, means
it, presents it. A finger does the like, and a sign of any
sort, to say nothing of a mirror. But they point only
for a mind, the mind that sees them; and then they are
object, not the seeing it. When we forget this, and substitute the analogy, we break the act of thought in
two: we suppose that a thought first observes what is

within it, and then gives this a meaning, which is the object without it. We invent the first act by doing one or other of two things. Either we separate consciousness from the states of consciousness, and it is nothing apart from them; or we separate them from their common function, and it is nothing apart from them. The first act does not occur, nor, therefore, does the second. When we say that the function of a thought is to point to the object, we should mean that the thought is itself the gesture, the finger pointing.

For this reason, and because thought can alter itself greatly for the same object, there is a better analogy from the hand than pointing; it is the usual one of grasping. An object is in my thought as an apple is in my grasp; it is in that simple sense that every sensation, idea, dream, judgment, embraces its object. And my grasp is not a thing. If I substitute a thing, and say that the apple is in my hand, I mean the same, and not that the apple has become part of my hand. And, when I say of an object that it is in my thought, or in my mind, or that an idea has entered my head, I still mean the act. There is no error in calling it a thought, idea, or by some other name. Coming from verbs they should be a protection, like 'in my grasp'. But the protection from thought, view, conception, dream, opinion, has not been very effective. 'Idea' gives none, having lost sight of its verb; and 'idealism' is beyond redemption. The nouns are used sometimes for the act, sometimes for the object, and sometimes for both. In practice the context is usually enough, even when any of the three might be meant, as by the word 'discovery', when it was said that "equating to zero was a greater discovery than the steam-engine".

A second ambiguity occurs when there is no

question of the mental act, and nothing is meant but the object. For it may be meant as an object of thought, or as in nature, or in some other connexion. A theory, a ground, a formula, mean only objects of thought, and not objects in nature, whenever we say that they are true or false; for facts are not true, nor their absence false. But we often intend facts in nature by the same words, and so their physical existence may seem infected. We call facts clear and obscure nearly as readily as we call them rare or universal. The ambiguity is harmless unless we assume that what is not physical is mental. And that is usual and fatal. If a physical theory is true, its object, though general, is in nature; if it is false, the object is nowhere; it exists for a mind, but is no more mental on that account than when it is true. The nature of an object depends on itself, and what it proves to be; if it is felt, that makes no difference to it. And there are plenty epithets like 'felt', *e.g.* seen, supposed, understood, debated. There is no general one in common use, because none is wanted. Technical writers find 'ideal' to be good enough, but it is too suggestive for other people. They, unfortunately, prefer 'mental', which is to stretch and spoil a good word. It is the only word for seeing, hearing, planning, and all their properties; if it has also to carry the light, the sound, the projects, and their properties, it loses its value. No one wants that, nor takes it for literal that chimeras and to-morrow are in our minds. Ideas, opinions, images, are not third things between the object and knowing it; there is nothing but the relation: the object as known, seen, debated. There need be no ambiguity when we speak of an object as being in or out of the mind, in or out of memory, and as being immanent or transcendent. An immanent object, an object 'in the mind', is just the real object so far as we

grasp, or take thought of it; and a chimera is as transcendent, not mental, as to-morrow is.

Of the two ambiguities from nouns, the one, which
involves the subject and his working, leads to no
error, but only to further question as in the instance
of 'discovery'. Only the other leads to error. The
error consists in assigning nouns like idea, view, argument, not to the object as felt or known, but to a third
thing.

§ 2. There is no such thing; it is a product of the
questions with which we turn from things to minds.
We ask how it can be the very things out there, or of
yesterday, that enter my brain and make themselves
known. If, looking at one thing, we all see it the same,
does not it, or the stimulus, produce its like in each of
us? And was not the book, as I see it, compounded
of mental and physical elements? These questions are
cause enough of the third thing; the nouns are merely
its carriers. How do they come to carry it, and what
do they mean when the third thing is removed?

The product of thought is knowledge; it is never the
known thing or object; it is being produced all the time,
and ends at the same time as the thought. What remains is the power to recover the knowledge with less
trouble, and to grasp other things by means of it, without having even to recover it. The power may be
called potential knowledge, in the sense of potential
energy, for both are named, known, and measured
from nothing but their fruit. The whole product that
remains goes into power; no further storing is needed
by the fact of memory. The potential is therefore the
problem, and its fruit is the criterion of any theory
about it. To make the potential consist of knowledge
deprived of light is quite idle. The theory that gun-

powder is a store of motion could only begin to be worth while when the kind of store could be stated.

The problem of the potential is not altered by altering the name of the products of thought from knowledge to ideas. Ideas have the advantage of saying 'pieces of knowledge' in one word, but they have two temptations against them. Like all abstractions with short names, they tempt us to treat them as things; and in their other, and better use, they mean known things, not knowledge. This lets them include and mix the known things with knowledge; ideas become pieces of consciousness, consisting of it; or else they inhabit it, and come and go. But ideas do not feel, they are felt. They are not kinds of feeling, and yet have no existence without it. That is why phenomena can be entirely physical, and the view the very landscape. The whole consciousness of them goes to the subject, and thence to mind. The colour and beauty go to the object, and thence to nature. And there is no duplication.

There is no ambiguity till we become curious about the fact that the properties belong to the object only in relation to a subject. Then we see from three grades of word where ambiguity begins. There is none from such words as colour and beauty, which make no reference to the relation. Nor, secondly, is there any ambiguity, when the words begin to indicate the relation, as when we speak of the view and its charm. Epithets like sensible and intelligible, attractive and dreadful, can go to the physical object as clearly as heavy goes. But, thirdly, we may want to go farther, and study the object in this relation only, just as we study its weight only in relation. The object is then called a sensation, a memory, an idea. Such objects are like weight in being independent of the other properties. They can be physical, or of any sort: an opinion, a ground, a principle, an error. There is no ambiguity so long as, like beauty and weight, they still do not include the other term of the relation, which is the consciousness of them. Its omission is as little peculiar, and also as necessary, as omitting the mass of the earth when weighing a ton. Then, when we bring in consciousness, the relation remains; the two terms keep the properties which they have only in the relation.

That is more important than choosing a fourth grade of nouns to denote the whole. These have to include the knowing with the known, the hearing with the music, and discovering with the discovered. Experience is the technical word, but, if it is to be used without ambiguity, it must reach its grade before the objects are omitted, and the remainder made the province of psychology. The other three grades have chosen their own words before psychology enters, because it is the course of conscious living that marks out their scope. The course goes back to animals, who have no words at all, nor other source of confusion; their minds are clear.

§ 3. But why insist on analysing into two factors, neither part of the other, with no common part, and their connexion unique? May not uniqueness, here as usual, mean our failure to analyse, and the third thing have escaped us, by our looking for it as a link? Why not see in phenomena not a link but a core? They would be at once mental and physical, mental in one set of relations, physical in the other. There would still be no copying, nor other duplication. A situation can surely be analysed in more ways than one; why insist on one way, and into two factors, and not another number?

Because we have no choice; for, so far there is only fact. The fact is that every thought makes the analysis for itself. Its function is to present the very nature of the object, often merely meaning it, and usually the greater part is unfelt. But at first the whole is felt. It may be a datum of sense, distinguished from nothing, identified with nothing, yet literally an object. It becomes the more an object if it has interest; it becomes a topic; and the act becomes a course, altering its grasp of the object or topic all the time. Like everything actual, thought has many aspects or analyses, but that is its own aspect, the one which makes it thought, and without which it would be none.

The core way of keeping the third thing is good in this respect that it will have nothing but what can be known. It has no need of Hume's fiction of a Nature that produces sensations and beliefs; and so it can distinguish and unite mental and physical more clearly than he could. What he called impressions and ideas are at once physical and mental. In their physical capacity they have rightly supplanted the old object which had to produce them. Locke began the supplanting; ideas were the objects, but in minds, and he gave the most important of them duplicates outside. Berkeley and Hume removed the duplicates, and their view has become that for physics; for it was merely to avoid the strangeness of calling things ideas that they came to be called phenomena. We had that already with the amusing protest that I quoted from Reid. But the new question is, Why do ideas not also supplant the subject in their mental capacity? They should, if the subject is unfelt. If he claims to be actual he must act, and be revealed entirely by his acts; he must claim them, and they him. One of them is the act of thought; and the core-question is, Why not let his act be just the mental aspect of the object?

When ideas supplanted the object, they took over

its functions, and wrought them all. But, when given a mental character, they take over no function of the act. They are said to act, but on one another, attracting and repelling one another, fusing with one another, and forming compounds. A century ago they began to be given a mechanics, and later a chemistry. The analogy was always rough, and has lost its ambition; the idea-masses, and the affinities, are no longer literal. The act of thought, on the contrary, does its work on the object, not on other acts of thought.

§ 4. The simplest instance is where the whole object is felt, and the clearest is where there is no question of a distance in space or time between a thought and its object. Let us begin with objects that are not physical.

The extreme instances are in dreams and day-dreams, romances, assumptions, and impossible things like a timeless change. Even there the objects are other than the thoughts of them. If I dream the same thing a second time, it is the same thing, but a new dream. My thoughts of all those objects are actual in every part; but there is nothing actual in the objects. And I can mean one and the same object, though my thoughts vary from fullness to merely a reference. Therefore in observing even objects so unlikely, in identifying, analysing, and pointing them out, my thoughts claim to know them, and not to be them.

This existence which every thought assigns to its object is nothing but the self-identity of the object. A griffin has a certain structure, whether one happens to be thinking of it correctly, or not at all. And a thought cannot begin to err by giving this existence to anything, nor by including anything in the existence, nor by ex-cluding. Truth or error begins later, when we identify an object with something else; and it is a matter for the two objects to decide. When, for instance, the object exists only for a mind, there is no error in being ignorant of that, but only in believing, as in dreams, that it has also other existence. When a thought is true or useful, its object is obviously independent of it; for, to be true, a thought must alter nothing; and, to be useful, it must report the very nature that matters. And a fiction offers the same field, once it is constituted. We call a fiction a mere idea; it exists only for a mind. Every time it is made an object, felt or meant, it is given this existence, with power to criticise its creator when he refers to it. It is independent of time, while the thought of it is not. When I recall it, I double every part of the act, but no part of the object.

Many things, though they exist only for minds, are so independent, that they seem as real as nature. Such are literature, a policy, a market, and every kind of institution. They remain like living species, while their generations pass; and yet they live and grow wholly by the minds of their present generation; if these failed them, the books and buildings would be their corpses. And science itself is like an institution. The pure sciences develop factors found in nature, first into ideal tools, but soon into structures that have an aim of their own, and a perfection or imperfection.

It is no great step from these practical and theoretical worlds to the threshold of nature. We have already left objects mainly created by us for those mainly found; and now we may add such objects as the beauty of things, and their meanness or grandeur, which are altogether found. For, if they are felt, they may have had to be learnt, but they are found, and not added as a fancy. Yet they exist only for minds. So do all objects like red, cold, sweet, properties of matter that are simply found, and neither created nor learnt by us at all.

As we pass to these things, we find an independence that lies not merely in their self-identity, but in a power to resist, and in the possession of properties yet unknown. To a less degree, however, this holds of dreams and fancies; for our dreams may be nightmares, and our fancies fertile in suggestion. And so we may put them all on one list, as having no active existence but for minds, acting only through them. Let us ask about their causes and effects.

And, first, negatively. Facts are causally connected in two respects. They may be connected as events; and the term cause commonly refers to the source of an event. There is no such relation between a thought and its object. A phenomenon is never the cause of its being felt, nor is any other object on our list. They do not produce a thought of themselves, having no active existence before it. Nor are they products of our thoughts of them; they are not made by our grasping them, not even those that we invent. We must know them if they are to act on us, or we on them, but our thought of them makes no difference in them. As the black of a morning turns to red, we see the turning and the red, but, like the black, they are not the cause of our seeing them. An act of parliament does not make itself known, though it refuses to be ignored; the object is never the stimulus. And, when I call the object mine, because I intend it, I know the thing I intend, and my course of action, but my knowledge by itself alters nothing.

In the other and wider application of the word a cause may persist with its effect, as when a wind fills the sails; and the dependence may be mutual, as when sail pulls on rope, and rope on sail. But neither in this way do the things on our list do anything, except as already objects of thought. And then all their action is by interaction with minds: they do nothing to one another. In a fanciful world things do what we like, but all at our hand; they do not take hands and feet; they cannot pass, for instance, from the fancy that they are vivid to an actual vividness. If we assume that hot is cold, or if we desire and decree that hot is cold, then hot is cold in those ideal worlds of error or desire, but there only; and what is done in them is all of our doing, though it be against our will. We can picture the stir of a battle, where the very figures thrust, and feel the fury, but it is we who are working them; we have all the fury that is actual. In dreaming we can believe otherwise, and are in error. So it is with our heritage of tradition and custom, of art, letters, and invention: though not created by us, it is only by us that they are kept alive and active. In practical affairs, in the most living spheres of corporate action, while the course of events is far beyond our individual creating, nothing happens but through individual minds; justice goes to sleep with the judges. The fields of pure science are still less created than found, and still it is only through minds that they flourish. Finally, where there is no creation, and all is found: if it be really the brightness that attracts the moths, they must feel it. That large division of nature, called the secondary qualities of matter, was set apart for no other reason than that they do nothing except through minds. Though they depend on extra-mental conditions, there is no interaction between these and them, nor among themselves. Their work is done through the mind that knows them, and after it knows them.

Once the object is thought, every one on our list may act and be acted on. And there are both kinds of cause: that of serial events, and that of mutual dependence. The sight of brown and gold produces a sense of harmony, or suggests a school, or a closer inspection; and, in general, the work done by objects on a mind is to induce it to deal with them. As a result, they become causes in the other sense; for, through our dealing, they affect one another in the sense that they are members one of another, like the parts in a play, in an army, or on a page of print.

That is our way with objects that exist only for a mind. They are not altered by being thought, and it could do nothing with them, if they did not have a character of their own. We might therefore open the list to things of any character. It makes no difference nor difficulty that they lead an independent life. But let us continue with those that we know completely, in order to see more closely the mere act of making object, and its grasp.

§ 5. In our ordinary knowing, every present object places itself in a greater; it is both an instance and a part. The things of sight place themselves most completely. They are therefore the most useful for examining our grasp, and its growth, especially the grasp and the growth of generality. And we shall be mainly concerned with them, when we ask how far we can penetrate nature. But hearing is better for our present purpose, because music, while complex enough, has all to be felt, and yet is all physical. Every tone has to place itself completely, and, though into three dimensions, there is nothing left over to claim that space escapes, and that what is caught is not the very thing that exists.

In the three dimensions—in the rhythms, the melodies, and the harmonies—every note has a different set of relations with its neighbours, and has to be heard in and with them all. The three are heard by normal ears from the outset. In the history of music the slow development of each, and especially of harmony, was due to want of material on which the ear could be trained. Slow though progress was, there was no slowing down, as if the native or natural ear could be exhausted; there was the reverse; it was like the pace of science. And, though the growth was under law, and therefore bound, far more than the growth of language, there was also increasing freedom. For many of us the development and the freedom fail to come; the world of sound has use for us, but little attraction.

That makes it the better instance of mental power. For, first, every other power to learn has also a different rate in different people; yet the course is the same. One child is a Mozart with a flying start, while another foots it, and makes little way; but the course is the same, being set by the object. And it remains the same though, secondly, having followed one branch, we are the less free to take another. It is then as with the language into which we are born, for we are born free to learn the click and the accent of any, if it is our first. The language of music is universal, but there, too, the forms, from which we have learnt, create a habit that makes it hard not merely to value other forms, but even to grasp them. And that though they are quite understood. "Music composed according to the Siamese or the Javanese scales, which divide the octave into seven and into five equal parts respectively, will sound absolutely incomprehensible to us, as no doubt our music would appear to one trained in those systems."[1]

The task is therefore typical. Look now to its achieving by listening and by hearing. Their connexion too is typical; it is an instance of the connexion between attending, and the grasping and appreciating that

[1] M'Ewen, *The Thought in Music*, p. 168.

depend on attending. They depend on attending not only at their start, but all the time, and not only on its effort, but better when it needs none, and none is felt. To attend is so essential to them that they have been called species of it. That, however, is not the relation; hearing is not a species of listening, but its purpose. The relation is of means and end; in order to grasp anything, to value it, to use or to alter it, we attend or keep it before us. In the affairs of daily life anyone can attend to anything. But there are many things that we cannot with all our will set before us; difficult music is one of them. What, in such a case, does listening do for hearing, and, in general, what does attending do for our grasp?

With easy objects it does two things: it keeps them clear, and it makes them distinct. It keeps them clear from invasion, or confusion with other things. It makes them distinct by clearing their factors from confusion with one another. For both purposes it can make a more effective use of external organs: we look, hark, sniff, in order to see, hear, and smell better. These additions are not themselves the attending; a painter and a psychologist may have to avoid them in order to attend; it depends always on the purpose. When the object is hard to grasp, a better use of the peripheral organ is not enough. The difficult parts are repeated, phrases are sought, and confusions analysed. Then there is tension, a sense of effort from a variety of muscular contractions.

But the aim of all the efforts is to become unnecessary. Then the two clearing functions of attending are being the better achieved; the music becomes absorbing, and it makes its own way. When, if it is absorbing, we still stiffen ourselves, or keep the strain, we detract from the attending; and, if we think of our attending, we do worse. We attend best when we are possessed by the object. Most of all we detract if, when the music is not only absorbing, but able to make its own way, we still search and analyse, instead of giving way. The means have to disappear that their work on the parts may have its value in the fuller object. Then the whole takes the parts in charge, and protects them. In reading, for instance, though we no longer spell, printers' errors are the more likely to be caught; in hearing we feel flaws and omissions, because it is the whole which they disturb. In general, effort is being released all the time for more difficult things, which it would otherwise be impossible to attack. That is a gain which we make through the whole course of knowing.

We inherit the power to make it. From our infancy the simple things of sense make themselves objects. It is an achievement of the race become natural, and so easy that we miss the age-long feat that it is. A thought points or refers to its object; it is the gesture of attending grown spontaneous; it lets the object display its value for whatever purpose we have with it. When the purpose is to know, it lets the object speak for itself, till, for instance, the atoms of a star record their condition now of ten thousand years ago.

§ 6. The working of our power to know is the same in whatever course of experience as it is in reading a book. The early part of the course throws light on the later; it does not have to be kept in mind, but our grasp of incident or argument as it comes depends on the grasp of what has gone; we know by means of what we have known. So the volume of our life writes itself. Our other powers there grow too, our power to do by what we have done, and our power to appreciate by what we have felt. The three depend on one another; there is not a triple plot; but the spirit, like the body, the more complex it grows, divides its functions the more definitely.

And it becomes the more intelligible. When we abstract knowing from the full working of a mind, it is torn from no conditions that must later qualify the account. They do not qualify, they specify. We can leave out the variety of interests which drive man and beast to their knowledge of nature; there remains the interest common to all knowing, the interest of our grasp. Whether a bare apprehending, or a full comprehending, it either satisfies or fails. If it fails to satisfy, and there is time, we do not act on the knowledge till we improve our grasp. The grasp-interest frees itself completely, when it becomes theoretical. We then speak of reason, and say that it must be satisfied; but there is the same impersonal demand in the simple acts of thought that are too inevitable to seem either acts or thought.

In answer to the question with which the lecture began, we have to add the later development which makes the start intelligible. The development is from mind as organ of body to body as organ of mind; it is from means to actual value. For no value, not even that of life, is actual, but for minds. There is a closer description, as we saw; the development is to and through objects as causes.

But, because our power to make an object of anything is so natural, we are apt to suppose it in the lowest creatures that feel at all. Nature is the home of them all; the different phenomena that it gives them it gives to guide them; why not as objects? Think of a spider watching all that enters its web.

That is better than merely to insist on the difference between sensing and perceiving, or objectifying, as

L

if the difference were by addition. But it forgets the long history of sensation before its quality became the quality of an object that had other qualities, a thing to deal with, part of a world. The historical record of the advance is in our nervous system below the cerebral hemispheres, and in the slow development and definition of cortical areas for sense and skill. The new or clear perceiving of things, which we and the higher animals enjoy without an effort, has to rely on so complex a foundation. In the lower or thoughtless feeling there can be variety enough, though all in organic sensations. They go from mere discomfort and restlessness up to those that constitute emotions, appetites, and the requisite movements. And the lowest creatures are affected by all the kinds of external stimuli to which we respond. But the taste, light, heat and cold which they feel may do their work like organic sensations, not local objects. The variety and the exactness of the motor effects require no more. And, when our own sub-cortical centres are dissociated from the later developments, any special sensations that remain are simple and diffuse. The thoughtless learning from such material is, at its lowest, the fixing of movements that bring relief, or give other satisfaction; at its highest we have the association of stimuli, as in the discharge of saliva where a sound or other sign produces an effect that at first was beyond it. Such learning is not a learning of external things, and of the body as one of them. But it is a preparation. We inherit the complex mechanism, and use it without effort, and without a thought.

Dr. Head's experiments in dissociation give an instance of the preparation, and another of the transition, which together bring out the difference. When a test-tube at 45° C. is applied to the skin, it can affect the nerve terminals there for heat, cold, and pain. "If these could all co-exist in consciousness, mental activity would be chaotic, and discrimination impossible. The struggle between these various impulses takes place on the physiological level, and the victor alone appears in consciousness as a sensation." Normally there is a sensation of warmth, but if the heat mechanism is out of action, the sensation is of cold, and if the cold one also, the sensation is of pain. The unwitting suppression is a forecast of attending, which always suppresses and unconsciously. The gain is developed when attending comes; the successful quality now maintains itself by its own interest, and by that of its new associates. It has the power of an object. This characterises the act of attending or making object, quite as much as in- hibiting and emphasising characterise it. "In fact an object might be defined as a complex of projected re- sponses; it is said to have characters, such as size, shape, weight, and position in space, which distinguish it from all others. The recognition of such features depends on physiological activities, the product of certain definite centres in the cortex. If these are unable to influence consciousness, the 'object' disappears, although its affective and qualitative aspects still produce their appropriate sensory reactions." The several qualities are not first projected, and then related; they are felt in relation, at once united and differentiated. "The unit of consciousness, so far as these factors in sensation are concerned, is not a moment of time, but a 'happening'. . . . It is the projected elements in sensation to which we owe our conceptions of coherence in space and in time."[1]

So much preparation within the living body was required before it was possible or useful to know a

[1] Head, *Studies in Neurology*, pp. 748, 754.

thing in space, and even, therefore, to know body or limb as a thing. It is a long way thence to the power of making an object of anything, whether sensible or not, physical or mental, real or nonsensical, concrete or abstract, complex or simple. Even the simplest is not so simple that the rest of our knowledge cannot make much of it. Every object that we set before us is set also in relation to other objects: to others of its kind, to others that depend on it, and to others on which it depends. They control our expectations, and come to light at a challenge. The whole setting has been learnt, and learnt by living it. The living has organised itself as our power to grasp, which is our mind as a thinking thing.

In the lecture after next we shall consider our mind as such a thing; but first we have to go farther with the service of thought to its objects in uniting them, and finding the unity to be theirs.

VII

SERVICE OF MINDS TO NATURE

§ 1. THE power to grasp physical facts varies in us all, but we all place them in the same whole of nature; the difference is in the completeness of our placing. It is a distinction that carries into every act of thought: there is always the pointing, or attending, and there is the grasping or comprehending. It is the comprehending that we care about, and isolate as intellect. We thereby isolate also the remainder, the making object, the attending, which we find so easy and inevitable. On occasion it forces us to notice it:

First, there are the objects of which we claim that we cannot grasp them at all: the soul, for instance, or God, or the aether. But we can make them object; we know what it is that we fail to grasp, and why; it is never because the object is real. Our making object also forces us to notice itself, when we compare the minds of animals with one another, and with our own; for we have to ask to what they can attend, and with what purpose. Because they cannot think of their minds, they have to be broken in to a behaviour. We are also forced to notice it, when we ask about the springs of our conduct, for it is objects that agitate them, and objects that they seek. And it forces itself, finally, when the relation between thought and brain, or thought and nature, puts the question how a thought can be true. It is true, you remember, on two conditions: the object must be independent of our thought of it, and it must be in our grasp. These are just our two factors; one is the making object or attending, the other the comprehending or grasping.

It is necessary, therefore, to generalise that beginning, which I quoted, where the object was "a complex of projected responses". The projection is not from one space to another, as if the thalamus felt something to be in the head, or elsewhere in the body, and the cortex, which knows better, placed it outside. Instead of a complex being projected into space, space is part of the complex projected. Our bodies are in it, the things in contact with them, and beyond; and, in their 'happenings', time is there too. No distance is created, nor discovered, between the perceiving and the complex perceived; all distance is in the object; and there it remains when skin and limb, and the brain for that matter, are known to be the means of perceiving.

The complexes that any animal projects may all adhere to the first model; they may all be spatial, for space continues to be of the first importance. But plenty of the topics that we project, or object, have no space; and among them are those that need space at the start. Music is an instance; it detaches itself from the source, and from our means of hearing it, even from our heads when we go through a passage in our heads. In perceiving we project not a matter into space already separate; we project space, and time too, as matters to employ, and to develop, with the rest.

When an object becomes complex or general, we grasp it by a part, and, as we grow expert, by any small and casual part. The line of division has no theoretical importance: it does not divide what has entered our mind from what has not, nor what is given from what is inferred, nor conscious from unconscious ideas. A thought seldom looks to the division, even when seeking

to be accurate, or to be adequate. This carelessness
ought to prevent us from dividing an object into part
that can enter our minds, and part that has to stay
outside and be meant.

It should also prevent us from criticising a view on
account of our organs, or on account of its history. The
only critic is the object. The division between felt and
meant coincides at first with the line between data and
inference. To recover the line may seem the proper
course when we are in doubt. That may be necessary,
if the object has gone out of reach, and we cannot use
it; often we rely on convictions whose origin we have
forgotten. But we base their force on their success past
and present; they rest on their ground, not on their
origin. And, as between the conscious and unconscious
parts of ideas, the division is important not because it
divides, but because it unites them.

For there is no significance of the division so great as
that we make it anywhere. Every creature that feels
knows the advantage; it learns to react on all sorts of
sign. We hold a situation by as little as a word, and it
is commonly by words that we hold anything in its
absence; for they are faster, and far more searching
than images. How effectively they hold can be seen
from the rate at which we read; thinking is quicker
still; and, the better we know, the fewer the words. The
matters that we hold and turn over, with less and less
help, can be of any size, weight, and complication. No
wonder they seem not themselves but their ghosts.

Whether we hold much or little in a grasp is no
speculation; it is always at the proof. The answer is
made by the course of thought or behaviour; it is
clearest when the course is broken by a challenge. There
is no mystery in saying that only part of the object is
felt, that most is merely meant, and that this greater

part includes both the factors which we know best, and those of which we know that we are ignorant.

We can distinguish, if we choose, between the part that is felt and the part that is meant. And, within the part that is felt, we can distinguish between the datum and the part that it is felt to mean, which is nearly always far more important. But, as a rule, the greatest part of all we take entirely for granted; we use it without having to recall it by word, or ghost, or at all. It is the fundamental part, and to say that we ignore it would be nearly as wrong as to say that we are ignorant of it. The datum, the conscious meaning, and the unconscious meaning, all three are in the object; they are in the situation that is directing our behaviour. Their difference has its importance, if we ask about the function and economy of consciousness. But the great thing is that the object, by which we steer a course at any time, is the whole situation, and not the few and fewer signs by which we learn to command our knowledge of it. Conditioned reflexes come in as correlates.

This fact absorbs three confident assaults on the kind of thing that we grasp. When I recall an incident of yesterday, can it be the very scene that is now before me? Has it been living overnight in my sleeping and potential ideas? And what if I slip in recalling it? If these are good against my grasp of yesterday, and force a substitute into my mind, they turn easily against my grasp of other things. They say that real things reduce to a suitable essence in order to fit a mind and be felt. The three questions appear fatal, because they appear final. They are not final, nor even first; they argue to our power of knowing from our means of knowing. But they are useful, and I shall now collect them, because the answers to them open easily into three general problems: the relation of ideal to other existence, the relation of vital to mental reactions, and the relation of truth to reality.

§ 2. The first assault questions whether a past event can possibly be the present object of my thought. It is the object of my present thought, and the thought grasps it without requiring either a substitute or a resurrection. But there is now an objection which did not come with the corresponding question about distant things. There it was enough that no distance lies between a thought and its object, all distance being in the object and the means. There is also no time between a thought and its object. But that is now the accusation. A thought can escape from space, but can it from time? Since it is in the present, how can its object be but present, and a substitute, if the real one is past?

There are two answers, and both are general, holding everywhere. The first comes from the relations that connect part of an object with its whole. When we learn that the sun is not a lamp some miles beyond the clouds, we do not say that there are two suns, the visible one and the real one. The disc that we see remains the sun, when we know the whole of which it is part, and when we see it through a cloud or coloured spectacles, or double. There are various ways of knowing one and the same object; we perceive, or imagine, or infer, or remember it. In each way we grasp it now by one factor, now another; and we may barely notice what they are, as we pass through them to the whole which they mean. They and their meaning make one object in virtue of the relations between them. We may be mistaken about the relations, and then the thought is false. It would often be false, if the factor were always taken for a quality or a bit; but a sign need be neither. To deny that I see the sun, when I see the disc, is to deny that

I see your past work in the garden, when I only see
its fruit.

That is the first answer. But, given the recalling
factor, what of the further part, or the whole, that it
means? Must this not be recalled or felt in some form,
usually pretty vague? We might repeat it in full, but
is the new object yesterday's one? To say that the two,
the new and the old, are alike is to have the question
over again; for we should have still to think of yesterday's event in order to compare, and say they are alike.
In all cases, vague or full, the new forms are as the
disc; there is no personation; they are our means of
grasping the object that they mean, because we know
their relations with it. We need them less the better we
know it. It is yesterday itself, not a present image, that
is held and is the sole object of my present thought. The
past is not the present object, if by the present object I
mean an image; but the past is the present object by
which I steer my course.

There is a general consequence, or rather two; for
both are important. One is that there is no real character in an object that prevents it from being ideal, that
is to say, an object of thought. The other is that even
the past remains alive and active, though only through
minds.

The first we have seen throughout. There is nothing
singular in the instance of time; its value is in the
strength of its assault. As it happens, we can see the
past; we see now the sun only as it was eight minutes
ago, and stars only as they were thousands of years
back. Nearly always, however, we have to imagine or
infer the past. Neither the image nor the statement is
taken for a substitute; they recall the very event; and
nothing but their purpose makes them true or false.
One may say that they stand for the whole; but they

stand on a ground that is commanding, and not because it is easy and we are weak; it commands the whole.

The very incident of yesterday, now entering into new relations, actively exists, though now only through a mind; hence history and its value. If dead bones living are a paradox, take to-morrow instead, and whatever is not yet. When I institute an object as my object or aim, it begins its existence. Because it is not yet existing in nature, or some other real place, I make it my object, and complete its further existence by making it real. My intention in doing, as in knowing, depends on ideal and real being characters of one and the same object. As, in doing, I make real the very thing already ideal, so in recalling I make ideal the very thing that was real.

§ 3. The second of the three assaults on thought is also met by the object. The past, it is said, you cannot really recall, for it left you nothing but a state of brain, or, if you choose, potential ideas. But am I to call the face of a penny physical because I see it, and the obverse mental because I have to recall and imagine it? They are both ideal and both physical. The error, instead of taking thought as thought takes itself, argues, from the means, what the object ought to be. It might equally well argue against our knowing real time at all. At any moment I feel a change, therefore a span of time, a past as well as a present; and a past is never present in the brain. The general error substitutes the correlation line for the living one. There is nothing singular in the assault being from time, but only that the shock goes so deep into the difference between physical and mental life; it goes so deep that, looking into it, we can see their connexion from the course of time. The coming of thought was the selecting, and then the enhancing, of a character already everywhere in physical life and its evolution. Seen on this great scale, it is quite in the course of things that thought handles not substitutes, but things in themselves as they are, were, and will be.

For, though the object of a thought is never the stimulus producing it, we saw that the object is cause, or stimulus, once it is object of thought. We are prone to liken the two, because both are stimuli, and so to lose the main thing: we assume that both kinds of cause are very simple compared with the body of energy which they excite. That is what strikes us when we look to the working of a living body. The whole body has some say in every response, and we are struck by such complexity in face of the simplicity of the stimulus; and by such unity in face of the complexity of the organism. For, in the history of living bodies, the unity grows greater with the complexity. The unity and the complexity constitute the individuality of the body, and this individuality is enhanced when mind supervenes. The unity is enhanced, for now a creature can seek to do what it does, and it does what it likes. The complexity is enhanced by the gathering of experience into knowledge. And yet the physical stimuli remain so simple. They are much the same for the highest and the lowest creatures, and in ourselves much the same from infancy to age.

But an object, as cause, far from remaining the same and simple, takes the power of its meaning. The meaning is so well organised, from the history of its gathering in our grasp, that any factor affecting us can command the whole situation. When we open our eyes all nature seems before us, and has nothing we cannot name, if we care. When things have lost their freshness and grown stale, we take their meaning for granted, though we miss them and are excited, when either sense or meaning happen to fail.

Qualities like visible and charming, though they live only for a mind, belong to the object, and not to the mind; it is the blue and not my feeling that is charming, and it is the blue that is visible and not my sight of it. Even the shapes that fear or longing gives to fancies belong to them. Form is as integral to works of art and letters, as their tones or whatever their matter. It gives us our grasp of the institutions that organise our spheres of action. It is everywhere in the mathematical structures that bring order to the chaos of events; and it is in the individuality and the values of the ordinary things of sense. When we pass from all these to self-acting things, we have it the more emphatically that to meet an object, or make object, is to find something with a nature of its own. And it never matters that part is given us by given senses, and part we learn by faculties that we have to create. The unity of a symphony belongs to it, like the unity of an argument, and both are like the unity of chord or circle, which we take at the first attempt. Their unity is one thing, there all the time, and our grasp of it another.

We have seen why there is no conflict between the two living analyses, between the conscious one, which we make all the time, and the vital one, which has all to be discovered along the correlation line. In order that an object excite us, it has to be known; in order to be known, there is reaction to a conscious datum; and the datum is reaction to a physical stimulus. But that is not the end; we have to continue. The physical or vital stimulus is only one of an endless number that are also present out there; it has been selected, as the body has been, in the course of ages. The body of every creature selects and reacts to the kind of world by which it lives.

This is the character in which we have likeness and continuity between old and new, life and mind.

The character grows with the body, but never with such a growth as when the world becomes the world of objects, which has grown and grows with the conscious organism, which is the mind. Whereas the body modifies itself to suit and use an environment that remains much the same, the conscious environment grows with the mind. It does this not only for individuals, but for species, and even for tribes; for it is inherited with the power to take possession. The higher the race, and the fuller the inherited tradition, the freer its members are to range farther. The immediate occasion, whatever it is, takes its force from a sphere of interest, the sphere to which it is felt to belong. So large is the object in even ordinary thought. But it can be as large as nature and all time. One's idea of such an object may be vague, poor, and therefore ineffective. But that does not matter. These very epithets, like true and false, do not apply except in one reference. They refer not to an essence in the thought, nor to the object so far as it is known, nor even so far as it can be known, but to the very thing.

§ 4. The third and remaining assault uses the world of difference that lies between a real thing and one that is not. It puts this against the fact that the thought of a real thing is quite like the thought of one that is unreal. When my memory has made a slip about yesterday, and I recover, the new edition is quite like the error which I drop. But if the error is idea merely, there being nothing real to drop, can the new and correct one be the very thing? Yes, if error did not feel like truth, there would be no error. But also there would be none, if I did not intend the very thing as it existed. It is

because I meant the same real yesterday in both
editions that the old one was in error, and the new one
can correct it. The third assault, like the other two, is
thus met by the object. It does not matter that the
object may only be meant; to exclude what I mean from
the object, would exclude judgment from the acts of
thought, and thereby their truth and error.

But let the assault be carried beyond truth to reality.
Let my present thought of the past be of the past as
it was, it is of the past as I then thought it. And, in
general, what can I make object of reference and real,
but what I have grasped and still retain? That forgets
the modest function of knowing, which is never to
limit things by its grasp. We do not suspect vision
though all eyes are so blind, nor memory though the
past is mainly forgotten. And reason stands on the
surer ground that, discovering defects, it can set out
the very factors that defy it. They have to complete the
things that it knows. Objects like reality, minds,
nature, all the worlds, are set out as things found, not
as doubtful assumptions.

The history of the meaning of these words, and of
words for great sections in them,—for thing, self,
matter, will, force, infinite, and the rest,—is a record
of our improving grasp on what they have always intended. They have always intended the standard object, the object of reference. Sometimes it is completely
known, sometimes it is not, but whether or not, its
constitution is complete. Otherwise it would not serve.
Even to-morrow is complete, so far as we can say anything about it that is true, false, or doubtful. The standard may be difficult to apply, but that is a matter of
reach. Even when the standard is of human origin it
may be hard, as lawyers know; and nature may be an
easy standard, though hard for theory and invention.

The very thing is the standard, though we can use it as criterion so far only as we know it.

For that reason, if we follow the new habit, and speak of nature as a conception, we have to distinguish between conceptions regarding nature, and the conception nature. The conceptions try to be true to one which is neither true nor false. On that account the habit is mistaken, or a pity. A physical theory is an object or conception of the first kind; it is intelligible in itself, but it needs nature to make it physical, and so far only as it makes nature intelligible. The distinction holds for all sections of the world, of which nature is one, and for their sections too, all of them objects of reference. The dividing is neither true nor false; it is good or bad, according to its value for the advancing of our grasp on the unknown causes that may make words change their meaning.

But the third assault proceeds with What then? Include in the object all that would complete it, can it matter that the real is an object of thought, if it is also an object of ignorance? It can, because our ignorance also marks boundaries on it. We cannot be ignorant of nothing; the unknown real still makes itself known, as malaria did in the long years of error about it.

But the long way from known to real thing looks longer the farther it goes. When little was known, there seemed little to know, and man was the measure of things. The characters of the real that were sought, and seemed at hand,—the self-moving, the permanent, the simple,—disappeared on approach, or grew abstract. Are we not as children chasing the sun? To-day, more than ever, the lines of knowledge are forced apart by the very facts on which they close. But they also prevent us from believing that we live in a cave, whether Plato's, or the cavity of the skull. The beckoning light is no longer sun nor mother aether, but general equations. It is because the ways on which we travel, every creature in its way, are already real.

There we have the answer also to the charge that, while our grasp and its truth are matters of degree, to exist has no degrees; it is yes or no. And the final charge against our objects takes us back to the beginning. Since to be real is no conception, and before any, can we not at least ask how in the world it can be known, and without bending to suit us? But a whole does not bend to a part, however they are related; and a distorted object has to prove itself distorted. There is no exception; the question is always about an object in hand, including how it came there, never whether a real, being real, can be known. Most things cannot be known, but it is never because they are real. When we doubt whether a thing that we infer can ever be known, it is already so far known, and our doubt is never lest the thing be real, but the contrary.

§ 5. Those assaults against the things in our grasp are often due to identifying known thing and knowledge. When the known thing is no fact, as in error or dream, the distinction is of no importance, and so both are thrown on mind as the rubbish heap. But the kinds of object make no difference to the analysis. Let us now open the list that we closed in last lecture, and add the whole surface of nature, the sensible world. All that is known there has been lived; it is complete in this that it verifies all the beliefs, or expectations, that creatures have who know no better. There are two further reasons that make the surface important. From it alone we reach the rest of nature; nothing is found below that the surface must not verify. The other reason is that, in next lecture, we are to be occupied with the

M

same section of oneself. A mind has the same working knowledge of itself as it has of the sensible world; and the consequence on the self that lies below is the same. Let us examine the physical character first of the objects of sense, and then of the objects of common sense.

Sensation has two functions in our knowledge of nature. As an event, it is the final criterion; and many of its objects are part of nature. It is a criterion by warranting the conditions on which it is known to occur; and in that function all kinds of sensation may be used. The qualities that combine in the group called a thing out there are its foundation members; the peripheral organs that receive their stimuli are skin and muscle, eye and ear. Taste and odour attach themselves to the group, as do qualities from senses more organic, like exciting, pleasant, fearful, and painful. Though sensory and qualities, these are not physical, for physical is a further restriction, a matter no longer of our organs alone, but of the nature of the objects or qualities. They are physical because of their mutual relations in space and time, and their mutual behaviour. Since their sense-organs are there too, phenomena prove themselves physical by the part that they play even in being felt. That is why sensation can be the final criterion, and why it does not wait for physics to say what is physical.

And that is why all question of the origins of knowledge is beside and outside the question of what is physical and what is not. We may seek the first mind of an infant, at or before birth, on the good ground that we seek the first quickening of a seed; but one might as well say "here we have the first pulse of life pure and unassisted", as "there we have sensation pure and simple".

It makes no difference. Our organs of sense alter little with exercise, and have to grow very little after birth. We are therefore able to ignore them, and to correlate the object of the sensation with the stimulus. It has the same advantage that we have in using our limbs without knowing the machinery. It has also the disadvantage of suggesting that our senses are mirrors. The error is easily rejected, but there are remnants of it. There is one if we exclude from the pure and proper object of sense the factors that cannot be correlated with factors in the external stimulus. There is another when we divide an object into data from sense and accretions from memory. For the additions are not by accretion, but a growth. When data take a meaning, they also change; they take within themselves a definiteness, and a complexity, that are new to them.

How can the objects of sense be physical, yet vary with our organs, and these vary in different creatures? How can nature be so different, and yet be one and the same world for an ant as for a man, seeing we all inhabit the same? We tell the sensations of another only by inference, and we infer them only from their causes or their effects. From their causes the inference is doubtful owing to our ignorance of the nerve conditions. There is better argument from their effects, but it is by no means perfect. One effect is the use of words, but they are general; a man can be colour-blind, not only without knowing it, but without giving it away. When one likes a taste that another dislikes, do both feel it quite the same? What pitch is heard when we fail to distinguish two neighbouring tones? And what can decide whether a second feels the same to us all? In a word, when we compare the objects of sense for different human beings, we meet a little of every difficulty that comes when we try to compare them with those that are

felt by lower animals. But the difficulty makes none
for the question what is physical; why is this?

Why is it that science is so little embarrassed, and
not only science, but creatures that have to judge one
another's minds? Because they ignore the similarity
of the objects, and pass to their sameness. Not to an
abstract sameness, as when, disputing about a tint,
we are at one that it is a colour. An abstract identity
leaves out the differences, and they are physical, and the
problem. It is concrete identity that is found by science,
and presumed by every creature. Also, if there were no
difference of sense-organ, and all saw and heard the
same, we should have to prove it one and the same.
Otherwise there might still be so many minds, so many
worlds.

Far from abstracting we take the phenomena more
fully. Their variety for different creatures, and at all
angles, proves to be wealth of nature. We add to a
quality which we feel the conditions on which it is felt.
Instead of looking into the mind to which it appears,
we look to the thing of which it is appearance. An
audience hears one and the same music, as it sees one
and the same player, though everyone is hearing and
seeing with a difference. When a stimulus gives rise to
different sensations by different organs, or in different
creatures, the phenomena are physical, for they prove
the place and function which they claim. Even those
from abnormalities in our organs may claim to be
physical, if they do not also claim to be normal. Their
claim is like that of the lengths of a stick seen in and
out of water. They do not wait for physics to prove
them physical, any more than we wait before excluding
the objects of our dreams. Whatever the number, the
variety, and the activity of sense-organs, we have
only to suppose them all in one monster to see them

reporting one world. He has an extension of the problem that each of us easily answers for the senses that we have.

Nothing that is discovered about the phenomena that are felt can correct them. The conditions in our organs never offer a reason why they give this sensation, not another, or none at all. The error of thinking that they ought to tell resists longer than the mirror, and therefore also has its remnants. We no longer ask whether a quality is felt through its like in our members, or through its opposite. But, if a thing is reflected upside down on the retina, how do we come to see it upright? And was it no answer that the image is reversed again, when projected on the brain? The question is in error, and no answer can make it good. Why is contact felt at the skin and not at the brain? We no longer answer: there is an impulse from the heart that drives the invading stimulus back to the surface. But is there nothing to answer? The nerve-cells concerned were once at the skin; why not say that, when they migrated, they left the sensation at the end of the fibre by a useful 'law of obliviscence'? And referred pains useful to the anatomist, and feeling in the fingers after the loss of an arm? There is something to ask and answer, but the question has to follow the fact, and ask for nothing but the means.

And so we pass to external phenomena, where we like the answer least; and thence to everything physical. When a quality is felt as not even at the skin, but beyond: if grass is not green till it is seen, and the means have all to be gathered in the brain, has not the green been transferred in the course of time from brain to grass? We cannot save even that remnant. For the reason that no one asks why the sense of green should come from so many and unlikely conditions, for the same reason there is no question why it is the grass that is green, and not the eye, or something else.

Sensations are events, and no event is at fault. They are often deceptive, but the deception is not in them nor their objects. There is none till we infer the conditions on which they are felt, or the conditions on which their objects exist. The colour-blind see as they ought to see. There are inevitable illusions, but there need be no more delusion from them than from a daydream. Phenomena prove themselves physical by their mutual relations, and by nothing else.

But the most important relations are dynamical. How can phenomena play the part in nature that we need, seeing they are not phenomena without a nervous system? We have cut them adrift from our minds, for we do not alter them by observing them; but how can we cut them adrift from our bodies? Our perfect monster would be in the plight. Let him have not only every kind of sense-organ, but a sense-organ for everything; and let his reason be so perfect that he can determine all physical events; yet the regret should remain, if it is good. There would be nothing in the self-acting system of nature that could not manifest itself. Any further clockwork would keep quite out of sight.

But also he knows nothing that asks for it. He determines the course of phenomena from their mutual relations. Their system includes the conditions for his feeling them, as well as the conditions for their behaviour; and because he distinguishes the two sets, he remains in their common world, instead of supposing a joint clockwork producer. Three means of escape from the veil of sense have been tried. The old loop-hole by way of reason was by a sense without an organ. That being closed, another way was to try and rescue the forces of nature. The third way was to take the veil for complete, but to press it on the features of reality, and reveal them so far. Our monster would see that, instead of being a pity, the veil is the thing to develop. He would also see that we do not need him, nor any other artifice. For there may be no other phenomena in nature than such as we know, and we saw that imagination does not really take us beyond their narrow range.

It is the more striking that the common-sense world with its things, classes, and laws, should consist of phenomena, that it has all been felt and lived, growing for us with our growing grasp, and that no belief is imported that is not an expectation of which sense can give proof. For animals this world is free from reflection and language; and, in spite of both taints, ours can be seen in quite the same practical character. Common sense is not so guilty as its language appears to say. It stands a poor examination on the meaning of simple words like thing, is, has, I, act. But it learns them not as definitions but as physical signs; it knows nothing of them but their applications; and so their implication is felt as merely a mutual analogy among the instances. When it says 'this thing has an odour', there need be nothing vague, let alone an error. When it says 'a stone broke the window', there need be no confusion till it is cross-examined; it is saved from confusion, as well as from error, by its ignorance. Instead, however, of making this defence, when new questions come to challenge the working knowledge, we may seem to have been answering them all the time, and wrongly. If a thing is hot to one hand, and cold to the other, can either quality belong to it? If the table that I see varies with my distance, is it not images that I see, and never the real table?

Such questions about a thing are never put nor

answered in perceiving it; they seek a notion of it. At first the notion is of a group of qualities and powers that hang together, or that need something to cement them and exert them. But that notion is not equal to the practical knowledge already in hand; it contains too little and too much. It omits the relations of things with one another, and especially their relations with our bodies. That would never do for our behaviour; it is the relations that guide us. And it says too much, when it deprives a thing of its observer. He is always present; he never asks nor knows what a thing is in his absence.

The cementing and exerting self with which he endows a thing is his own. It is his way of grasping the independence, the spontaneity, and the power beyond his knowing that he finds in every thing. He does it in the only way available: he lives the thing. It is a venture of ignorance that prevents no later learning. When we learn the machinery we do not leave his way; the machinery is not a rival explanation. Science puts his way aside, as it puts colour aside, and the rising of the sun, when it dismisses the observer. But literature keeps it and art makes it fundamental, using the strength, grace, caprice, all the characters of individuality, with the same right that it uses colour and sound. If science follows nature, so does art. There need be no confusion of the two; and at their source there can be none, for they are not yet distinguished, far less mistaken for each other.

There is the same contrast between the practical knowledge of oneself and the first notions that collect it. The practical knowledge makes no confusion of mind and thing, whereas the first notion pictures oneself as a kind of thing. Mind and thing are kept apart because they are kept in relation.

Therefore our principle of conscious living does more

than exclude later questions, and make ignorance a refuge. It sets to the later questions, and their notions, the whole body of living knowledge for their data and criteria. It sets not merely sensations, because they are the final criteria; it sets the sensible world. Nothing has been imported that must first be removed. When we animate a thing in perceiving it, we animate the whole; we do not instil a core of life or will; all belief about it is open to correction by sensation. That is why there was nothing to control the long controversy about the substance of a thing, and how it stood to the thing's qualities and powers. The substance was rightly regarded as a work of reason by those who thought it a discovery and those who thought it an imposition.

In perceiving we select any spatial group of qualities to be a physical thing. The tangible qualities are so important in practice that without them we may call the group a thing, but we hardly call it a body or a substance. It is the visible qualities, however, that take precedence for knowing; we speak of every kind of quality as if we saw it; we call it an appearance, a phenomenon, a view. Other creatures rely on other qualities; "in aerial insects sight is the directing sense, in worker ants it is usually smell, in spiders it is touch, in caterpillars it is touch and taste combined" (Forel). The groups that they select for a thing are doubtless very different from ours. But every group is physical, a thing in nature; and every creature verifies its own things with its own body.

The groups are all actual; and, when we want to distinguish between what is actual and what is real in them, there is no mystery; it is a matter of degree and purpose. Each quality has aspects, and, when we call one aspect the real one, we merely set them a standard; we refer them to the aspect that we should feel at the best distance, or through a microscope, or in clear air, and so on. To this easy meaning of real we add only a little when we quit the aspects of a quality for the quality itself, and ask what is qualified by it, or of what it is the appearance. We answer by giving the whole group, or by giving the factors that are most constant. Either may answer all that we ask, when we ask what is real or appears. We add more to the meaning of real, we ask for more, on finding that some factors are indispensable to the group. There are first the time and space, and then the tangible properties, if there are any. Because of their practical importance we call the tangible the real qualities, and the others their phenomena; to be real is to be palpable. But they are all still qualities, phenomena of one another. Finally, it unsettles nothing if three are selected—volume, density, and weight—to be the defining qualities, which together, and as related, make a thing a body or substance. We should object only if they were taken for the whole body. Thus far, if we leave the sensible world, we keep in touch, and continue the way of life without the chance of a quarrel.

But we enter on a new course when we take a factor away from the group in order to study and combine the variety of its instances. It is then as if a thing; and we slip easily into the error of thinking it a thing. The error grew explicit in the substantial existence of forms, essences, life, principles, energies. Though the error could persist for some time after it was exposed, the make of our minds, or of our brains, could hardly be blamed; the common notion of the laws of nature, for instance, can easily lose the error. But there are still older notions, and they have been thought to have their roots in perception itself: our common notions of time, space, matter, and the unity and the power of a thing or a particle. They have been thought too deep to uproot.

As we look back from present science to past, it is more from light to dark than from truth to error. The laws that were found in nature are ill-fitting, and the forces in them are always more, and often less, than the facts require. The farther we go back the more we find this, till we pass the notions of common sense and come to its perceptions. The course has been continuous, and it suggests that here we are still in science. It would follow that, as later science displaces earlier, so part of perception may be displaced, or, if inflexible, may be twitted with its age and inertia. Nothing of it is displaced in fact. Explanations come and go, but it remains, and remains the demand on all that follows. We are often mistaken when we perceive, but we are corrected by sense and not by science, though science finds the instruments.

That will seem too easy an answer at the present time, when we may appear to be sent still farther back than from perception to sense, by the phenomena which confirm the quantum theory of the atom and the general theory of relativity. But the sensible world speaks only for itself, and it does not ask the rest of nature to be like it, as it would if the rest had to be imagined. And, far from sense losing control by its uncertainty, it was a measured vacillation there that gave the cue for the profoundest reach at present from the surface to the depths of nature (xiv. 5). All the oppositions between the sensible world and nature proper will be found to come into the general one between flexible and rigid, which puts the essential question to minds and lives.

VIII

THE MENTAL SURFACE

§ 1. In conscious life at any time the variety, complexity, and intensity may be great, or they may be as little as we hope they are in helpless creatures. The changing complexity, though we feel it all, is always greater than we can notice without the cunning of psychology, and the abstract handling of phenomenology. The absence of elements can be far more exciting than their presence, in the feeling of oneself no less than in the feeling of familiar objects.

The unity of a consciousness at any time may well be such that to change any element is to affect all the rest. That, however, is only evidence; it holds more or less for all unities, all of them objects; but it rather misses than points to the subject unity, which is nothing if not felt. It is felt all the time, and has only to be noticed, not to be demonstrated. The evidence would lead astray, if it appeared to argue some law of conservation for consciousness. The law is to economy instead, and the economy is greater the wider we are awake; consciousness is not preserved, it is a process.

To notice the unity, consider what you feel when you open your eyes; the elements of the scene are equally separate and connected. Open your ears as well, say to music; there is the same, though the separation and connexion are no longer in space. And the elements of scene and music live together without confusion. Add whatever feelings of yourself you find in looking and listening, your interest, alertness, your temper also, and background of mood; they are all there together, as connected as they are separate. There need be no sense of effort; when there is, we have the same, and the same when your noticing of your consciousness gives it a new direction, and so disturbs it all. To separate is to connect, and even to identify is to separate; it is the nature of consciousness, and the virtue of the first syllable of the word. Since neither word nor unity means that where no difference is felt there is no feeling, the third syllable goes farther. It adds that consciousness is not an agent but an abstraction, the common character of its elements, not their unifier. And then finally: its elements are entirely varieties of it. Not only has it to be felt, nothing else is felt. There is no difference between it and its varieties, but only between its varieties. To ask whether the subject remains one all the time is to ask about both consciousness and its varieties. Let us continue with the varieties:

Consciousness at a time, which we have been considering, is only a cross-section. The actual course has a direction, intended or not, towards an end that will end it. The end may be a better grasp of the object, a fuller appreciation, or its alteration; but the course to each end needs the three kinds all the time: grasp, appreciation, and action or direction. And there are stages in the course, each also a course, though economy shortens them towards instants. The felt elements are more again than we should notice on reflection without help; but their full number is trifling compared with the kind, as well as the number, that are taken for granted. These have all once been felt; now they work without being felt, proving their presence by the disturbance that they make when they fail to work. Their power is such that the conscious part is only the steering which commands their power. The very end that guides the steering can take itself for granted, once the course is well set. The answering neural development remains quite unlike it, and has a complexity infinitely greater. Thence to longer courses, occupations, and the whole course of a life.

It is not the worlds which open out that develop; they are discovered. It is minds that develop, and their growth can be followed from the advancing responses with which they enter into fuller possession. The worlds that we possess, and that possess us in what we take for granted, we have lived. We dissent on first hearing that; and the reason is important, for it carries us farther. The advance of physical life from accepting to seeking continues in the advance to conscious life, which makes object. It continues from making object to completing the object. Seeking is adventure still. It occurs no less in fear than in daring; and, in the unexciting range between, it is habit, where words carry on and we seem to retire. To believe is to expect, and expectation is from what we have lived already.

The adventure completes objects and occasions into their worlds. At first into one, space taking them all. After they differentiate, they continue to keep all completings or presumptions that nothing has corrected. That is why we seem to be completing nature, though it is the universe that is differentiating into worlds, including the world of minds, and minds themselves. The resistances that we have met, and are to meet, are due neither to stubbornness, nor to any inherited structure, nor to nature, but to the forecasting or completing, which is of the essence of life. It is by no worse cause, when the universe differentiates into worlds, but not well enough yet to show their connexions, that we call

them all aspects. We do it in deference to space and our
first notion of a completed object, or thing.

§ 2. There is no mystery in a mind's working knowledge of either self or thing. Few ever seek to define the
two words, and all are confused and fail when they
begin. It is because our knowledge of them does not
need to define them, and, everybody having the same,
because denoting is enough. Nor is there error in the
knowledge, none that does not correct itself without
a notion. The adventurous completions can be distinguished when the two begin to be defined; and then
it is obvious where completions come from, and why
they do not interfere. It is only after notion or definition
that they interfere, and that error begins. The fact is
not so clear for minds as for things, but there must be
no doubt about it, for we are to use it as final. As the
sensible world is final in correcting all working beliefs
about it, so the course of a mind corrects all working
beliefs about itself. The only difference is that its beliefs in itself are far fewer, though as frequent. Being
working beliefs they are again easy to separate from
the completions. They are still easier to separate from
the accretions that come with defining. It is the completions that matter.

They are seen at once for a thing, because physics
found it hard to replace them, and still finds individuality
a problem. The 'energetic' reform removes, from the
group of qualities that make a thing, the substance and
its force that had been imported to work and unite them.
We take a thing's grasp of its variety and power from
the feeling of our own variety and power; the substance
is a kind of subject, and the force a tendency, or will.
They are completions, not accretions; for, besides the
clinging together of its properties in one place, a thing

is seen to have invisible powers that work as one. To open out this borrowed unity was for ages thought the way to open up the thing; but the ingenuity spent upon it was never rewarded with a discovery. The loan from our mind still remains in things, but not for physics. For physics there is a different individuality belonging to the thing itself, which becomes intelligible in proportion as the clinging together opens out, and reveals the relations that make the thing a body, and systematic. This individuality is not borrowed, and it persists to the end, far below the living and lifeless bodies on the surface of nature. The surface bodies keep the individuality that is borrowed, for it repays. We do more with things than understand them and put them to use; they have intrinsic value, native to them when we live them as objects; it is developed in all art. The contrast is clear in the contrast between science and art. Things are understood in the general forms by which we grasp them; they are appreciated in the individual forms by which we are absorbed in them.

In differentiating mental from physical self, mind from physical thing, the accretions made on reflection are again easily distinguished from the prior completions. The completions are physical, due to minds being shown by their bodies, and to our own mind feeling itself in the behaviour of its body. The completions neither puzzle nor interfere, till reflection arrives. It puts questions good and bad on their account; but now consciousness alone has to answer. If it has to play the part that the surface of nature plays for physics, it has to develop itself to answer the questions when they are good, and convict them when they are bad. At first the task looks unlikely for the same reason as for phenomena, and then it looks a piece of unreason on quite another account. The same blight of being a product

fell on feeling as on objects felt, blocking the 'new way'
for it as for them, the way that freed them to speak for
themselves. In addition there came doubt about the
'reliability of consciousness'. The doubt removes itself
by the same means that remove all doubts from the
physical surface. But there is the piece of unreason. Is
it reasonable to presume consciousness to be the surface
of a subject with a unity of its own, which excludes any
possessed by its objects, in particular by nature? By
nature in particular, which includes our bodies, for we
should have two selves; but also by all their worlds,
seeing that we live, grow, and discover ourselves by
working in and on them. Why should consciousness
presume a unity for itself, and one that excludes them
and theirs?

§ 3. The answer is that it presumes nothing, and has
no need. The need found on reflection is from sources
that cause the felt unity to look trivial, and be overlooked. Yet it marks the difference between philosophy
and science, and its overlooking is the cause of their
confusion. When the properties of consciousness and
the properties of an external thing are differentiated by
excluding their mutual borrowings, that does not set
the question of their connexion, neither the individual
nor the universal question. The accretion that knowing
duplicates puts it wrongly, and for both. It puts the
individual question between the connexion of mind and
brain. It puts the universal question better by not losing
the object; but the duplicating still distorts. It makes
consciousness the surface through which reason in
nature is in contact with reason in minds.
   When science parted from philosophy, leaving the
whole to it, while it proceeded to occupy the parts,
what did it leave? The task of putting the parts to-

N

gether, and then of telling what is real? That brought the attractive conflict whether the real proves itself in the best performance, or in the indestructibles. The attraction has caused the alternative task to be over-looked; and it is the real one. The real task left with philosophy is not set by the sciences, but by the fact that all their findings come through consciousness. They left, and they leave, this fact behind, because it makes no difference. It makes none to psychology any more than to physics. The attractive conflict between worth and permanence being only increased, the felt unity of consciousness can still appear negligible. But the fact says more: all conscious creatures live and adventure within the felt unity of their conscious life, using no assumptions that have not fallen within it. The same remains true in advancing, or entering, the sciences, and in their advance to the freedom of their provinces. We may say with Bergson that, whereas the savant has to try and reach the unity of his province, the philosopher starts with the unity of his. But the unity for which the savant tries is offered him on the surface, and is reached in grades of increasing unity, at every deeper level.

That is what we substitute at the mental and the physical surfaces when we remove their mutual borrow-ings. We have a mental world consisting of minds like the sensible world consisting of things; for in both all has been felt. If we go below the minds of vertebrates, we go below the world of clear things. As we pass from the well-organised parts of any state of mind of our own, to the sporadic elements that are always present, so we may pass to lower minds, still inferring organisa-tion from behaviour. We cannot reach a stage so low that consciousness loses unity, for it would not be feel-ing; and perhaps not even one so low that a creature

is in several minds at once that have no bearing on one
another.

§ 4. When it is we who are in several minds, they
force us to feel their common self or subject. The feeling
is not emphatic unless it is forced; but, if absent, it is
always within easy reach. We know it so well that we
ask: Why not begin with the real sameness of oneself?
Why infer it from the unity of consciousness? That way
appeared so proper, it was made a ground against
the existence of a mind or self that the felt self can
break down, and sometimes break into two, or more.
Such a ground is no longer taken against the existence of a physical thing; and a self would have just
as little use for an unchanging substance to keep it
whole.

As it is late before we begin to distinguish the sensation of a physical quality from the quality, so it is late
when we begin to distinguish between our sense of self
and ourself. Here too when we separate, we begin by
duplicating; we connect them by their likeness, and
account for their likeness by making the real self a
stamp, and the feeling its impression. That failing, we
cannot leave them unrelated, if the feeling of self claims
to be true; for it can be false, just as can the feeling of
a physical quality. The relation between myself and
my feeling of self is the same as between a piece of
music and what I hear, or between any other thing and
what I perceive. Since the feeling of self is not a copy,
there is no invariable factor among my hundred feelings at any time to stand for I; and there is no question
about the presence or absence of the feeling in lower
creatures on the ground that they do not say I. Nor
need we look for the feeling of self in a feeling to which
the rest are attached, or which attaches itself to them;

there is no label that we may know them for ours, and not forget ourselves.

Shall we find it in a feeling always present? The sense of familiarity is promising, for, the more it is disturbed, the more we feel strange. Not novelty disturbs, but its conflicting with our expectations; before they are challenged they are quiescent in the sense of familiarity. That sense knows itself a resultant; it is not an item among the hundred, but a feeling of their mutual belonging; change their belonging, our expectations will change, and change our sense of familiarity. If the familiarity of the whole is not the feeling of self, is it a familiar part which gives the feeling? There is always the group of body sensations; when we feel fit, they keep to so familiar a range that we do not analyse them, and hardly know what we feel. It is when this bodily group feels unfamiliar that we complain of not feeling ourselves; and the strangeness, if persistent, may go the length of alienation. Like the whole, the group has unity, and feels its bearings, for it enlivens or depresses all the rest. This bearing on our outlook and inclinations gives us yet another sense of self. They are affected not only by the organic group, but by the hopes and worries that we make ours from whatever source we know them to come. And, most clearly of all, the sense of self comes when we are active in controlling the current of thought, and in keeping to a course of behaviour.

In all these complexities we have a sense of self. Why is it that we are baffled when we try to extract it from the whole web, and from any part? And, if we pick it out of each part, or from the wholes at one time and another, and place them together to find their common colour, why are we baffled again? The customary group of organic sensations might serve as a

common dot, if any mark were needed, but it does not
do the work; we want the working feelings of self that
each group requires. Their work varies with the task;
to extract a common thread, the feeling of acting and
yielding, for instance, would merely abstract. Take any
actual instance and we see what baffles us: it is that the
other threads come away with it. For without the feeling of self, these either change or disappear. When they
change they are a matter to which the feeling of self
has been form, as a square is the form of its lines, life
the form of its body, and a sentence the form of its
words.

We feel ourself, as we see and feel a thing, now from
one of its appearances, now another. We do not see a
shape and colour, and infer the thing; we see the thing
in seeing them, never the whole thing, but the thing as
a whole. We learn the power so to see. A painter learns
also to analyse what is learnt; but he does not undo it,
and recover his early mind; he paints no more than he
sees; and the meaning, which makes the difference, is
fixed and felt in the purely sensory values. For ordinary
seeing the meaning is practical; we read the field of
light and shade, without knowing how, into solid things
in empty space; if we try to prevent the reading, it persists against our will. Again the lesson can be analysed,
but no science requires its unlearning. Quite the contrary. Finally, the thing which we see does not consist
of the qualities and powers that we have felt; it includes
also the powers in the thing that have taught us our
ignorance of them. And always, when we perceive it,
we take most of it for granted, developing our grasp of
the part that has interest at the moment.

The whole of that can be transferred from a thing
and its appearances to a self and its feelings. They are
its appearances, though they are not of an object to a

subject, but only of the subject. The real self is learnt from them as the real thing is learnt from perceptions. Their self is common to them, as the thing is common to all perceptions of it, and it is felt in them as a thing is felt. The correspondence continues if the thing is living, growing, and decaying all the time. Whenever we say I, the pronoun denotes the living self. Like every concrete name it distinguishes its application from that of all others, and then is comprehensive. It comprehends mind and body; and we should be puzzled, but hardly more than with a living thing, to say what factors are indispensable, and how much of mind and body may fall out without the self collapsing. We denote the appearances by the predicates of I, just as we do the appearances of a thing. And a self, like a thing, does not live and grow by being known. Nothing benefits by 'know thyself' but knowledge; for the difference that the knowledge makes to oneself is no other than the difference that knowledge makes to the future of wool. Self grows by living, by being subject, by feeling, desiring, thinking, doing. That is what we make object; we interrupt the course of the subject, but we do not distort it, when we make it object, unless we forget that.

When something is said to fill our mind at any time, it is to the exclusion not of everything, but only of the thought of other things; for the more we are absorbed in a thing, the more it attracts us, and the less we are likely to enfeeble the attraction by watching our excitement and its feelings. Let a piece of news, or a visible danger, come like a thunderclap; we meet them with a welter of organic sensations. As the object defines itself the welter soon defines itself into a complexity of emotions, none the less definite that we do not name them, nor separate, but only live them: astonishment, fear, doubt, submission, hope. The confusion has polarised itself into them, as our self-experience, and the news or vision as our object-experience. The two vary with each other, our emotions with the thought, and it with the real factors that give us concern. The means by which they develop are past experience, partly remembered, mainly not. If we could remember all, the self-experience would not constitute the self, any more than the memories would constitute the danger. Subject and object have always taught us our ignorance of themselves; their unknown properties or powers have proved their existence from those we have known; they have proved themselves necessary.

§ 5. That is the superficial account of oneself; its facts are on the surface; it has no belief about them that they do not verify directly. Its reputation has been as bad as that of the corresponding common-sense account of things. There are three grounds against it. First, the polarising into subject-experience and object-experience does not coincide with the division into mind and thing, for the object-experience remains with mind. Secondly, when a self is left with body and mind, is it not left as two? And thirdly, what are those powers in oneself that produce thought, emotion, and behaviour, but the names of faculties that merely classify?

These grounds against the superficial account go beyond its profession. It speaks of nothing but our conscious living, the living of oneself apart from all notions about it. Like the common-sense thought of a thing it assigns nothing to the self that cannot prove itself. The account is superficial, because the facts are superficial. Physics does not question it, nor do the three problems. They come when we push home the notion of oneself as a kind of thing; we do it in order to find its facts more intelligible. And, because the notion

is good where it goes, its three failures to go farther
open the way from the superficial to the deeper relations.

The situation for the investigation of mind is therefore like that for the investigation of nature. The three
problems are so comprehensive that their solutions give
and suffer a variety of challenge. That is one reason
why the three are still treated with reference rather to
theories than to the facts that are felt. But it is also
because the facts did not appear to be final; and for two
reasons. One is that there are beliefs among them. The
other is that the feelings of self are out and in, as if
unimportant. But these two reasons, that begin by
making light of the facts, end in revealing two characters in them that are fundamental.

Our feelings of self contain beliefs which, though
practical, have been challenged. The sense of freedom,
called the freedom of the will, has been thought an
illusion, which bare logic is enough to expose. And there
is the challenge to all effort, that it cannot alter the
course of nature. What is there to protect our beliefs in
the freedom and the value of effort? It may be no great
protection that we do not create the feelings, and cannot
discard them, however we condemn them. But the
ground is good that no one wants to discard them; for
desire is part of the field of fact for which every theory
must account. The field is the course of experience, here
the course in directing and forecasting itself. Because
it verifies itself, it is not merely firm ground against
theories; they have to cover the ground.

We soon learn to distinguish the changes in the
sensible world that depend on our minds, and to distinguish their two kinds: those which alter the course of
nature, and those which do not, being merely a shift in
our grasp, or appreciation. The evidence for both is

the same, and the same as for the continual change in which we have no share. My arm obeys my will, but it may fail; and a name defies me to recall it at night that comes easily in the morning. These limits do not reject, they expand our knowledge, making it more precise. A man feels now fit for anything, and now the grasshopper is a burden; he can be in every kind of temper. All comes out in the variety of his reactions, and is made precise by experiment, whether the source be mental, as hope or fear, or whether it be physical, as fatigue, poisons, or the weather. All kinds of circumstances make a difference, and, as often as not, without being felt; but they have to be absorbed in the mental structure, and the structure has to prove itself in response to a situation. Many conditions can impair and destroy it, but they cannot force it to choose, nor prevent it from choosing, but as it chooses. The beliefs of a mind about its power cannot be handed over to any theory that does not let them prove themselves. And the acts that prove them condemn whatever principle would make them impossible.

But would they not put even logic on its defence, if they could prove real freedom in choosing? And, when they are self-deceived, cannot experience confirm the deception, and leave it life-long? These questions, like their physical parallels, require the rescue of working beliefs from reflections. To feel free refers to the alternatives offered me by my cause at any time. The situation, like the juggler's, is able to assign a task to the means without knowing them; the task itself would be ill-done, if any knowing of them interfered. When I toss a coin, and feel free to call, I am not submitting to my ignorance of what I shall say, but using it. The other question is simpler, because it throws no challenge to theory. Self-deception, however long-lived, is like every deceptive sensible appearance which only drastic events can undo. The love of country that proved itself selfish had met nothing drastic enough to define it better; whereas maternal love in animals proves its purity at once, despite its early passing.

The correspondence of the surfaces continues when we begin to describe subject and object apart from their being felt. As in describing absent things we provide them with an observer, so we provide minds with occasions or objects to which they respond. As we endow absent things with aspects, so we make minds contain ideas, desires, even emotions, all unfelt. There is no error nor artifice in either case, for we are not asking about the state of a thing, or its interior, when there are no aspects, nor about ideas and impulses when they are asleep. Obvious questions though these are, they do not occur in the business of life. When we put them, they are as disturbing about minds as they are about things. They are the more disturbing that mind has done so well; it has succeeded so well in separating nature from itself, and itself from nature, that we think experience must be due to their coming together. On the contrary, we have to go back to their separating.

§ 6. Standing there we see the three objections to the surface account of oneself. The surface is too superficial to answer them; but it holds the data and the criteria for all three and their answers. It begins by removing a common but fatal confusion between two separations. The living subject does not polarise his experience, but keeps it all to himself, when he makes object; his intention is to find the same behaviour in things felt or unfelt, and understood or not. The other is a later separating, used by psychology, as when it asks how a scene, or an argument, feels at any time, and how the same

ne, the more fully it has been known, is used with less
nd less feeling of it. But the primary fact is the
depositing of the object for reference, and for heaping
up its known part and its unknown.

Though no feeling is deposited with the object, the
object is deposited. Is that not some sort of idealism,
where things are ideas? Only if 'deposit' imports anything of a physical act or extract. The word merely
looks back, where the better words look forward: objectifying, pointing, grasping. They are better because
they are mental in the first instance, and, copied into
nature, are clearly metaphor. All objectifying is a feat,
a function of life, and therefore ill done at the start;
objects are at first ill-defined, for only other objects ever
define them. Next, our early and commonest objects
being sensory qualities and therefore physical, we are
apt to think that images, expectations, and other later
objects contain a defect for not being physical. On the
contrary, to our actual or forward look all objects have
natures of their own, and whether these are sensory and
real, or fiction, is for them to prove. That being clear,
we have a total deposit, more or less connected, and of
a mind handling it. But all that a man deposits, heaps
up, and becomes able to mean, he has felt.

Whence the objection converts itself into a strong
unlikelihood. Can objects that are deposited be entirely
nature's, for instance? Can phenomena, and can they
prove it, seeing they have nothing but their connexions
to take us below the surface? How can these reach the
depths and the final system of nature? The unlikelihood will collect the prejudices about minds and about
nature that we have to discard. They are erroneous
forecasts from the two surfaces in the first place, and
then from successive stages in the analysis of the
physical surface.

§ 7. We are to begin where the long failure to penetrate the material particle was taken to be final. There our mental life, though still thriving against reason, could still appear to be as parasitical as Hume saw it to be at the surface. An addition, since his day, had been made from the study of evolution; though nature as we know it could not be real, and science rested on contradictions, everything in nature, and in our mental and social worlds, was evolving, and dissolving, on one and the same set of principles. It was a poor substitute for their being real. Had Hume known the principles and included them in his long discussion, where reason convinces him that the conscious way of life is artificial, he would have ended as emphatically: "I may, nay I must, yield to the current of nature in submitting to my senses and understanding. But does it follow that I must strive against the current of nature, which leads me to indolence and pleasure? . . . If I must be a fool, as all those who reason and believe anything certainly are, my follies shall at least be natural and agreeable. Where I strive against my inclination, I shall have a good reason for my resistance, and will no more be led into dreary solitudes and rough passages." [1] While reason condemned us, it could also be bound, being never but the servant of sense for our knowledge, and the servant of passion for our behaviour. The addition of the principles of evolution went into the dilemma only to make it worse: not only passions were products, but reason also was now a product from countless generations. The defenders of human dignity were willing to believe it for the minds of animals, and therefore appeared to be fighting a rearguard action for the mind of man against the course of evolution. But a conflict between life, however low, and reason, however

[1] *Treatise of Human Nature*, p. 269 (Clarendon Press).

high, means that reason is at fault, and turns it back to make a fuller analysis. There is the same turning value in the conflicts between a mind and its means, between mind and necessity, between mind and its history, and in the conflict between mind and nature, where the more there goes to the object the worse for the subject, the more to nature the less to minds.

We shall be far more willing for a fuller analysis of the mental surface when we have seen the effect on the surface of nature, and have seen the nature of our shifting grasp. While the physical surface has been establishing itself more and more completely, the forecasts that reason took from it have been surrendered one after the other, till not one is left. They have found themselves too narrow, and because they had been copying, though there was no intention to copy. Instead of being copied, the surface has been analysed and derived. Hence there is nothing negative in the surrender of the predictions. And, with the surrender of the mutual independence of time and space, nature for each of us has found its place in universal nature. Such a well-defined place we should like to find also for our minds. Towards this, nothing is so important as to have their place well defined with regard to nature, which excludes them.

The three objections to the mental surface, the three questions that it raises and cannot answer, are answered by the three factors that constitute the mental causal system. The felt object is the fundamental one, and its weight or value depends on the whole which it is felt to carry. That is how the question of reality rises for minds, and why it has to be answered by the object alone; the other two questions go out of the account. They have to answer for the power of minds; that for brain looks for depth to the correlation line, that for mind or subject looks for depth to the living one. The two occur for nature in the two ways that we shall carry farther for minds. While the sensible world leads to the whole of nature, the leading depends on correlating sensations with external stimuli, which are the peripheral ends of the correlation line. That is one way. But the lead is given by the living line. Following it we see nature to be partner with the organs of our grasp, including the organs that we create. The partnership is an articulation, not an echo. Theories prove, when they succeed, that they can be as physical as the eyes and brains that we inherit. But that is a hard saying, and meantime it is enough to have in mind the two advances from organic to mental life, one the development of nature into a world of objects, the other our power to follow them, unhampered by our past, inherited or acquired.

PART III

THE FIRST OF THE THREE PROBLEMS
FROM THE MENTAL SURFACE

IX

FROM SURFACE TO DEPTH IN NATURE

§ 1. A PERCEPTIBLE thing, a grain of sand for instance, takes a logical as well as two physical analyses. The physical ones find in the particle an unexpected order and complexity; the logical one finds another. For the very notion thing, though the thing be a particle, and even if the particle be whittled down to an event, involves many notions. They are nothing if not coherent; they offer to be portion of an organon or logic out of the total organism of which language consists.

The logical analysis puts no restriction on the physical two. On the contrary, its grasp grows larger, better knit, and more competent, through them. The reverse would follow, if nature were logical not in itself, but by conforming to forms of thought. The inherited forms would differentiate in our life histories, and come out in the species of notions, and in the forms of the sentence. That has been a current view, but it is a remnant of the error that things conform to mind or brain in order to enter and make themselves known.

A thing, being concrete and particular, carries more notions than anything universal that is not concrete. In Hegel's organon, for instance, where the notions develop from partial to concrete, the notion Thing completes itself as an event, or, as he calls it, an Accident; a Thing is an Existence which rises from a Ground; it is Essence come to Existence, Force to Expression. Others come in, and all remain, when

Things advance themselves to Substances, whence, the notion still finding itself partial, they pass from being Substances to being Accidents of a common Substance. These or other such notions in the notion of a thing should be as flexible, if as firm, as our grasp. If they lose their coherence, or if they persist when they are obsolete, they become the familiar vague demand which nothing will ever satisfy. It forgets how words begin for everyone as pointers, and why they come to spell disaster. In the order of the notions I have mentioned the first one, the ground, remains first, because the others have to profess to stand on it by completing its demands. Essence, force, substance, and the rest stand on good ground, when they specify the demand. But, as a science improves its grasp, the outlook may so alter, and with it the demand, that the old notions and their questions are discarded. If they are then called metaphysical, it is for no better reason than that physics has abandoned its offspring, as it abandoned the substance of heat, and now the substance of light. The new grasp gives up the notions that would hamper it, but they remain with their names, because words do not readily die; they and their questions remain to cloud the horizon with an ignorance that no knowledge can dispel; that is all.

But must not, or should not, a logical system prevent the disintegration of its notions, let alone their abandoning? No, it cares only to be systematic, and it does not care to be left to itself, but to be used for dissecting out the systems in nature, because they are systematic. If its ambition is to be merely a frame, the same for new pictures as for old, it easily makes itself abstract enough. But it can do better in two degrees. The instrument or organon, which Aquinas completed for analysing and grasping a thing, was made from knowledge little better than perception. The claim is made for it that the whole revelation of things lifeless and living, which has been made since his time, fits into it. If by not altering, that would be poor; the frame, like a bottle, would be indifferent to the difference of system that filled it. If by the instrument being able to alter itself to fit the new knowledge, that is better. But there has come a still better ambition. A notion is the means not merely of grasping but of seeking; and it secures an improving hold by taking one that must yield a better, if it fails when pressed home. That is the ambition of the royal road which we are to follow.

We see it in the two kinds of physical analysis of a thing, and thence of all nature. Before the opening of the atom they were still at enmity, though not as at the start. But it will be enough to look at the early life of each, and its improving outlook, to see the course to be continuous and the quarrel to be no more mental, nor fault of human reason, than when it came to be between energy and atom. One is the analysis into qualities, the other the analysis into atoms.

§ 2. The analysis of a thing into the qualities of a matter is other than that which we make in our every-day sentences. In them we make the whole thing subject, and its factors are the attributes or predicates. It was long before explanation took the form of separating the factors into matter and qualities; Plato was the first to name the notion of quality, and Cicero the first to bring the name into Latin. The notion of matter was harder to name, because, being a residue, its properties were negative. Matter was incalculable though inevitable, without limit or definition, and therefore beneath real knowledge. It was also without real being, for it was inconstant and incoherent; whatever possessed it, or whatever entered it, lost unity, as everything did that possessed or entered space. The positive career of the matter-factor began when Aristotle found its name. The name gave it one of the two functions of the old animating self: matter became the subject of the qualities. With that it inherited the potentiality beyond our knowing which we find in every thing. But the potentiality was not energy, hardly potential energy; it was capacity, like the capacity of a metal to become a seal. The other and active function of a self was withheld: matter did not animate the qualities. They animated it; they made it a thing, and could raise it in the scale of things. It still kept out of real knowledge, as iron or gold remains out of the impression made by the seal. For matter could not penetrate our pores to reach our minds; only the qualities or forms could work a way in, and be wrought in the soul as in things.

The sensible world is unable to resent this reading, strange though it seems to us, and stranger that it kept the field against atomism and mechanism for two thousand years. The reading seemed the work of our native reason, which, at first praised, then came to be deplored. Being sure that the stuff of a thing does not enter our minds, we readily think it an indefinite matter which, taking one form, becomes wood or metal; then metal to be the more definite matter which, by taking a further form, becomes iron or gold; and then iron to be the still more definite matter which, taking further form, becomes a key or a sword. Though lasting so long, that notion and its grasp are from nothing native to our minds, but from the problem. The notion seeks what is permanent, and the answer is at hand in the arrangement of genera and species that we learn in perceiving. There a genus is the constant part of a

species, and the qualities of a thing manifest many
species, which are permanent in the degrees to which
they are generic.

The analysis led to the problems of the schoolmen.
They also led to the pursuits of alchemy. All metals contained the same primitive or essential metal; there was a
primitive acid in all acids, a primitive salt in all salts;
change the qualities of a metal, its colour for instance,
and the metal would come the nearer to being another.
The answer was a likely answer, and is likely to common sense, because the problem was not known as we
know it. It contained three errors, which we correct by
saying that phenomena do not need correcting, that
things are not self-dependent, and that they have not
a natural motion, and a natural state or place, to which
they tend. But at first the three appear to us all to be
fact. That is why the classes, which we learn in perceiving, seem a more likely quarry than the laws, and
things at rest than things in change.

Though the analysis could lead only to classes, and
so far did not explain, it explained nothing away. Of
its grounds against atomism this was the first and the
sound one. In the end it bred an atomism within itself
that should not explain away, a chemistry of qualities.
This led by its failure to the chemistry of molecules.
But that was not all. The qualities, or forms, being
already separate from matter and one another, brought
the separate sciences; and they gradually lost the manifesting of secret essential qualities, as they were seen to
depend on their connexions. Their indefinite matter had
an easier passing. It had been usual to endow matter
with quantity, and, when the notion of mass became
definite, mass became the quantity of matter. Finally,
with the reduction of qualities to motions, matter and
qualities fell to being masses and their motions.

The abstract analysis could then come to a working agreement with its old enemy, the analysis into atoms, an atom being now distinguished by its weight or mass. But the gulf remained as absolute between mass and motion as it began between matter and qualities. If the essence of matter was the first of the seven riddles of the world, the origin of motion was the second. The gulf, however, was doomed as a gulf, when the origin of rest became the same question as the origin of motion. And it was clearly a myth that motion should flow from one thing to another, the last of the abstract fluids. It was time for mass or matter to disappear as a subject, and become a quantity of inertia. The subject left the ghost of itself in the notion of a bearer, a "vehicle or receptacle of energy", the vehicle being still inert, passive, "the body of the physical universe, energy its life and activity" (Tait). But the vehicle having properties of its own, the 'properties of matter', it became no more than a convenience to distinguish the load of qualities from the conveyance; both had become energies. The gulf disappeared, and the metaphors that filled it, when a mass was found to vary with its velocity. Soon every kind of energy was found to have mass, and mass to be energy. That is how the analysis of a thing into matter and qualities has ended. We have each of us to recapitulate the long story without its length.

The ending of a thing in energy ends nothing in the perception with which it began. On the contrary, there is a return to our daily judgments. The subject is again the thing itself, which unites the factors, and is not one more, as matter was. In perceiving we know their union as just their joint occupation of one place, and their behaviour in unison. All the other relations, within the thing and without, add themselves, and correct nothing:

'We may define matter as a complex of gravitational, kinetic, and chemical energies, which are found to cling together in the same space" (Ostwald).

§ 3. Nature is a community of things, every thing a crowd of things, and, the smaller they are, the fewer their sensible qualities and their differences from one another. May not growth and dissolution, and the coming and going of structures and their qualities, be the collision and collusion of invisible particles too fine to be corruptible?

It has been thought that in the long run we can be satisfied with nothing less, and that the demand and the fault are inevitable, coming from perception, where every cause is a thing, as well as from our own work, which is all push and pull. But the blind force of the bias cannot be great, if the weight of Aristotle could counter it so long. And nature had as long a time to instil the opposite prejudice that matter is always divisible, being always in space. If we are born to bias, we should be inclined both ways. But again all difficulty is with the problem, not with our minds. And there is none of it in the problems of perceiving; continuity and discontinuity are compatible there, and there we have no question which of them is final.

When the question comes, it has been thought not merely to defy, but to break, the foundation of reason; for we have to say yes and no to both alternatives, though they are contradictory. But the atomic theory, like perception, can refuse the question. In its first intention the theory did nothing but imagine the imperceptible world as if it were perceptible. "When the chameleon puts out its tongue to catch the fly, we see the agent of attraction; when the electrical body attracts other bodies, how can it draw them to itself if not by 'innumerable rays darted out like tongues'? Beyond the world of our senses lies another, identical in kind, but too minute for ordinary perception; if our senses were magnified, these invisible agents would start into life; we should see the tiny thorns wherewith the nettle stings us, and perceive the corpuscles whose unsuitable shape makes the object painful to our sight.''[1] There was no question of discovering particles without parts. The theory keeps everything in space; that is the virtue, which made it welcome against every theory whose factors cannot be imagined. Yet there is less reason for surprise that it suffered so long an eclipse than that, so late as the seventeenth century, Gassendi could still revive the original form of it. Invisible copied visible; the surface was expanded instead of cultivated; the roots were like the flower.

There had always been a doctrine of the elements; and, in that century of writings on logic, men so different as Bacon, Gassendi, Descartes, and Leibniz compared them with the letters of the alphabet, and made it the task of science to resolve the language of nature into these and their compounding. The atoms of Democritus and Epicurus had been rejected, because together their variety was too great for an alphabet, and singly they were too simple. They threw off the endless variety of qualities, but they replaced it by an endless variety of shapes. Every difference of quality was represented ultimately in the atom by a difference of surface and size; the bitter taste of a thing came from atoms that were small, smooth, round, and furnished with hooks; "what is sour is angular, twisted, minute, and thin"; the shapes that give black are rough, irregular, and unlike one another; those that give red are spheres, like those of heat, but larger; "we redden as we become

[1] Brett, *The Philosophy of Gassendi*, p. 79.

heated'', and so does iron.[1] The failure of such analogies led to others that also failed, until the problem itself was seen to be in error; there is no likeness between object and stimulus. That result seemed at first a misfortune, and still its upsetting quality is not recognised. But there is no resistance from our minds, though no error can be older.

The atom has been released from that original duty; but it had three more. The theory undertook to account for the indivisibility of the atom, for its compounds, and for all change. The three were first explained by selecting from perception. An atom was individual because it could not be divided, and it could not be divided because it held no empty places; for, in their absence, there could be no disruption from within, nor penetration from without. Compounds and structures were due to cohesion and pressure. Change was due to impact and pressure. This theory of the three by selections offered so little resistance that the story of its failure is the history of its development. The development came in the reverse order on the royal road. It began in the explanation by impact and pressure, whence it passed to the compounds, and finally to the individuality of the atom. The explanation by impact and pressure had not been challenged. Before Galileo mechanical problems had been statical, and weight the common measure of the forces engaged. He discovered the notion of force, and its measure, by separating the inertia from the acceleration of falling bodies. When the discovery of the law of gravitation showed this to be world-wide, the two factors were formulated as the first and second laws of motion; and the third law, which had been the statical basis, could now proceed from one kind of equilibrium, in which no work is being done, to all kinds, and to the

[1] Stratton, *Theophrastus*, pp. 123-135.

equating of all work. Of the three the law of inertia was most welcome to the atomic theory, which had endowed every particle with an intrinsic motion, though whether straight or circular had been a matter of choice, and it could always be rotary. The law was welcome, because it supported the theory against the two traditional views that motion needs a force other than itself to maintain it, or else that it is a state which oozes away like heat. But the second and the third laws attacked both the plenum and the void. The interstellar voids were lost when gravity was found to cross them, a heavier load than light and heat, which could still be thought to shoot their way across as particles. The aether entered; as its difficulties grew, it became a charge against our minds, which, being brought up on matter, could not grasp it.

Then the charge went farther. The new notion of mass was not all hostile to the atom. Though mass could be divided indefinitely, it was additive, inde-structible, and indifferent to qualities. And the centre of mass confirmed the old advantage that the internal transactions of a thing, or system of things, may be ignored in dealing with the interaction of masses; a planet may be treated as a particle, and treated exactly. But the very advantage brought out the adverse; there is never merely mass. However small the particle, it needs an internal structure to account for the distribu-tion of energy at every collision. The third law would be satisfied, as Newton pointed out, if opposite motions cancelled one another, and were merely lost. But energy is not lost, and so the theory found that collision and cohesion, far from ending the dynamical question, open it. The plenum fell with the void. The discovery of gases, and of the means of measuring their pressure, and accounting for Boyle's law, though it began by supporting the theory, soon gave trouble, and ended in being fatal to the solid particle. For the simplest particles have most elasticity, and, on the theory, they have none. Hence the charge against our mental capacity again, and now because our minds were brought up not on matter merely, but on solids. "The gaseous form of matter is the true basis for the explanation of the solid form, and not, conversely, the solid form the explanation of the gas. . . . The true relation between the molecular states of matter is the exact reverse of that universally assumed. The universality of this assumption indicates that it is due not to a mere chance error of reasoning, but to some natural bias of the mind. The question arises therefore: What is the origin of this prevalent delusion respecting the constitution of matter? I believe the answer to be exceedingly simple, and important in proportion to its simplicity. One of the fallacies to which the human intellect is liable is that the intellect tends to confound the order of the genesis of its ideas respecting material objects with the order of the genesis of these objects themselves. . . . The first form of material action which was apprehended by the dawning intellect of man, was the interaction between solids, and it followed that the difference between the solid and the gas was apprehended as a mere difference of distance between the solid particles."[1]

§ 4. But that is the proper course. We proceed from what is first for us, and our own physical action, and go to what was, and is, first for nature. Therefore the course is by analysis. By the analyses of mechanical and statistical theory, a superficial system, pressed on a deeper, defines the deeper problem. The kinetic theory

[1] Stallo, *Concepts of Modern Physics*, pp. 174 ff.

of gases, ignorant of the interior of the particles, and regarding them as if they had none, and then as if they were 'perfect', forced them to open; and the theory of radiation, which came to meet it, had a similar history. They saw themselves, and all nature, pass into the electromagnetic system. There, far though it is from the surface, they saw sense able to recall theory, open a new prospect by means of the quantum of action, and establish a final control by the 'uncertainty principle'. Looking back we can see that nature was accepting the grasp, and insisting as well as we, but it could look more alien than ally on the route. The early outlook of the gas theory was into the picture of increasing chaos.

The royal road may well appear far too hopeful, though clear of the old horizons. There is no question of lifting the barriers of sense, but of cultivating within them. The route is to the roots of phenomena; it has to cause their cultivation from every level; and from each to the next it becomes more general. Will so narrow a surface let the route become entirely general, and reach the final roots or concrete system of nature? And, if the barriers of sense can be forgotten, can the boundaries of theory continue to define the difficulties against them, and thereby open a way? It was not to be expected, and no one expected it. Yet it is the way of life. The opposite way is to turn within, and look out from our equipment. Seeing our natural endowment so unequal to the task, we think the course of knowledge to be our cunning in fitting nature to our range; system looks a summary and ours, as if, the more we grasp as one, the more we must let go. That is the morbid route; we reflect on ourselves, and see that we can do no better than our capacity, and that nature must come down to it. But the healthy quest, the working one, fits our range to nature's, till we rest and reflect.

Bonds and their bounds then appear everywhere, but there is never anything to undo.

To count the particles of the air, and measure the weight and the size of one of them, to count the average number of its collisions per second, and measure the distance between them, and the speed that it makes, these appear great feats, because nature has put the particles and their behaviour so far beyond our senses. Their number in the usual unit of any gas runs to twenty-four figures, of which the first three are certain. Understanding has gone such a distance beyond sense that the credit seems ours, and nature a sleeping partner. But we have to thank her for dividing into systems, even for failing to do it completely, and leading us by correction. Understanding thrives on her stepmotherly treatment. We should be at worse fault about the partnership, if we made the common error about extending the bounds of sense. But there are consequences of the error.

We can see the situation best from a typical instance. There have been many ways of approaching the size of the smallest material particle in order to measure it. We may put them in three sets, each with its moral:

§ 5. One way starts by calculating the viscosity of a gas, because an equation of the kinetic theory then gives the mean free path of its particles. Or the start may be made by measuring its heat conduction, or, again, the diffusion of one gas in another. The mean free path is the radius of action which the centre of the particle has before the particle meets another. The liquid phase offers a further means because the particles adjoin, their number in the gas phase is known, and their volume in both gas and liquid. Or, the free paths in a gas being geometrical cylinders, and their number known, their total volume can be calculated, and so their radius. Or the correction to Boyle's law at great pressures can be developed. A different way measures the dielectric constant of the gas directly, or from its refractive index, then assumes each particle to become a conducting sphere, and so reaches the radius. And a film of oil, or metal, may be made so thin that it has only the thickness of a molecule; the volume of the material being known, and the area over which it spreads, the thickness or diameter follows, presuming uniformity. All these pioneering routes converge on a diameter for the particle of one or two hundred-millionths of a centimetre. There might have been as little use for the length as for the north pole on reaching it; but, by converging on it, the routes establish one another; and, making other junctions at the terms common to their equations, they draw lines across the virgin wilderness. There is no question of carrying the bounds of sense across the waste, but of cultivating a small perceptible field in order to realise its power as fragment and product. The distances that are actually brought to sense, and measured, do not seek to come anywhere near the minute length which has to predict them.

Newer routes look more ambitious; they not only go nearer, they are so picturesque that they look ocular proof, copying imperceptible size and behaviour in perceptible dimensions. Hence their aim is easily mistaken. The Brownian movement has been followed in air and liquid, though the moving particles have a diameter of only a ten-thousandth of a centimetre. The feat can seem also a failure, because the experiment reaches only a ten-thousandth of the way. That is the mistake. In cultivating the field of sense to discover and measure the wastes that lie beyond it, atomic or astronomic, there is never the aim to copy the size. No one has more right to speak of a feat than M. Perrin, whose patient work made the liquid route. He marvels that man can reach and measure a particle so small that it is as lost in our body as our body would be lost in the sun; but also that nature's gift of the gram-molecule is so fruitful and unrestricted. After the gas theory was extended to liquids, the Brownian movement came in as a product, and then an instance, of invisible collisions. It became possible to examine the behaviour of the particles of a gas by taking, instead of gas, the behaviour of an emulsion containing spherical grains of one size and mass, large enough to be visible, and small enough to make their chaos visible. When the temperature is kept constant, the emulsion reaches and keeps an equilibrium where, at every level of the liquid, the number of grains keeps itself the same. The number diminishes with the height, the difference being due to their effective weight, and calculable from a formula like that which determines the pressure of the atmosphere according to the height above sea-level. Thus gravity arranges into calculable layers the forces that balance themselves against it at their several heights. The radius of the grains can be calculated from the time that they take to reach an equilibrium by overcoming the viscosity. And a mean value can be built up by taking the positions of a grain at regular intervals of time, and projecting them on a horizontal line at the level. By such work at microscopic limits four different ways were developed of reaching the number and dimensions of the far smaller and speedier particles in a volume of gas. A similar use of gravity and viscosity was found through the cloud method of reaching electrons, a mist being formed on the sudden cooling of ionised air. The fall and rise of the cloud's droplets can be put under electrical control, which opens a route more exact, as well as more picturesque. "It was only necessary to get a charged droplet entirely free from evaporation into the space between the plates of a horizontal air condenser, and then, by alternately throwing on and off an electrical field, to keep this droplet pacing its beat up and down between the plates, until it could catch an atmospheric ion in just the way I had already seen the water droplets do. The change in the speed of the field would then be exactly proportional to the charge on the ion captured" (Millikan). The microscopic speck of oil or mercury is held in view like a star, and may be followed for hours. The charges on the drop have each an identical effect on the time of its motion; and, being equal, they not only measure themselves, but give the weight of the drop. "The device is simply an electrical balance in place of a mechanical one." Five years previously a balance had been made that "succeeded in weighing objects so small as one-millionth of a milligram, pushing the limit of the weighable down at least ten thousand times" the finest result of fifty years before. "The work which we are now considering pushed it down at least ten thousand times farther, and made it possible to weigh accurately bodies so small as not to be visible at all to the naked eye. For it is only necessary to float such a body in the air, render it visible by reflected light in an ultra-microscope arrangement, charge it electrically by the capture of ions, count the number of electrons in its charge, and then vary the potential applied to the plates, or the charge on the body, until its weight is just balanced by the upward pull of the electric field. We made all our weighings of our drops, and the determination of their radii, in that way."

The third kind of route is unmistakable, for it goes from small to large: from electrons and their radiation to the sizes of atoms, and to the distances between atoms in molecule and crystal. There is the same partnership with nature. "We can take directly from the hands of nature the diffraction apparatus necessary for Röntgen rays in the form of one of her masterpieces, a crystal of regular growth" (Sommerfeld). No artificial grating was nearly fine enough then to diffract them, so that at first they did not seem to be light. The moral is not that nature is good and wise enough to hide a stile at every barrier, but that phenomena can be cultivated from great and greater depth. It is not the number nor the fineness that counts. The thousands of lines in the visible spectrum of iron are as fine as they are abundant, and are used as a standard; but the two that Moseley cultivated from its x-rays had far greater value. Bohr's original theory of the atom had to predict the length of the diameter of hydrogen, and from constants that had been determined with no thought of such a thing. It then undertook to say how the diameter varies on excitement, till lengths in atomic interiors became as important as in solar systems, and then overturned the theory.

We might have gone for our instance to large instead of small. Instead of a diameter of two hundred-millionths of a centimetre we might have taken one of two hundred million miles, which is about that of Betelgeuse. Again there were approximate estimates on a variety of grounds, and again the feat had increasing importance, till the interference fringes of the light from the star were caught by an interferometer on Mount Wilson. The light which fell on the instrument a few years ago had left the star in 1760, and had been coming all those years with a speed of millions of miles a minute. It is easier to admire large things than small; but the same light could also record the diameters of the single atoms of the star.

Those persistent waves of light enforce the morals from the connexion of surface and depth. During the long strife between the two physical analyses it was agreed that, whereas qualities occupy one and the same place, two things or particles cannot. Everyone thinks the same till he finds that waves of light have all the properties of things (xii. 5), and yet occupy one place, blending and parting without resistance or confusion, each behaving as if no other were there. To keep our view we first ally them to waves of sound, as if they were made of particles. When they refuse, our failure reflects on our confident unconscious reason, and we see that we have merely been forcing the surface on the depths. Next we separate the two by the simple conscious reason that the surface came late, coming only with our senses. But, the two having to be joined as well as parted, we arrive at the main trouble; and again reflection finds the cause to be that we have been presuming the last word, giving it now to the historical order, copying it unwittingly from our individual lives. That presumption, which everyone makes, is also wrong. The situation clears up always in that way, being purely physical.

It remains purely physical throughout the depths, with their levels, boundaries, or degrees of system. A system so concrete and fundamental as that of light we are willing to assign entirely to our partner. But abstract and tentative systems we prefer to take as ours and imposed. That would not matter, but it makes us liable to error. Vaguely the error is that our impositions ought to imitate the surface. More definitely it is that they should aim at framing models, as if nature proper must be imaginable, though not by us. Finally the error stands clear when models have to give place to mathematical organs; for these, being created and far too

weird for the surface, look especially ours and not
nature's. The error will be met by converting the
partnership, and all notion of sharing, into the articulation of organ and nature.

Pass now from the barriers of sense to the boundaries
of theory. We are to follow their order in the analysis of
the material particle, keeping the single systematic
route, and setting out from the simple kinetic theory of
gases, which was thought for so long to have the last
word, or the last available one.

§ 6. Gas means chaos; the first analysis makes it
a simple mechanical system, in which only the kinetic
energy of translation is considered. Hence no property
of a particle is taken but its mass, and its mass is
taken to be indivisible, to be constant for all speeds,
and to occupy no appreciable room. The hint of system
came from the surface in the empirical gas laws, and
the system came clear with the discovery that the
energy in a gas, as a gas, is measured by the temperature. Every particle collides many million times a
second, and every encounter redistributes the energy.
How that can happen without loss, the theory does not
know; the question looks past the mass of the particle to
the properties that keep it whole, and perfectly elastic.
At first it also ignores the spin from collision, the
viscosity, the cohesion, and other attraction in the
encounters. It assumes that the thermal capacity of
every gas is the same, and the same at all temperatures.
The value of the theory is not that it may defy those
things, but that it can force them to the surface, where
it can profitably cultivate them.

The cultivation consists in securing the same temperature for a gas and its vessel, then disturbing the
equilibrium by altering the temperature, volume, or

pressure, by known amounts, and measuring again at the new equilibrium, where the distribution of the kinetic energy has grown uniform again through the collisions. The absolute scale of temperature (indicated by one of the empirical laws) having been fixed, where a degree is always to measure the same amount of energy, the theory yields the gas law or equation, which connects the mutual variations of Pressure, Volume, and Temperature, by means of a constant: $PV = RT$. It says that the product of pressure and volume is constant, however they are varied for the same temperature, and that the quotient of this product by the number of degrees absolute is always one number R, which is the number of units of heat, or units of work. Except for being so simple, the four factors being directly measurable, that is typical of the whole material advance. The theory then proceeds to establish its credit by seeking and meeting the numerous obligations that a mechanical theory must bear.

It meets them so well the ancient hope was revived that the theory might pass to all matter, and it did pass from gas to liquid, and non-crystalline solid. The hope was also a despair that nature should consist of such a dust; but what better was to be expected from the origins of phenomena, and the inevitable structure of understanding? And so the early intention, in correcting the theory, was to make it more equal to the chaos, till the corrections began to open the particles, and expose their electrical system.

This deeper system was already indicated on the surface among the several kinds of push and the several kinds of pull. Besides repulsion from impact as in a gas, there were the magnetic and the electrical repulsions. Especially there were the five kinds of pull: gravitational, magnetic, electrical, cohesive, and chem-

ical. All obey the inverse square law, but they are
effective to very different distances; and, while gravitation, the first and weakest, goes farthest, the last and
strongest of them goes no way. The five were problems,
and it was more than doubtful whether our minds could
cope with them. For the first three, acting across empty
spaces, had somehow to be borne by an aether for which
we had no sense. The last, the chemical pull, defied
minds for the opposite reason. Were the atoms in a
molecule a mosaic, or did they occupy the same place
like two or more qualities? And cohesion, the most
familiar pull of all, had always been hostile to the very
notion of an atom. The five attractions were beyond
the concern of the kinetic theory, but, by taking over
the empirical gas laws, in order to make them necessary
or systematic, it took over, and defined, the exceptions
to them. They are the exceptions to the laws of Boyle,
Avogadro, Charles or Gay-Lussac, and of Dulong
and Petit.

§ 7. The simplest is Boyle's law that the product of
the volume and the pressure of a gas is constant for
any given temperature. There are two great departures
in fact: one everywhere, the other at the points of
liquefaction. The universal departure is due to the
omissions in calculating the volume and the pressure.
The correction for the volume is that quite four times
the volume of the particles must be subtracted from the
volume of the gas, in order to find the amount of free
room. The correction for pressure is that they are not
quite free in the room; for they have a mutual attraction. It is other than the attraction of gravity, and the
temporary drag of viscosity; it is their cohesion. The
amount of this drag was brought into the simple equation by Van der Waals, together with the correction for

volume. He argued that the drag must be proportional to the square of the density of the gas, or the inverse square of the volume. The two corrections hold for all gases in all conditions without reference to the other bonds within and between the particles. The difference that they make has to prove itself in the discrepancy between the simple equation and the actual behaviour. The discrepancy is made visible in the shape of the isothermal curves which trace the product PV as P increases. The uncorrected equation makes the curve a straight line parallel with the axis of P. The actual curve differs, and the more the lower the temperature, the line first falling till it reaches a point where it begins to be parallel, but very soon rising up to a check at the point of liquefaction. The fall and the rise are as expected by the two corrections in the equation; for, while each correction ought to tell more as P increases, at first it is the inward drag that ought to tell most, and then the size of the particles. Their effects are antagonistic, and the two do not come apart from each other to be measured apart. Nor is either quite independent of high temperatures. The correction for cohesion assumes that they keep their average number, not breaking up nor combining; and it ignores any repelling, or merges it in the attraction. All that is the kind of fact that looks a defect. And again, except for being so simple, being all diagrammatic, the method is typical of the whole material advance. Much finer general corrections have been found, but the method remains of making them serve. It is suggested by the form of the corrected equation, and by the difference in the curves for different gases. Let us first continue with the curves.

While they look alike, they do not nearly coincide, when they lie on one another at the same temperatures. But they do coincide, when they are attached at their critical temperatures. By reason of this new check from its own cultures, the theory becomes far more comprehensive. A critical temperature is the point above which a gas does not liquefy under any pressure. It is different for different gases, and the difference may run to hundreds of degrees. There is also a definite pressure, and therefore a definite volume, at which they will just liquefy at the critical temperature. The three—the critical pressure, volume, and temperature—fix the common point from which all gases can be read in corresponding physical states. Two gases are in corresponding states of pressure, for instance, when they are under pressures which are the same fraction of their critical pressures.

The parallel in behaviour continues beyond the liquefaction points; the theory could discover that a liquid is just a highly compressed gas. The parallel is made visible in the isothermals which picture Boyle's law directly, plotting now volume against pressure. The curve ought by the law to be continuous at every temperature, a hyperbola lying symmetrically between the two axes. That is nearly true only for the critical temperature. Below it there are two breaks in every curve; one is where the gas begins to liquefy, the other where the liquefaction is complete. The portion between is a straight line parallel with the volume axis, which means that the pressure remains the same though the volume contracts. When the volume has contracted to the point where the gas or vapour has all become liquid, the curve resumes, but far more steeply: there is an increasing demand on pressure for every small contraction of the liquid volume.

That straight line between the two breaks marks out a theoretical and practical field of its own. At each point of it there is an equilibrium between gas and liquid, and the mechanical theory can be seen to pass from its application to gas to its application to liquid. There, on the vapour condensing, the particles keep their individuality, they have still the same energy, make the same collisions, suffer the same drag of cohesion, and, from the drag, the surface of the liquid takes its tension and shape. The lower the temperature, the longer the straight lines in this picture. If the ends on the left are united, and also those on the right, the uniting lines meet at the point which determines the three critical quantities. As the point is approached, the surface of the liquid phase becomes flatter, and it disappears altogether at the point. Proceeding beyond the point the theory accounts for the permanence of the gas phase at all higher temperatures; it means that the greater speed of the particles can no longer be balanced by their cohesion, whatever the pressure.

Because everything in the pictures is measured, they are a record of the cultures on the surface from the statistical and mechanical systems in which they are rooted. The mechanical one seems to be properly nature's, and the other to be a cunning that nature lets us use in lieu of reaching the real roots, the collisions, one by one. At the end of the material development we shall find that view reversed. There the collisions reduce to others very unlike them; and statistical laws, from being superficial to those of cause, become fundamental. Important as that correction at the end is for physics, and for life, our question of mind as life has no less interest in the uncorrected course. The statistical system has been a typical growing invention, an organ of understanding, which neither copies, nor creates, what it gives us to understand.

When statistics and the records fail, and the equation is thrown on itself, it carries the development farther,

and again by means of the two corrections. They let it
find the three critical quantities by merely transforming
itself. That seems a trick with which nature and actual
substances can have no concern. But the trick is inevitable, if the form of the equation is good. And the
form is good, if the correction for pressure is proportional to the square of the volume. The product of the
volume by this imported factor makes the corrected
equation a cubic one for the volume. The three values
mean that a fluid substance, at any given temperature
and pressure, may occupy one or other of three volumes.
The empirical picture does not object. In the two-phase
part, it is true, there are not three but an infinite number, and so that part is out of account; the instrument
does not dictate except when it must (xii. 5). But all
the rest of the field comes in. There, whether as liquid
or as gas, there is one and only one volume for every
temperature and pressure, except at the ends of the
straight lines, where there are two: one where the gas
is ready to condense, the other where the liquid is
ready to evaporate. A cubic equation can fall in with
this; for, where there is one real value, the other two
are imaginary; and, where two are real, there must be
a real third. This third point has data to determine
it; they even give an independent way of developing the equation at the critical point. But look at the
two end values; they approach each other the higher
the temperature, and, at the critical point, they become
one. That lets the corrected equation take the form of
a cubic equated to zero; the volume, the pressure, and
the temperature can be expressed in terms of the co-
efficients; whence the corrections are brought to book.
We see what it means to push a theory to its limits. The
critical state becomes critical both of the theory and of
the corrections. The theory proved itself, and found

how far out the corrections are, and how their ground needs developing.

That being done, the simple equation can pass from the corrected to the 'reduced' equation, the law of corresponding states. It takes the values that are found for the temperature, the pressure, and the volume of any fluid substances at any one-phase point, and divides them by their respective critical values. Putting these quotients for the three simple terms, we are back in the original form of the equation: the product of the pressure and volume, divided by the number of degrees of absolute temperature, is always the same, the absolute gas constant.

One reflection from the cycle that the theory went through is that nature does not become intelligible by conforming to our constitution; we do not bring things within our range, but pass from ours to theirs. They have no concern with human standards. The cycle takes up our human range, and makes it universal by defining the part that it is. Every other great advance in physics has also found that our outlook on nature had been too narrow, and for one reason: we had made the whole in the likeness of the part. We have to proceed from the part, but through other relations than a likeness. Here avenues were opened that groping would have taken long to find; they led, for instance, to the conditions at which helium could be liquefied, and to the correction for cohesion as the means of creating the conditions. "It is not at all easy", as Nernst said, "to form a conception of the boldness of this equation." He used to summarise the situation in this way: "There are certain undoubted deviations between the theory and fact, but the results of the theory are so undeniable, and the region of the phenomena which it claims to control is so extensive, that it would be a very profitable prob-

lem to follow the deviations". Now "I am of opinion
that it is possible now to state with certainty the cause
of the breakdown of the theory of corresponding states
even in the simplest cases; it is to be found in the re-
quirements of the quantum theory".[1]

There is, for our gathering, a boldness in the gas
theory more general than this. The theory attacks the
chaos with so simple a weapon, and one so superficial.
It assumes that pressure, volume, and temperature
form an independent system, though it knows that each
depends on factors which it ignores. The system is a
resultant, an index, but it assumes that nature may be
good enough to make the index self-contained. Where
nature fails to do this, the theory is said to fail, and
need correction. But the failure is within its purpose,
and the corrections are its fruit.

There is the more welcome fruit of agreement, as
when, pushing into dilute liquid solutions, the theory
finds that the particles of the solute exercise a pressure
proportional to the absolute temperature, and nearly
the same as they would exercise in a gas of equal
volume. And again these gains are the greater that,
in pursuing them, the theory meets and measures a
check. It is the check from electrolytic dissociation,
which goes past the cohesive to the chemical bond.

The two general corrections to the gas theory do not
reach that length; they remain at the threshold. The one
which opens on the particle's power to cohere, like the
one which opens on its diameter, is connected with
other routes converging on the same place. And these,
coming now from within, as well as from without, have
given to collision and cohesion, as well as to size, a
meaning quite unlike the solid one familiar to our
senses. The volume of the particle is that of an electro-

---

[1] *Theoretical Chemistry* (tr. 1923), pp. 237, 262.

magnetic field, the collision is its invasion, and the drag or cohesion is electrical.

What becomes of the motions of two particles during their collision? We cannot answer by dividing the motion among their parts, as if they, too, were now colliding. The precise answer cannot be made, but it is no longer because the field must be final, and end in desert. It is because the desert within a particle has become so orderly that the simple answer of an exchange of energies now appears to be meagre. Cohesion, puzzling and hostile to atomic theories from the first, has lost its ancient mystery to electricity. The gas theory can absorb the growing values, as the free path shortens, till, from being only a correction, the energy of cohesion matches that of translation; it does so in liquids and non-crystalline solids. There the molecules move and diffuse within the range of molecular attraction; and the tensile strength at different temperatures can be measured. The meeting of the two forces is at present being explored through the corrections which appear where the material is passing from one phase to another, and in other ways. They remove one of the main instances on which it was believed that science must rest on contradictions, because of our minds. "We cannot truly represent to ourselves one ultimate unit of matter as drawing another while resisting it. . . . But we are compelled to the belief," and so "these universally co-existent forces of attraction and repulsion must not be taken as realities; they are modes of the unconditioned as presented under the conditions of our consciousness".[1]

§ 8. Besides this distrust of minds and phenomena, two grounds are taken against the reality of our laws

[1] Spencer, *First Principles*, § 74.

of nature: that they are theoretical, and that they are statistical. Avogadro's law would fall to all three. Yet it has continued to be the "almost inexhaustible horn of plenty" that Nernst called it forty years ago. Its gifts are not least when they correct. The law itself is not corrected; for, being statistical, it merely rules out the temporary deviations from an average. The corrections which it discovers are the permanent deviations: they are the associations and dissociations that put at fault the law of Gay-Lussac. By counting the molecular bonds that are ruptured in solutions, Avogadro's law comes on those which point from the structure of the molecule to the structure of the atom. And then it passes from structure to energy, each correction asking about the new energy that appears in the rise of pressure, and disappears in the fall. And so it challenged the gas constant, and the law of Dulong and Petit, whence it found the route from the energy of the molecule to the energy of the atom.

Chemical discovery had gone far before such a route could reach its facts. There was no clear distinction between atom and molecule till 1860. Discovery had to make its own theories, but, pushing their victory, they then defeated themselves. "We say that nations maintain themselves by the very means that established them, but we have to say the contrary about chemical theories. They see their existence threatened by the very problems that led them to victory" (Ostwald). The dead ends were disheartening at the time, but they look better in the retrospect, when the course can be reversed, and the highways run from theory to fact. If any route had a right to go all the way, it was that which was opened and carried through the carbon compounds. They are far more, and more complex, than all others, and their atoms were seen to arrange themselves on the

plan of a constant valency, and a geometrical distribution. But inorganic compounds, while admitting the
route, kept out of the way. Van 't Hoff, writing in 1901,
says that, when he was a student, chemistry was "pro-
nounced by our master to have reached a dead end, and
to be without visible prospect of a new advance. . . .
Chemistry was looking for some Newton who should
discover the laws according to which the atoms were
held together in their molecular configuration. No
Newton of this kind arrived, yet it was only a few years
after Kekulé's unfortunate utterance that there arose
the conceptions of stereochemistry. By means of stereo-
chemistry, the real existence of the atoms being assumed,
not only was their mode of union described, but also
their relative positions in the molecule were determined.
. . . We remained, however, and after twenty-five years
we still remain, unacquainted with the laws which
control these relative positions. Perhaps by the new
conception of electrons we may be on the eve of getting
a clearer knowledge of the conditions of the atoms. . . .
During these twenty-five years, however, investigation
still proceeded, although in an entirely different direction. It did not advance by the elaboration of symbol
architecture, with atoms as bricks. About fifteen years
after Kekulé's unfortunate expression, a second child
of hope, the new physical chemistry, came into being."
It thrust the kinetic theory farther into liquids, reducing
the mystery of osmotic pressure, and weighing all kinds
of molecules that will not volatilise. Absorbing Raoult's
laws it brought the vapour-pressure, the freezing, and
the boiling points of solutions, within the theory, and
could use them to discover and measure abnormalities.

One of these is the abnormal pressure due to the
splitting of some of the molecules of an electrolyte into
ions, which have the gas effect of separate molecules.

And so the three molecular bonds—cohesive, chemical, and electrical—now appear in their common character. For the dissolution of a neutral molecule into ions occurs in the solution before the electrical field is imposed. The field merely uncovers the fact by directing the ions to the electrodes. First, then, may not all cohesion be electrostatic? Next, the number of charges carried by an ion is proportional to its valency, and marks the difference in the chemical behaviour; may not, then, the chemical bond be identical with charge? Finally, and strangest, must not this, the electrical bond, be granular, to suit the valency?

§ 9. The energy within a molecule comes out and defines itself, as the structure does, by forcing the kinetic theory on the chaotic facts at the surface. Such are the facts of specific heat. Their chaos was made the more striking by the regularities that were found on cultivation; Joule found the mechanical equivalent of heat from the specific heat of water, and Mayer by taking the difference between the specific heat of a gas at constant pressure and at constant volume. The old unit of heat, the calorie, became so many units of work. There was no suggestion of an opening into the gas molecule; the regularity was too good. But the specific heat of solids did better. It was found to be an additive property, the specific heat of a compound being the sum of the specific heats of its atoms; and Dulong and Petit had found their law. They pointed out that the product of the weight by the specific heat was much the same for all atoms in the solid state. This product, the atomic heat, is the number of calories that will raise one gram-atom one degree; they pointed out that, so far as was then known, the number was about six calories at all temperatures. Later it was found that six is far out for certain other solids, and that it varies for all, rising and falling slowly with the temperature. Then, extending the range farther, it was found that regularity came again, as we saw it come for the corresponding states of a gas.

Thrust against the facts, the kinetic theory distinguishes the quantity of heat that goes to the energy of translation. This helps to measure the remainder, the energy that it has ignored. And, in the solid state proper, the particles have no energy of translation, and so the whole is remainder. Look first, then, at the difference in the specific heats of gases. The simplest indication comes from the number of atoms to the molecule. Their atomic heats are not additive, as in the solid; but an indication is given by the ratio of the specific heat at constant pressure to the specific heat at constant volume. Within the theory a degree of temperature in all gases means the same quantity of kinetic energy of translation; two-thirds of it should appear in the pressure and volume; and their product, divided by the number of degrees of absolute temperature, gives the value of R, the gas constant, which comes out at nearly three calories under standard conditions. This would be the specific heat at constant volume, provided the energy of translation took it all. If the gas is allowed to expand against the standard pressure, the work that it does during the rise of one degree requires two calories more. Therefore the ratio between the specific heats ought to be 5 to 3. When part of the energy that is added does not go to translation, but into the molecule, both terms of the ratio should be affected alike, and the ratio become less the greater the molecule. And, in fact, it is about 5 to 3 for monatomic gases, about 7 to 5 for diatomic, and about 9 to 7 for triatomic. But there are exceptions already: they grow with the number of atoms to the molecule; the ratio varies with the temperature; and it does not vary if the gas is monatomic. These vagaries all become definite, and open a way into the molecule, when the obligations of the theory are pressed home:

For a mechanical theory of the encounters cannot confine itself to translation. A gas molecule should have two other energies from impact: an energy of rotation, and an internal energy to receive and repel. The theory has to divide the added energy among the three kinds, and within each kind. The amount that goes to the translation of the average molecule goes in equal parts to the three co-ordinates that describe its motion. Rotation has also three directions, three degrees of freedom. The remainder goes to the internal energy of the molecule; and there is no remainder, if it cannot enter the atom, nor therefore if the gas is monatomic. When the molecule has more than one atom, the share to internal energy goes to their oscillation about their common bonds. As this is a constrained motion, the energy divides itself equally between the actual and the potential forces in the swing of each atom in the molecule about its mean position; and so here there are two units to each degree of freedom. Finally, let each of the three channels be as open to the incoming flow of energy as their directions are, being independent. Then the three calories that go to translation should go one for each direction, rotation should have three, and the residue, going within, may possibly vary with the number of atoms, and assume a higher figure when nearing the temperature at which the bonds within the molecule are broken.

Such a scheme, if its purpose is mistaken, condemns itself at once; for nature is not so artificial. The grasp of the organ that we create would appear to force an

Q

alien order on the real disorder, to suit our needs. But that is not the case. Far from forcing things to be simple in order to be intelligible, the theory presumes that, though consistent, they are chaotic. It then finds that they are not so chaotic as it thought. By forcing its own superficial order it brings out the real one.

In the specific heat of a monatomic gas it brings out two facts. One is that no other gas accords with the theory in having a specific heat that is independent of the temperature; there the number of calories remains the same even at the highest reach of temperature hitherto employed. The other fact is that the number is only 3, which is the number needed for the energy of translation; there is nothing for spin, nor for internal energy. The simple theory, which knows only translation, would be perfectly satisfied if only the full theory were not flouted. Both would have to fail (xii. 5); but the two facts do better.

The first one, independence of the temperature, means that monatomic molecules continue to distribute the increasing energy among themselves, without either taking toll of it, or breaking up. Argon has been tested to 2000° C., and even in that intense agitation the particles hit like weapons that will not wear down. If that were all, the horizon would be dark, but it would not be chaotic; for the interior of the particle would be anything but a copy of the chaos outside. The fact, however, is not final, but a matter of hitting speed. At a far higher speed than can be had by way of heat the nuclei of helium break through the defences of other atoms, and report their adventures on a photographic plate. Their speed is ten or twenty thousand times greater than in ordinary gas, but the chaos is not the worse confounded; they break through the chemical surface and report a deeper order.

The other fact makes another breach that was even more unexpected. Let atoms be so perfect they return all the energy of the collisions, how can they return it all to translation, as they do? For it is a negligible chance that, when two bodies collide, only their speed and its direction are engaged. They should spin one another, and, if the monatomic molecules were free to spin, their three degrees of freedom should share the energy equally with translation. They take none of it, and so the missing three calories make as measured a problem as the actual three. It is no answer that in a gas there is not the kind of contact that we see and feel; there is all the contact that there ever is. The theory knows also that it need not look for help to the shape of the particles. Now it also knows how the mass of an atom is distributed, and how the core is protected by enveloping electrons with their own reaction to collision. The theory could enter these things in its equation, forecasting the distribution of new energy. But it checks at the fact that they do not enter at all, when the gas molecules are atoms.

There is this advantage in the failure of the theory that the problem for other molecules becomes more definite; for it may be assumed that atoms, when they combine, remain unaffected. The calories that go to internal energy keep to the bonds between the atoms without penetrating farther. With the interior of the atom out of the way, the figures could give good hope of order. When the molecule has two atoms, the calories rise from 3 to 5 at ordinary temperatures. The oscillations about their rigid bond could just claim the addition; but would leave none for spin. And, when there are more than two atoms to the molecule, the prediction from the degrees of freedom to oscillate was out more and more. The early promise of order died always away.

That is why the figures have been less tantalising than those of the atomic weights. If the weights are frayed, the heats are in rags; they were taken to echo the real chaos of the world. Until the other day the weights gave that impression too, resisting the efforts to tidy them into whole numbers, which most of them were just missing. The heat figures were foreboding, as well as forbidding; they supported their confusion on the degradation of energy; their ragged state was only to be expected; must they not reflect the final confusion? But again the gloom was outstripping the reason for it by assigning the wrong function to sense and instruments. The figures are a triumph of cultivation within our native range of sense; and they do not copy their roots, any more than do the lines of the spectrum, which go far closer. Since weight has become no longer final, the decimals that fray the weights have taken quite another character. So also the specific heats begin to yield, when seen from their farther side, the side of radiation. Their reading will be less dramatic, and far slower than the isotopic reading of the weights; and their rags may not be so instructive as the rag of hydrogen; but the situation is the same.

It is therefore an advantage that over so long a range the interior of the atom does not come into the reading, whether for molecule or for solid. It comes in at high temperatures, where the atomic heat of metals rises well above the Dulong and Petit rule. But it was the failure of the rule at low temperatures that pointed the way from gross to radiant heat, and so to radiant energy in general. At very low temperatures the gas theory fails altogether, for it cannot command even the energy of translation. The specific heat of monatomic gases falls below three calories, and gradually dies away; an amount of energy that would barely raise the gas one degree at ordinary temperatures raises it many. Other gases behave there in the same way, called their degeneration. And now this failure, and the precise figures, are of increasing positive importance. It is not because averages and probabilities have been superseded as merely ours, but because they are more final to nature than the particles. The failure went farther, and could seem to condemn more than our grossness, and our having to rely on statistics. In solids the atoms, though separate, are anchored to one another; the only energy concerned in a rise of temperature is their oscillation or vibration; and it has apparently three degrees of freedom, and takes two calories for each. Well though that holds, the number of calories falls with the temperature at different rates for the same atom, and for different atoms. From the early rule of six it falls to none at a point well above the absolute zero; in diamond at a temperature as many as fifty degrees above it. With such a collapse the theory might seem to end in contradiction, and the classical system to condemn itself as only ours by the very perfection with which it fits our ordinary range.

The horizon began to lighten when a corresponding collapse appeared in the classical theory of radiation, to which we now proceed. The gas theory would not have been idle, however, nor have confined itself to bettering its approximations. By pressing on the facts it was proving that its grasp could open and follow the object instead of merely impressing itself. At least no one will grudge to Nernst his claim that "the quantum hypothesis could have been completely developed from measurements of specific heats, and from the atomic weights, melting points, and atomic valence of the elements, independently of any optical measurements, though these are far more reliable".

X

THE CYCLE THROUGH STRUCTURE

§ 1. THE theory of the distribution of radiant energy had no perfect particle as had the theory for the distribution of molecular heat. A perfect fluid, called the aether, was assumed instead, conveying in all directions the energy emitted by matter, and offering it back when matter was met again. But what prevents matter from draining away, there being so little of it, and so much aether? Its gross energy as a gas is prevented from frittering by the particles, but what of its loss as radiant energy? The tangible world would have gone into the blue and beyond long ago, if its energy could spread and break, like waves of water, into ever finer and weaker quantities. The check was first found through the check to dynamical theory, and its presence everywhere was confirmed by cultivation.

Cultivation is far closer than for gas energy; and the means of measuring, if more difficult, are far more exact. The chamber constructed for experiment with radiant heat has the same purpose as the one for molecular heat. A statistical equilibrium is reached again at every temperature. The chamber can be so perfected that all the energy becomes full or black radiation, the walls emitting to the cavity the very lengths of wave that they are absorbing from it. Experiment found how the amount and the distribution of the energy depend on the temperature; and thermo-dynamics followed, and found the laws for amount and for distribution demonstrable or necessary. The instrument could grope from such a grasp. The amount of heat radiated per second depends on the fourth power of the absolute temperature. At each temperature-equilibrium the whole heat is distributed over a great range of wavelengths. The extremes among them, the short and the long, always have least; most of it lies between. The range that does best, even the length that does best, can be found. The advantage passes to shorter lengths as the temperature increases; we see it when a hot body begins to glow and rises to white heat. Wien found that the most effective length at each equilibrium depends on the fifth power of the absolute temperature; and from that he could infer a law of corresponding states, or distribution of wave-lengths.

But the main law could not be found: a law to connect the energy and the wave-length. One was found that has the support of the longest waves in the range, and another that has the support of the shortest; but the two equations were in direct conflict, and the great body of the energy defied both. Planck found a formula that could include the two as cases, but only by presuming that the exchanges between the vibrating elements in the walls and the vibrations in the cavity were not continuous, but in quanta. "Even if this radiation formula should prove to be absolutely accurate, it would after all be only an interpolation formula found by happy guess-work. I was therefore, from the day of its origin, occupied with the task of giving it a real physical meaning, . . . until, after some weeks of the most intense work of my life, clearness began to dawn on me, and a view that I did not expect revealed itself in the distance." Dynamical equations had always presumed that energy is taken and given up in all quantities, no matter how small. But radiant energy does both only in multiples of a well-defined quantity.

This quantum is defined by two factors: by a unit of energy per second, and by a multiplier. The unit, Planck's constant, h, is as tiny as we shall see; its multiplier, n, is the frequency. Hence, the higher the frequency, or the shorter the waves, the greater the stroke of the work that produces them. To produce blue the vibrating electrons have to work in units of energy twice as great as they need for red; and for x-rays they have to use quanta several thousand times as great. Far from copying the waves of gross matter which fritter away into shorter, to grow shorter is now not to fritter but to climb. The rule is universal, and not merely an addition that removes the discrepancy between fact and the classical theory, though also that. Of the formulae obtained for the distribution of energy "all those which do not contain h agree with Newtonian dynamics, while those containing h entirely disagree. The formulae of the quantum theory all agree with experience, while those of the classical theory only do so when they agree with the quantum theory also." [1]

Confining itself to exchanges, as between wall and cavity, the new theory could at first hope to keep continuity for the radiant energy itself. But the hope soon went: the energy is not only born and absorbed in quanta of the unit hn, it exists only in the units. The quanta of heat and light became like the particles of a gas, and were as capable of statistical treatment. This extension, begun by Einstein, was directly against the wave theory of light. Experiment supported it in all that it could predict, but continued to support the wave theory as well.

The new situation, being more fundamental, is the

[1] H. A. Wilson, *Modern Physics*, p. 81.

more drastic for our question whether all nature involves itself in our phenomena. The answer continues
hopeful for one part of the question: whether nature
is all a system of phenomena. But the presumptuous
part remains: whether the whole system can be reached
from our phenomena. The horizon, though clear of the
dust, shows again a contradiction, with phenomena now
supporting both views. Did not the solution lie in the
aether? "We must free ourselves from the materialism
which will acknowledge nothing in the world that sense
does not show. Behind the world that we see there lies
another; it is true that we feel its work; but our equipment for knowing it is very incomplete." [1] That familiar
reflection could still come. Though we shall find its
direction to be wrong, we may well adopt its words
about our equipment. But no one let it account for
any particular dilemma; no piece of ignorance knew
itself well enough to be final, though a new situation
soon came in view that held more than ignorance. The
dilemma that light is both particle and wave presented
a horizon that was the reverse of the one from the gas
theory. There theory was clear about itself, and saw
chaos ahead, where sooner or later it must fail. The
new horizon was, and remains, the reverse: it was no
longer the facts that were refractory to theory, because
they were out of reach, but theory that could not reach
the well-defined facts.

§ 2. The influence of light on metals was first observed when the electro-magnetic explanation of light
was still young. The fact was found as the electrical
effect of ultra-violet light on charged and uncharged
bodies, and then as the positive charge which light gives
to all metals, if its frequency is high enough. A few

[1] Wiechert, *Der Äther im Weltbild*, p. 43.

years later, when electricity proved itself corpuscular, and a positive charge to be a loss of electrons, the effect was seen to be a stream of electrons driven out by the light. Soon there came Lenard's discovery that, while the number expelled follows the intensity of the light, their speed depends only on its frequency. There is no mutual compensation between the two factors in the cause, the frequency and the intensity of the light, nor between the two factors in the effect, the number and the speed of the electrons expelled. Everywhere else an amount of kinetic energy had done its amount of work in an infinite number of ways, but not here; the light may be strong or weak, and come from near or far, it does not matter; the speed of any electron that it expels is the same. Many are expelled or few; that is all the difference.

An exacting test is in the range of visible light, where the effect is least; for most metals respond only to ultra-violet frequencies. The culture from lithium and sodium which Millikan made within the visible range, required apparatus that he describes as a machine shop *in vacuo*. He was able to measure there the several masking effects of the experiment itself, and then to determine that frequency of the light which releases the electrons from the grasp of the metal, but just fails to give them speed. Then, as the frequency is increased, the speed begins, and increases according to a simple fundamental equation. The electrons coming off do not all have the same speed, because they have had different adventures in coming clear, and they come away at different angles. But, if Einstein's equation is good, there is a maximum speed. It can be found by imposing either an electrical or a magnetic field. By imposing an electrical one the positive potential is found which, applied to the metal, brings the speed to zero; it is the product of the charge e of the electron by the number of volts v. This quantity ev matches the quantity of kinetic energy $\frac{1}{2}mu^2$ which it prevents. The equation says that each is also equal to the cause: to the quantity of light energy that expels the electron. This quantity is also the product of two factors: Planck's constant h, and the frequency n of the light, less the frequency which is just able to expel the electron. Allowing for that, we have $hn = ev = \frac{1}{2}mu^2$.

The three pairs illustrate the variety and the minuteness of the quantities that measure one another in this far field. In the first two pairs, we have four quantities, of which three—the frequency, the voltage, and the electronic charge—are each very closely determined, so that the fourth one, h, must profess an exactness equal to theirs. It is a small but constant fraction of an erg per second; and an erg is so minute that about forty-two millions of them go to a calory. The constant fraction of the erg is so small that the significant figures do not begin till the twenty-seventh place after the decimal. The experiment on both metals agreed on that first figure and the next; and they are the figures that Planck first gave on quite other grounds for the quantum in radiant heat. If minuteness measures our mental power to penetrate, and the willingness of nature, we need not look farther than those four quantities. And the third pair is like them: the mass of an electron and the square of its velocity. The velocity that it gets from visible light is only about a thousand kilometres a second; and its mass at that speed is an even smaller fraction of a gram than Planck's constant is of an erg. The minuteness is reached because nature remains, at the finest, not only logical, but systematic or intelligible.

§ 3. We have a greater interest in the equation. The

three kinds of energy—radiant, electrical, and mechanical—are here not equated merely but united. They offer to be factors in a more concrete system that should absorb their private difficulties. The classical system had developed itself to include every kind of material motion on the assumption that the mass of a moving body is independent of its velocity. That being found at fault for high speeds, the effect on the mechanical system is profound: it has led to a certain identity of mass and energy, and to a certain unity of time and space.

But the radiant system stood divided against itself, as in Bragg's parallel: "It is as if one dropped a plank into the sea from a height of 100 feet, and found that the spreading ripple was able, after becoming infinitesimal in comparison with its original amount, to act upon a wooden ship in such a way that a plank of that ship flew out of its place to a height of 100 feet". When a light-wave proceeds on its way, it keeps the quantum with which it was issued; for, when it meets and collides with an electron, presumably free, to which it loses energy and momentum, it remains a unit, a quantum of lower frequency, and proceeds in its new direction in accordance with the equation. As was also said at the time, the equation "stands complete, and apparently well tested, but without any visible means of support. These supports must obviously exist, and the most fascinating problem of modern physics is to find them. Experiment has outrun theory, or, better, guided by erroneous theory, it has discovered relationships which seem to be of the greatest interest and importance, but the reasons for them are as yet not at all understood" (Millikan). That is our road.

We have also interest in the equation because of the two erroneous ways of reading it, and because the energetic way now does better than it expected:

The equation unites three quantities in three forms of energy, and says that the quantities are equivalent, and the energies interchangeable. The reading that needs no knowledge infers that there is, therefore, one quantity of one energy, or Force, beyond our knowing. Such is the familiar way to the final gulf. But the energy which is one and the same in the three quantities is nothing but their equal value for work. The other erroneous reading is that one of the three forms came first, or, there being no beginning, that one of them is the only real one. That was rejected by the energetic view, partly because the form called mechanical had been selected, but also because there had never been only one form of energy. The first contention is good, but the other has been qualified by two advances beyond the hope, or despair, in the energetic view:

First, there is one final form, electro-magnetic energy, and the others are compounded of it. Unless that is understood, it would be right to say with Haas that the notion of the transformation of energy, so useful for half a century, has become an error, there having never been but one form, and it a known one. The other advance we are about to see in the development of the photo-electric effect. The energetic view followed the radical sweep, you remember, which left nothing but the course of phenomena. The course consists of the beginnings and endings of courses that are out of sight. Instead of trying any longer to unite them beneath the surface, the endings were to be equated to the beginnings. That was all that should be expected. Our equation says nothing about the hidden course of events between cause and effect, the impinging light being cause, and the issue of electrons the effect. Between them lie the surface atoms of the metal; and the early framers of energetic were unfriendly to atoms. But we are still on their way, if the cause and the effect, the beginning and the end, reach towards each other. That is what has been found; they meet within the atom; the equation holds at every point across.

§ 4. No exception was found when x-ray light was identified; and, the unit of its action being so much greater, the full fact could be followed. The process could be reversed from photo-electric to electro-photic, a stream of electrons being now cause, and light of proper frequency the effect. The stream has been cultivated up to the x-ray tubes of to-day in which the particles are attracted across a vacuum to their target with a force whose range has gone down to ten volts, and up to hundreds of thousands. The work done is always the work of individual electrons; the frequency of the light that they produce from the collision increases with the potential applied to the tube; there is a highest frequency for each potential; and, from the measurements of this frequency made by several investigators using a variety of targets,[1] it can be seen how well the value for h is confirmed. It is mainly as effect that the light is followed on our course, because its cultivation in spectra has been so fertile.

As cause it has also been highly developed and fruitful. Monochromatic rays of sufficient strength are directed on the target, and expel electrons of which a stream, escaping through a narrow slit, enters a magnetic field; there they are bent, and registered on a photographic plate, in groups corresponding with their velocities on entering, and therefore with the different levels of energy in the atoms from which they are driven. Calculations[1] of the levels by this method, and

---

[1] Richtmyer, *Introduction to Modern Physics*, pp. 495 and 517.

by the other, show the close agreement of the two. "It is remarkable", as M. de Broglie said, who first completed the experiment, "that results based on the measurement of a length and a magnetic field should coincide so well with the results of x-ray spectroscopy", and so establish its right where that route is not available. The available range has been great enough, however, to let the readings become general. And, after the Bragg spectrometer, with the four quantities in its equation, made the wave-lengths measurable, a commanding precision has been reached. In comparing the lengths with a standard one, the error may be only one part in a million. Even in comparing intensities it has been claimed that the error can be within one part in ten thousand. Commanding such precision, two discoveries that had been made began to develop rapidly. There was Barkla's work with primary and secondary x-waves; it concerns the interior of atoms. The other was the Laue photographs of the diffracted waves; it concerns the crystal unit of the atoms that diffract them.

The unit is the three-dimensional space pattern in which the atoms combine. It is gathered from every aspect by rotating the crystal, or from the single spectrum of the powdered crystal. Whatever the substance, and whether its atoms are of one kind or more, the pattern repeats itself throughout, and contains the whole. It provides that bridge to the properties of a solid which the way through gas and liquid could not reach, nor could chemistry; why, for instance, diamond is so hard and graphite so soft, and why ice takes more room than water. The way back from it to liquid and gas gives new importance to known properties like melting points, and the elastic resistance to compression. Pictures have begun to show, from the different intensities of their radiation, how, in the joint structure of two atoms, each maintains its individuality. The fact had been known from their line spectra since 1860; it began 'spectrum analysis'. Especially there is new power over valencies, including those of organic compounds whose crystal unit has molecules, not atoms, for the terms of its pattern. "The crystal unit ranks in its uses, and very possibly in importance, with the atom and the molecule; for, whereas the general limitation to the properties of substances in the gaseous or liquid state is really severe, . . . we are in a position to consider all the physical properties of the crystal as dependent on the structure of the unit, and, ultimately, on the force exerted by each atom; in other words, on the structure of the atom" (Bragg).

The structure of the atom revealed its own plan readily. The light produced by bombarding with electrons in the x-ray tube, gives a continuous spectrum; but, in addition, if the voltage is high enough, it gives a spectrum of lines. They are due to disturbance at deep levels within each contributing atom of the target. There is the same scheme of lines whatever the metal, and there is a characteristic difference for the different metals. The scheme consists of groups of lines called the K, L, M, etc., groups, coming from as many levels of energy whose electrons are disturbed. The K lines mark the deepest; they record the waves of shortest length or highest frequency, whose quanta of energy are therefore greatest. It was a natural expectation that, the heavier the atom, the higher the frequency, and even that the difference might be regular and characteristic. But it is seldom that cultivation can hope to yield so much at once, and so precisely, as the lines in Moseley's pictures, proving both.

They move towards higher frequency from atom to

heavier atom, and by a step so regular that the new doctrine of atomic numbers became fundamental: an atom is now characterised by the number of positive charges in its nucleus. Since a normal atom is neutral, this is also the normal total number of electrons in its extra-nuclear levels, K, L, M, etc. Hydrogen has one of each, a positive charge balanced by a negative one; uranium has 92 of each; and the others fill the places between. The atomic weight is met by the presence also of a neutral part, an equal number of protons and electrons, in the nucleus. An atom's mere number on the list becomes more fundamental than its weight and its permanence, which had been final. These had both been at a stand against the periodic table, partly by conflicting with it here and there when pressed home, but entirely because they could not account for it, neither for its division into periods, nor for their cross-division into columns. The table now stands on the manner in which the extra-nuclear electrons from 1 to 92 distribute themselves.

Again the old basis, here the weight and the permanence, finds itself to be more important than when final. The advantage remains that an atom can be identified, however ionised, and whatever its intake and output of energy; for the weight of electrons and their energies is negligible against the weight of the nucleus, and the nucleus is adamant against their adventures. But the advantage is hardly less that the nucleus breaks to severer assaults than theirs, and is unstable in the families of radio-active atoms, breaking of itself. As the steps of descent in them came to light, two facts were pointed out, which might be found for stable atoms as well: the group-displacement law, and the existence of isotopes. In addition, the break-down gave the three unexpected rays alpha, beta, and gamma.

R

§ 5. The five pointed to five characters in the structure of every atom, and were developed to display them. It is a very picturesque part of our route, because the theoretical and the practical instruments are so immediately one. But it ended in a worse conflict than ever between the works of the two instruments. After making unexpectedly easy so much that had seemed hard, the picture did the reverse when pushed farther. The farther road had to become more royal than ever to take the cycle back to the surface through a series of revolutions. These undid still nothing of the past, nothing that had proved itself, only predictions. But predictions come not only from accretions that know themselves for theory, but from the completions that think themselves final, nothing having caused them to be analysed. Three are worth a halt:

Nothing could well make a more striking finish to all thoughts about physical structures than that their elements are atoms needing nothing to combine them. And no addition could well be more striking than that the internal structure of every atom is like that of a solar system, and that all the structures are analysable into that of the simplest. But, while that final picture was still making its way, as if merely into complications, I heard Rutherford remark on the curious apathy of people about it, whereas he used to wake in the morning wondering whether it could possibly be true, notwithstanding the proofs. No doubt one completion causing the apathy is that while known atoms are the bricks of every structure there is also the cement, if not also the design, and perhaps both of them forces. But I think there is also the completion which made the synthetic philosophy so acceptable; we are familiar with it in the separation of laws from things, whereby things obey them. Seeing that real laws are universal, having no exceptions, why wonder that they are the same for large and small? These two are explicit.

But a third completion is less aware of itself. It gives nature a course, like the course of a life, putting it into time and into space, instead of putting them into nature. One of the revolutions, finding the junction of space and time, expands nature to a concreteness that makes every course abstract. Yet, knowing that also, the completion sees a miracle in the coming of consciousness, and therefore more than a miracle in the picture of an astronomer identifying an atomic event of a million years ago. If it is a real event that he deposits from the present on a pre-human time, the date, and all such conditions of his thought, put no more restriction on his power than on his belief in twice two. You might think, if that is clear for our problem of the deposit, that the fact would be as clear for the general problem of our place. But again the completion is made, and in a way so familiar that it may seem the reason for my halting at the splendid display of structure. Gifford lectures are expected to extol the mind, and reduce its misgivings. We may well think the better of it from the display. But the casual character of the five pointers can also give pause. They came by chance, from rare atoms of a still rarer action, and from so small a particle that it has only a millionth part of the invisible volume of its atom. And the advance has increased the two old sources of misgiving. All the fields of sense have gone out of cultivation except the visible one, where the cultures have reduced themselves to dark lines and coloured. And the immensities have dwarfed us, as they have grown. What does it matter that a mind can reach and measure an event so far back? Why pride ourselves on grasping the policeman who has us in his grasp? But the halt is to test not our faith but still our sight of the fact; for we do not see it, if we think that the last word is with the policeman.

Let us resume the course of penetration and its passage from statistical to individual elements. We shall follow the five pointers from our partner, and their conversion into instruments, practical and theoretical.

§ 6. Gamma-rays are of light; they are shorter than any but the shortest x-rays, too short, as a rule, for the crystal method to measure. But their penetrating power was easily measured, and a method has been developed of securing their lengths from their passage out of the nucleus through its own envelope. This lets the photo-electric equation apply as simply as possible: the gamma quantum is equal to the energy spent in detaching a κ electron plus the energy that the electron takes up and carries to a magnetic spectrograph. The results agree that in the nucleus there are ordered energy levels with discontinuous transitions between them. It is not yet certain how the gamma-rays depend on the nuclear shocks that expel them, but further sifting of the data can decide.

The same is true of the speed-records of the electrons that shoot out with them, and constitute the beta-rays. Though they are particles, their speed is always comparable with that of light, and has been reported up to 99.8 per cent. The high speed, and the long range of speeds, varying with the kind of atom, began the two revolutions that have transformed the foundations and the theatre of physics. The high speed brought out the fact that, the higher it is, the greater the mass of the speeding electron. The long range brought out the rule for its gain in mass. And soon the rule became inevitable, not because the body is an electron, and not because the speed is so high, but merely from the observer and his means of measurement. The classical theatre had presumed that a mass remains the same whatever its motion. Even common sense, from the day that it began to theorise, believed that, when masses and speeds are measured from moving points of view, the results have to be discounted; for, if they did not agree, what else? The answer could have come long ago, if there had ever been a doubt. It came as the special theory of relativity.

The alpha-particle offers more about itself. It is identical with the nucleus of a helium atom, consisting of four protons and two electrons holding each other so firmly that no terrestrial collision has yet been found able to break it. It breaks from its origin with a velocity that is usually the same for one kind of radio-active atom, and is not the same for the different kinds. The range of variation is from 5 to 7.5 per cent of the speed of light. Though the speed is far less than for beta-particles, the energy is far greater, for a proton, and there are four, has 1835 times the mass of an electron. The particle can penetrate other atoms with a result that Rutherford made his ground for the nucleus-and-envelope structure. Combining the main results till then (1927), "we can form the following picture of a radio-active atom. One of the neutral alpha-satellites, which circles in a quantised orbit round the central nucleus, for some reason becomes unstable, and escapes from the nucleus, losing its two electrons when the electric field falls to a critical value. It escapes as a doubly charged helium nucleus with a speed depending on its quantum orbit and nuclear charge. The two electrons which are liberated from the satellite fall inwards towards the nucleus, probably circulating with nearly the speed of light close to the central nucleus, and inside the region occupied by the neutral satellites. Occasionally one of these electrons is hurled from the system, giving rise to a disintegration electron. The disturbance of the neutral satellite system by the liberation of an alpha-particle, or swift electron, may lead to its re-arrangement, involving the transition of one or more satellites from one quantum orbit to another, emitting in the process gamma-rays determined by quantum relations."

Besides leading to their origins, the three rays, like the crystal unit, came from our partner's hand, more penetrating than could be manufactured, and showing the way to make equal and better. They penetrate by collisions, and so place their three fields beside that of gas collisions. The gamma-rays join x-rays in sounding the envelope. "If you want to know how many matches there are in a matchbox, you rattle them. You hear a noise of a strength that depends on their number. It is the same with the electrons in an atom" (Gerlach). That sounds an unlikely way to count, but the quantum restrictions make it good; the number came out the atomic number, the diameter of the electron could be determined, and the character of the kernel near the core. The beta-rays offer an exploring service that is as definite and orderly; for electrons also differ by a single effective character, and their work is the work of each. The character is merely its velocity or, therefore, its kinetic energy; but an atom imposes quantum conditions just as on the light that would excite or ionise it. When the energy of the attacking electron is below an amount which every atom fixes according to its kind, there is no disturbance, just as there is none from light of too long a wave. When the amount reaches or exceeds this excitation potential, the atom takes from it a quantity that exactly raises one of its own electrons to a higher level; the invader retires with the balance;

and the atom, at once returning of itself to normal, radiates in one or more quanta the quantum that it absorbed. Each level has its own excitation potential. When light is the invader there are corresponding conditions and results; it retires in waves of greater length. With a greater speed still, the electron ionises the atom, and again at critical values; each atom and each level has its own ionisation potential. When light is the ionising invader there is the photo-electric effect in that detail. The cultivation is being carried through an increasing number of atoms, the discontinuities in the curves and the photographs marking the number and the place of their several potentials.

The experimental difficulties tell how really full is the empty space in which gas particles collide, and across which the collisions within them have to deliver their records. Neither the parallel effects of wave and electron, nor the increase in their penetrating power, nor the variety of interiors that they explore, found a way to the better unity of wave and particle, which their simplest instance made the standing problem. The quantum theory, when pressed home, was unable to meet and define an exception.

But it took over the exceptional phenomena that had been waiting to come into better cultivation from a deeper ground. As always, they had been valued at first and cultivated because they were rare, but in the end because their value became universal. Fluorescence had long been known to be due to a light of higher frequency than its own; and there were exceptions. Now it became the visible instance of the general fact; the atom after a large excitement returns to normal by emitting the energy in steps; and the exceptions are due to the invaded atom being excited already. The very rarity of fluorescence is at present being used, to measure the time, the hundred-millionth or so of a second, that an atom takes to recover. The instance from larger and longer damage goes farther. The electrical conductivity of flames and their neighbourhood, explored from Faraday's time, was rather a thing apart, before the nature and the sources of ionising were discovered. Now, on the contrary, it follows that most atoms outside our earth and its moon must be living in that abnormal state. The chaos of collisions between the independent perfect particles of the gas theory is little to that between atoms in every state of dishevelment, electrons of every speed, and light of every length. They are all of them selective, and yet their collisions are all coming into the theory.

If the field of the gas theory is advanced at the fine extreme by wave and electron collisions, the alpha-particles advance it at the other, taking it beyond the range of chaos on earth to the frantic fury in the stars, where atoms may lose their envelopes altogether. Here too the single particles can be followed; they are identical with helium atoms that have lost their envelope. When a pencil of them hits a prepared fluorescent screen, there are flashes, which can be separated by a low-power microscope, and counted per second or minute. The distance from the source is known at which the particles are still able to produce a flash, and, because the power is the same for the same source, the space between can be filled with different gases at different pressures and temperatures, and the stopping power determined from a standard one. Solid films can be interposed, and their resistance measured from the same standard. The power to produce a flash ends abruptly; the particle has been falling to the speed that lets it seize and hold the two missing electrons; it becomes a normal helium atom, joining the levelling dance of the gas theory with a speed still many million times that of its neighbours in the air.

The difference in the adventures met by the particles of the pencil causes it to spread. The vast majority are deflected very little, though they pass through thousands of atoms. But a few break away at large angles. They are too many, and the angles too great, for the chance that the same invader is forced in one direction by many small encounters. That was Rutherford's argument: the large deflections must be due to an electrical resistance of such concentration that its diameter should be only about a million-millionth of a centimetre. His view was more than confirmed immediately afterwards by the Wilson photographs of the tracks of the particles, each the even track of destruction by ionising, which they leave behind them for a moment. Some of the lines bend sharply as if broken, and sometimes a branch appears at the break. The real angle of the two limbs marks the recoil of the two colliding masses, and is found from simultaneous photographs. The masses can be calculated from it; and, if they are masses positively charged, their equation can be tested. A third ocular witness arrived with the discovery of the x-ray spectroscope, when Moseley proved the regular shift of the spectral lines with the increase of atomic weight. The three cultures in rapid succession concern us owing to their directness and their independence. The first and crudest, by the screen scintillations, is not superseded; it has contrived to distinguish the nuclear charge on different metals by the angles of scattering; but especially it has pioneered a farther province:

Far beyond the range of alpha scintillations others that are weaker had been observed. They were now proved to be made by protons driven directly forward, and the protons to have been driven out of hydrogen molecules by the very few head-on collisions that could have occurred. On other gases being tried, protons were driven out of nitrogen, and proved that their speed could be greater than when driven out of hydrogen, and that, instead of going forward, they were coming off at all angles, often at angles greater than a right angle. The new province cultivates this result by bombarding different atoms, especially in solid films where the absence of hydrogen can best be secured. The first clear results were from the six of odd atomic numbers from 5 to 15, one of several indications of the nuclear structure. Other atoms have yielded, and a further culture has been introduced at the Vienna Radium Institute by the use of a microphotometric means of identifying the sources of the two scintillations wherever they occur; it lets expelled protons of short range be identified. Work with it has brought the belief there that the nuclei of all atoms may yield to the bombardment, and that already the angles and the velocities of the proton tell against the simple view that it takes up the whole shock. There is an explosion, it is thought, from whose products the whole structure of the nucleus may yet be gathered. Rutherford looks rather to the use of much higher voltages: "I am hopeful that I may yet have my wish fulfilled: a copious supply of atoms and electrons which have an individual energy far transcending that of alpha- and beta-particles from radio-active bodies".

§ 7. And, without either exploding or splitting, the nucleus has analysed itself for all atoms in accordance with our fourth pointer. Every radio-active atom shares its place in the table of atoms with one or more others; ten of the final twelve places accommodate forty-four. Had they been caught separately, each place, instead of containing a pleiad, would have seemed single, its elements uniform in weight, as in all other properties. For, once mixed, there had so far been nothing that could sift them. The possibility had already been tried for stable atoms, as a way to whole numbers for their weights; but no chemical analysis, nor search in different specimens, had been able to realise it. The discovery came unsought, from neon, among the cultures by which J. J. Thomson was analysing the positive ions produced in a discharge tube. He developed the perforation of the cathode, through which Goldstein had collected them, into a longer and finer canal, through which their energy might take them, and then carry them, as a straight stream, to hit a sensitive plate. The particles of the stream differ in speed, in mass, and in charge. To analyse it he imposed an electrostatic and a magnetic field so set that, when imposed simultaneously, they must bend the stream into separate courses which must meet the plate and mark it in parabolic arcs. The relative distances, lengths, and intensities of the arcs mean three separate characters in every course. Close to the strong arc from neon a weak one always appeared on the side next the axis. The well-proved atomic weight 20.2 might therefore be the weighted average of 20 and 22, and itself the weight of none, provided the lighter of the two kinds were ten times as many as the heavier. From confirming this reading, Aston proceeded, after the war, to alter the apparatus into his mass-spectrograph. After securing a better stream it imposes the fields in succession, arranged at angles that make ions of one mass converge at one spot. He found that placed at a higher angle the plate takes the spots, and that they lie on straight lines very nearly, forming a mass-spectrum. A third method produces nothing so picturesque, and is the more typical by the small surface evidence of the deep stream. For its final record, from Dempster's apparatus, is merely the amount of charge that the ions deposit on emerging from a final slit. The electrical and the magnetic fields, through which they have passed, are together built on a simple equation to give the measurements that the equation requires. The electrical field has a potential difference in the neighbourhood of 900 volts, and the whole intention is, by varying the strength, to follow the variation in the amount of charge deposited. The apparatus aims at the theoretical condition: the charge deposited gives the number of carriers, and they give the difference in their masses, because the product of mass and voltage is the same for them all. The speed of the ions has to be controlled before entering the electrical field; it is done by a development of the hot-anode method of producing them. By this method a supply in all kinds of atom is found for Aston's apparatus as well, of which he has recently constructed a new edition[1] with each detail improved. "The new instrument has five times the resolving power of the old one, far more than sufficient to separate the mass lines of the heaviest element known. Its accuracy is 1 in 10,000, which is just sufficient to give rough first order values of the divergencies from whole numbers." The previous accuracy of measurement, 1 in 1000, had been sufficient for the divergence in hydrogen, and had confirmed the belief that there is another source of the fraction in atomic weights beyond the main one from the mixture of isotopes. "Since the neutral hydrogen atom is one proton plus one electron, the masses of all atoms would be whole numbers on the scale H = 1. The measurements made with the first mass-spectrograph were sufficiently accurate to show that this was not true. The theoretical reason adduced for this failure of the additive law is that, inside the nucleus, the protons and

[1] *Proceedings of the Royal Society*, A, 115, p. 487.

electrons are packed so closely together that their electromagnetic fields interfere, and a certain fraction of the combined mass is destroyed, whereas outside the nucleus the distances between the charges are too great for this to happen. The mass destroyed corresponds to energy released, analogous to the heat of formation of a chemical compound. . . . It is for this reason that measurements of this loss of mass are of such fundamental importance, for by them we may learn something of the actual structure of the nucleus." And already from that loss for helium, and from the equation of mass and energy, the chemical question of the formation of molecules had passed to the profounder question of the formation of atoms, and been taken to the stars. In the formation of 4 grams of helium from hydrogen the energy released amounts to that which would raise 200 tons of water from freezing to boiling point.

§ 8. The last of our pointers from radio-activity is the group-displacement law. The law anticipated, for the resulting atoms, the principle of atomic numbers, which followed soon for all. When the resulting atom is due to the loss of an alpha-particle, its nucleus must have two positive charges fewer than its parent had; when due to the loss of a beta-particle, an electron, its nucleus must have one more than its parent had. These differences of themselves, and only they, were able to specify the column in the periodic table in which the new atom placed itself with corresponding properties.

Next, the list of six inert atoms, which had been completing itself, made the division of the table into periods intelligible, and so far its columns. Helium is the first of the six; it has two positive charges in its nucleus, and therefore an envelope of two extra-nuclear electrons. The last is radon, with 86 of each. Though very radio-active, it is inert like the rest, because the number of electrons constituting the envelope is able to take so stable an arrangement that it remains unshaken by the presence of other atoms of the same or other kind.

Finally, and the important thing: the periods pass from arranging the list of 92 atoms into arranging the envelope of each individual. There the periods become levels of energy. A level or period, on completing itself, is inert; it is beyond the reach of chemical compounding. Chlorine has 17 electrons for its envelope: 2 occupy the deepest level, corresponding with the period which ends in helium; 8 occupy the second level, corresponding with the period which ends in neon; and the remaining 7 are the shell, or outermost level, the electrons available for compounding. Were they one more, a third level would complete itself, and the atom be argon; the unchanging charge on the nucleus keeps it chlorine; but the nearness to completion counts in the presence of another atom with which it can combine. If the other is sodium, it captures the sole occupant of the sodium shell, leaving the sodium with a neon stability plus a positive charge, and having itself now a negative one. If the other is another chlorine atom, the electrostatic bond is not available; but each atom, by sharing one electron with the other, reaches the strength of a shell of 8. Though this bond is called co-valent, and the other electro-valent, it is equally electrical. How the sharing holds is part of the general question how electrons hold themselves a stable system, as they do at every level, though they must repel one another.

The bond is a factor of the joint structure, and only a factor, as the difference between diamond and graphite brings out, where carbon combines with itself. But it is where carbon combines with other atoms to form the enormous variety and size of organic molecules that the reach of its 4 co-valency is seen with the fact of being only a factor. Isomers are extremely numerous among them, molecules which, though identical in the kinds of atom that constitute them, and in the number of each, are very different in their geometrical, optical, and other physical, as well as chemical properties. Like bricks ready for any structure, the atoms in those large molecules might well seem to need integral or molecular bonds, in addition to their superficial own, and especially when they are the molecules of living bodies. But the only kind of chemical bond still outstanding is found in inorganic molecules, and is no longer thought to be other than between atom and atom. It is the bond called co-ordinate, found on molecules whose valencies are saturated already; and they will not reduce to the co-valency of a mutual give and take. It may be that they will reduce to a co-valency where the pair of shared electrons is given by one of the two atoms, and accepted by the other.[1] But it is also on our route if that "represents the last resource of a dying theory", and if "the problem of valency must follow, not precede, the solution of the more general problem of atomic structure, so that the problem of the number of electrons in any chemical bond will be the last solved of the problems of chemistry".[2]

§ 9. With that we pass from structure to its working and its maintenance. The force working the electrons of the envelope was requiring as yet that each maintain its place like a planet. That was hard for those of the shell, through which all chemical compounding is made and maintained; for the electrons combining two atoms

[1] Sidgwick, *The Electronic Theory of Valency*, ch. vii.
[2] Main Smith, *Chemistry and Atomic Structure*, p. 125.

had to compass two suns. The dilemma, lying deeper, again did not interfere; which is the main thing. It is an eminent instance of the proper meaning of the saying that science only pushes difficulties farther back. The 'only' is in error; they are pushed where they belong, and where alone they can be met, if still there.

The dilemma did not prevent the advance of chemistry and physics from reaching the law of atomic structure, and the architecture of the whole envelope of every atom. We now proceed to the planetary theory, and the pressure by which, like every good analogy, it was able to reject itself, after defining the opening to the farther field. And, since I quoted the variety of work that converged on the law of corresponding states, so here on the farther and far greater cycle of structure: "The law of uniform atomic plan has been deduced from the evidence of radio-activity, the evidence of general and specific chemical properties including valency and co-ordination, the evidence of the widths of x-ray absorption bands, the evidence of the wave-lengths of optical spectra, the evidence of the wave-lengths of x-ray emission spectra, and the evidence of the wave-lengths corresponding to the heads of the bands of x-ray absorption spectra".[1] It belongs also to our route that, as the hard-won inferences of mineralogy and stereo-chemistry on molecular and crystal structure were corroborated, so chemistry lost nothing. The few details that were altered surprised it only for its having missed them. The remarkable thing was that the surprising number of isotopes leaves the old atomic weights in possession. They remain the combining weights, which was all that they had ever proved themselves to be.

But more had appeared to be proved by the seeming finality of chemical action. It had been a charge

[1] Main Smith, *Chemistry and Atomic Structure*, p. 194.

against our minds that the properties of compounds could not be derived from those of the elements, nor therefore the evolution of the earth, its life, and minds, but only their superficial history. When it began to be clear that chemical action involved only the outer structure of particles, there remained hope that the core might hold the secret of living bodies. But the common belief was that chemical action is profound enough for anything. Its compounding appeared so searching that even feelings might emerge from elements which had none; psychology watched new mental molecules arrive to prove 'creative synthesis'. This familiar refuge was lost when chemical compounding lost its profundity, and affinity lost its mystery.

But the discovery that all structures and forces in nature find their element in the atom, which contains every kind of them, suggests that the advance is into abstractness, if also into generality. Think of the kinds of machinery that I have mentioned for cultivating phenomena from streams of electrons or protons. Their very virtue in creating a stream, in guarding, bending, and dividing it, supports our solid pictures of it. Yet the image of every particle is as metaphorical as the charge or load that it bears. Is not the stream a fiction and a substitute? No more than a sketch or a portrait ever is. The stream that proves itself can be just as easily separated from the metaphorical part that makes it a picture. There is no fiction in grasping by means of a picture, unless we presume that nature consists of phenomena. That crude error tends to linger, and to betray itself in doubtful words like percept and concept, though the fault is not theirs. But it may linger without ambiguity. If a proton cannot appear, nor therefore be pictured, is it not abstract? And, if we knew all that it does, is there not still what it is? No, it is what it does, and can do. Nothing is the less concrete that we have no sense for it. But when we have the proper sense-organ, and the stream is too fast, and the particle too fine? The answer for baffling quantity or complexity, as for absent quality, is that nothing is the less concrete and particular that it is outside our range of picturing, which can never be better than the range of sense.

When now we pass from structure and picture, this question of abstract and concrete has to be taken very much farther.

XI

TO THE FAILURE OF THE FINAL ANALOGY

§ 1. THE range of electromagnetic waves has been measured through sixty octaves or more, stretching from beyond the longest waves for wireless till, approaching the single visible octave, there begin the lengths from within the atom. They begin with those from the peripheral electrons, and shorten through nearly twenty octaves to the x-rays from the K level of the heaviest. That is the range for our route. Beyond it are several octaves of gamma-rays from the nucleus, but it was the extra-nuclear part of the atom, the envelope, through which our way next went. After crowded adventures in pressing home an analogy, now the planetary theory, the way came by its failure to the deeper unity of particle and wave, which is the present end of the material development. We are still to keep to our route, as this route, instead of seeing it the advance, as it also was, of general electromagnetic theory.

The difficulty has not been from want of data, though they have had all to be cultivated. None was cultivated till early last century, when the cue came from the improving dispersion of the spectrum of sunlight. Breaks appeared in it having the shape of the slit through which the light was pouring. They mark the lengths of the missing waves from the sun's interior, missing because they have been caught and kept by atoms in its atmosphere. When these robbers exhibit their own incandescence, they produce, at the same places, bright-coloured lines. It is the place of the lines that carries the meaning. The lines from iron atoms in the sun can be seen beside those from iron vapour in the laboratory, and can be seen to coincide with them. They run to thousands, and yet the places, or wavelengths, of several have been so precisely fixed that they are used as a standard; and the official standard, the red line from cadmium, has its length fixed to eight significant figures. The number, the spacing, and the intensity of the lines from a single kind of atom mean that the countless millions of them that are contributing, one by one, to the picture have among them that variety of action. And the permanence of the picture means that the variety has that average, or equilibrium, in the given conditions. It is what we had for the pressure of a gas, for specific heats, and for full radiation: a fixed order from the chaotic elements being so many.

The lines began to be actively cultivated for their value in chemical analysis, after it had been seen that an atom produces the same lines in compounds and apart. They tell the presence of known atoms in quantities far too minute for other methods; and they have begun, or have guided, the search for atoms unknown. The second stage of cultivation led from that massproduction of lines to the contributions of the single atoms. I mentioned the value and the difficulty of cultivating the x-ray lines from deep levels of heavy atoms; the outer levels and the lighter atoms are far more easily excited. The lines that these produce are in the visible range and its neighbourhood; their crowding makes them hard to resolve; and those that form series have to be selected from the crowd by observing their joint behaviour when conditions are varied.

The pursuit of series from different atoms began to be active after Balmer's discovery (1885) of the one in the visible range from hydrogen. In time other series from it were found, one in the ultra-violet, and two in the infra-red, and they all came into a general formula consisting of the Rydberg constant and the Ritz combination principle: $\frac{R}{1^2}$, $\frac{R}{2^2}$, $\frac{R}{3^2}$, $\frac{R}{4^2}$ etc. The constant R is the line whose wave-length is 109677th of a centimetre; the figure claims to be accurate up to nearly one part in a million; and its derivation became critical for the planetary theory of the atom and its successor. The combination principle is that the difference between every two of the terms in the formula identifies one of the lines in the hydrogen spectrum, and that every line can be expressed as one of those differences.

Though it is the unit and the simplest of atoms, twenty lines have been identified from experimental hydrogen, and over thirty from the states that it can take in stars. Besides the line spectra from atoms, there are the flutings, or band spectra, from their molecular bonds. They consist of close-packed lines, which have begun to be cultivated from diatomic molecules, in order to reach the distribution of new energy, which we saw that equipartition fails to give. The practitioners express the same confidence that light can lead them through atom and through molecule, as I quoted for its power to lead them through the crystal unit. "A complete knowledge and understanding of line spectra would provide a complete knowledge of the structure and properties of atoms, and similarly a full understanding of band spectra should provide an adequate interpretation of the structure and properties of molecules, the goal of chemistry" (R. C. Johnson). Whether they can keep theory in control will be our question. They flattered the planetary theory so directly that ten years of cultivation were enough to let the working model of an atom define every orbit by four mutually independent numbers, and so uniquely that an orbit could be occupied by only one electron at a time. That remained after further cultures rejected the model; it was quite as a child rejects the chairs by which it has found its feet, and learnt to walk.

The lines that are seen in the spectrum are the precise products of as precise causes in atoms. The lines are also products of as precise causes in eye and brain. How is that possible? Just as, thirdly, the lines are the precise products of spectroscope and camera. There is no distortion of the atom's work by brain, any more than by apparatus.

§ 2. The series in hydrogen lines were purely empirical discoveries, and arithmetic found the formula which unites them. Their source must be periodic motions, a different set for different kinds of atom. At first they were taken to be vibrations of the atoms themselves. When the normal Zeeman effect on the lines came to be proved (1910), they became vibrations of the electrons. And, when the nuclear character of the positive charge was established, their vibration was first replaced by two motions: a planetary one about the nucleus, and an instantaneous move of the electron from one fixed orbit to another. The planetary motion secured the stability of the atom by there being no radiation from it. The orbits were as if "stationary states, waiting places between which occurs the emission of the energy corresponding to the various spectral lines. . . . The radiation of light corresponding to a particular spectral line is emitted by a transition between two stationary states; and we are not justified in expecting any simple relation between frequencies of revolution of the electron and the frequency of the emitted radiation." Unlikely though the theory was, Bohr showed it in that first *Essay* (1913) to be systematic enough to make very critical predictions that were correct. For us it repeats the situation with which we began in the kinetic theory of gases, where the pressure of a simple, but entirely measurable theory forced the inexplicable factors to define themselves. "I shall not attempt to propose an explanation; on the contrary, I shall try to indicate a way in which it appears possible to bring the spectral laws into close connection with other properties of the elements, which appear to be equally inexplicable." These were two: the quantum in heat-radiation, and the power of the electron to maintain its energy in the normal atom.

As the attraction of sun for planet is countered by the speed of the planet, so that between proton and electron was countered by the speed of the electron, the electrostatic law being the same as for gravitation. Electrodynamic law, however, is quite adverse; it requires the electron to radiate and lose energy all the time, seeing its motion is all accelerated. But then that would conflict with the very existence of the atom, and with the spectral record. As the electron lost energy, its orbit would contract, and the record would show a continuous band instead of lines at favoured lengths.

Bohr turned the two defects into postulates: let the electron revolve without radiating, and let the number and the shapes of its possible orbits not be infinite and arbitrary, but at fixed axes. Then, when the hydrogen atom is absorbing energy, its only electron is exchanging one orbit for a greater; and, when it loses the excitement, and the electron falls back, the quantum surrendered gives the line found in the spectrum. The number of lines, and their intensities, mark the number, and the prevalence, of the different falls occurring in the crowd whose record is being taken. The list of orbits corresponds with the possible differences in the series $\frac{R}{1^2}$, $\frac{R}{2^2}$, $\frac{R}{3^2}$, etc. And, since every line is determined by one of the differences, the steps between them grow less as the denominator increases. This comes out in the lessening distance between the lines as they near R, till they seem continuous, and are harder and harder to part. There the theory joins the old one, just as the simple quantum does when the wave-length increases. The new picture commends itself in other ways, even by the atom growing bulkier the more it is excited, and behaving still in steps when its planet is at a thousand times the normal or unexcited distance from the nucleus. The picture also takes up the separation of the four hydrogen series from one another within the general one; and it says why the normal atom can absorb a length of wave that it cannot emit.

But the fundamental strength or weakness of the theory rested on other obligations, which it could not but profess to meet. For, though revolutionary, it placed the orbits on the formal foundations of the old or classical theory:

First, it had to profess to tell the diameter of the hydrogen atom, and in a way so new that it could use none of the many ways that I mentioned. The angular momentum of the electron in any of the prescribed orbits is a multiple (1, 2, 3, . . .) of h divided by 2π. When this multiple is equated to the general expression for angular momentum, and the expressions for the equal attractive and centrifugal forces are introduced, an equation emerges for the radius or semi-axis. The radius must be equal to a quantity in which the only physical elements are three constants, viz. the mass of the electron, the elementary charge, and h. The result

gives a length for the normal atom which fits well with
the best results of the old approaches. The orbital
velocity also comes out, and therefore the kinetic
energy of the electron, as a function of the same three
constants.

But the severest obligation on the theory follows its
other impossible postulate, the electron's leap from
orbit to orbit. The theory cannot refuse to take up an
equation that requires it to tell the wave-length of R,
and thence that of every line, in the following way. The
kinetic energy of the electron in each orbit is equal to
the energy that can expel it from the atom. The more
the electron is already excited, the greater its orbit, or
level of energy, and the less energy it needs in order to
go free. The orbits are therefore distinguished, and
connected, by the ionising energy that each needs; and
they have a common standard in the amount for the
normal orbit. The energy that is lost in falling from one
orbit-level to any other, near or far, is the energy that
is recorded by a spectral line; it is in one quantum. This
quantum hn, h times the frequency, is equal to the
kinetic energy lost by the electron. If the theory is
right, any other expression for this energy, divided by
h, is equal to n. One containing the same three physical
constants, as for the radius, ought now to give the n of
the common standard, which is R. The theory stood
the test, a thing not so surprising as that the precision
of the three commands a fourth so precise.

The obligation then went farther. Bohr pointed out
how the expression equal to R, and therefore R itself,
ought to alter for other atoms than hydrogen. There
was a crucial instance in lines hitherto thought to come
from hydrogen, though they broke the whole-number
rule; might they not come from the electron of ionised
helium, whose R should be multiplied by 4, because its

nucleus has twice the charge and attraction? This proved itself, and the formal demand became general when the atomic numbers were established: the square of each number from 1 to 92 should be the multiplier of its R. In return the complex atoms made a unifying gift as remarkable, and imperative, to hydrogen. The series of lines from each of their K, L, M, N, . . . levels have their equivalents in the four hydrogen series named after their discoverers. And yet hydrogen has never but one electron at any time to make the fall to a lower level.

Like the gas theory, the planetary theory grew in value not by adding factors to make it more equal to the facts, but by developing their necessity, and again by first removing the calculable simplifications. Those crucial lines bear a value that could hardly come from helium, if their R had the same value as for the hydrogen lines. The mechanical reply came at once, and was right: the electron does not revolve round the nucleus, but both round their common centre of gravity. The constant value for the mass of the electron has therefore to be multiplied by a factor proportional to the mass of the nucleus; "the value of the Rydberg constant increases with the increase of atomic weight, . . . in perfect agreement with many years of spectroscopic research" (Reiche). In Moseley's work, which came immediately after the theory, the atomic numbers, plotted against the square root of the frequency, gave nearly a straight line. The 'nearly' became inevitable, and important, by marking precisely the sub-levels of energy found from the notable breaks of the absorption curves. They can be so well determined that, from corresponding levels in a range of atoms, taken in their natural order, the straight lines became "so perfect, that the ionising potentials can be quite accurately obtained from atoms for which they have not yet been determined, . . . by simple extrapolation along the lines " (Millikan and Bowen). The self-development of the theory, notably its magnetic demands and their applications, were meeting the ever more exacting demands that poured from the spectra without question.

How was a success so remarkable to fail and do better? When exactions began to define the failure of the theory, would they open the secret of the impossible leaps, and the impossible non-radiating orbits?

When the concentric circles of the early account are generalised into Kepler orbits, the energy at each level remains the same with the diameter, now the major axis. But it should vary a little with the degree of eccentricity. This is defined by an angular quantum number, and a radial quantum number, together equal to the total quantum number which is that of the major axis. As the total number moves from its normal 1 to higher energy levels 2, 3, 4, . . . the number of possible ellipses at each level increases. Their difference in form and size involves their level in differences of energy, which, though trifling, should measure as exactly in the source as in the spectrum; the electron should vary in mass with its different enormous speeds, and the orbit of each must be revolving in its plane at a great calculable rate, forming a rosette. And so, instead of the fall from level 3 to level 2 emitting energy of one wavelength, there should be 6 possible falls, and the same number of lengths. There being only 3 in fact, the system had to search itself again. It found a selection principle in the conservation of the moment of momentum, requiring the angular quantum number to change by one unit only in any fall; this reduces the 6 to 3. The theory had to do more. Besides their shapes and sizes, orbits have inclination; "from the continuous manifold of possible planes the theory has to lift out a discrete number of routes distinguished by quanta. . . . The simple character of their derivation, and of the results, affects our minds almost like magic" (Sommerfeld). But the magical mapping invaded no secret of the leap.

§ 3. Nor would the other secret open to Bohr's magic wand, as Sommerfeld called the principle of correspondence. The principle went so well we might have expected it to arrest itself at a well-defined entrance, leading deeper. For, though 'illogical and fantastic' to its critics, it was rational in the sense of systematic, and its correspondence was the very analogy that bears fruit and retires. That is why it interests us. At the end of the formal development, we shall also come to an eminent instance. But there the outlook was not blank as here, looking towards the material end. For Einstein could see the farther system into which the old law of gravitation might lead by its error, and there find itself more intelligible. The gas theory, too, had known the system into which its impossible postulates might break. But, that theory having broken through, and found the electromagnetic system universal, what sort of field could lie deeper still to take over the new impossible postulates, and make them intelligible? Nothing deeper appeared to be known. For the aether was hopeless. Borrowing all its properties it had borrowed the quarrel between quantum and continuous, and between particle and wave; the aether was merely ready to borrow any settlement as well.

The settlement has come from two directions, from both by reason of the pressure. They had been overlooked on account of two presumptions that we all carry from the surface. We have always presumed that wave is superficial to particle, consisting of particles; and we have always presumed that statistical or average facts are merely ours. The issues are therefore the main concern, and the route will soon be forgotten. But its value is not the less for us, and is greater that with the issues there has come a formal development, which can forget all cruder obligations, and confine itself to the spectral lines. The unrecorded gropings would themselves be worth regarding, down to those that a snail feels, when it puts out another horn because the first one has failed.

If the snail feels at all, it would not be ludicrous to identify and contrast the three factors in its causal system inspired by the rain, with those of the explorer groping through equations or apparatus, who feels that they are reducing him to the snail's condition. We might look at the feeling factor, which, in the snail, takes nothing for granted, and in the explorer so much; but it would be to separate feeling from the deposit, the object that he tries, and that fails or succeeds, here the equations or the apparatus. They are handles to so much of nature, and the explorer's grasp of them is another matter, competent according as it is sensitive to their power, whether failure or success. On the road here again we have the failures that began by succeeding. The successes remain; they have to be found again on better ground. The road is forcing itself into new country, therefore by analogy, and finds itself baffled by being unable to define the hindrance.

§ 4. The analogy that Bohr developed into the correspondence principle stood on the ground that any quantum theory of the source of the radiation from an atom ought to be a "rational generalisation of our ordinary electrodynamical conceptions". These would give the hydrogen lines to the frequencies of the periodic motion of the electron, their serial order to harmonics of the motion, and their intensities to the amplitudes. The new model, though analogous, looks entirely different. Instead of one compound motion in each of the myriad atoms that give the lines, the new model for hydrogen has a myriad independent motions, each a leap, one leap in each atom. The crowd of atoms is divided afresh every moment into as many classes as there are lines; in each atom of a class the electron has just left the same higher for the same lower level; and the intensities of the lines tell the distribution of the myriad into the classes. The model does nothing but classify, for the leaps have no connexion. But the lines have connexion; they mark always the same selection of spectral terms between which they are the difference; they have always the same relative intensities; and there are always intervals that they mark one by one, which they combine at the same time for one stride. They are statistical results, for no atom keeps its class; and, since it can be in any of the possible classes, the relative intensities of the lines mark the relative probabilities of the leaps. The life-time statistical picture of a single atom corresponds, therefore, with its actual present picture on the classical theory. There the lines came from one compound motion in each atom; and, as that compound is always analysable into a Fourier expansion, the correspondence principle made a "rational transcription" of the old individual components to the new statistical ones. Its critics called it an illogical blend, because the two sets of components have nothing in common. And its promise of reaching a new law of corresponding states was not good. The new critical point was to be where the correspondence nearly amounts to coincidence, and where alone the transcription could begin. The point is where the leap that gives a line is from one great orbit to a neighbour so near that the formula for the line series calls the difference between them negligible. There the line's frequency is nearly the electron's number of revolutions according to the old theory; not a very promising place from which to carry much far.

Yet the principle went far. It found the quantising rules for the orbits and leaps to be the same as the direct planetary route was proving; and it could reach towards the intensities of the lines, or probabilities of the leaps. When a crucial test arrived in the effects that foreign fields produce on the lines, both routes went farther than the classical one, and, of the three, the principle went farthest. There had just been found the very definite effects (Stark) of a strong electric field. The classical way had no means of accounting for them. The new one found a quantum formula for the splitting of the lines, for their spacing according to the energy levels from which they come, according to the shapes of the orbits there, and all according to the intensity of the field imposed. And only the principle was able to predict the relative intensities of the lines, and reply at once to the changes in polarisation. Strong and weak magnetic fields have effects on the lines that are more various and are still a growing challenge. The answers to meet it continue to be as fruitful as when they began. The effect that was found first, the normal Zeeman effect, came at once into the classical theory, when Lorentz used and proved the new electrical elements. Later he preferred the new reading, because it was able to account for the 'anomalous' effects as well. And they have proved themselves the more fundamental; but "the perfect agreement between final results obtained in two such different ways for the normal effect betrays an intimate, and certainly not an accidental correspondence". The principle deserved better than to work "like a foreign body in the quantum theory". No better was to be expected from the ground on which it was working; it quantised the energy only at the beginning and the end, and there in two such different shapes as light and the leaps; light at one end was balanced by leaps, or phase-areas between orbits, at the other. And, all the time, light had to be left continuous to secure the interference by which it was to measure itself. A drastic step could be taken by quantising once for all through the general phase formula, making continuity merely appearance.[1]

But the use of trouble is to go through it; and the principle kept the model to the two elements of the general quantum theory that somehow make one: the oscillator with a train of waves whose energy and momentum are in quanta. First, the leaps and their probabilities, by corresponding with harmonic oscillators, could let their cause be regarded as an interaction of the electron revolving with known energy against a radiation field. Critical data for that answer came in from the Compton effects of collision between electron and wave; since the effects, when the electron is free, could be used for collisions where the electron is bound with known strengths. Then the data grew too critical, but not to destroy; they could encourage the energy equations to smooth out the crudeness of the model. The two postulates, impossible apart, were taken into the duality, the stationary states going to the radiation field, both being continuous, while the leaps took up the quantum characters.[2] Coming in together as complementary, might not state and leap manage even to exchange their functions, and cause the leap to

[1] Sommerfeld, 4th ed., pp. 762, 817; Wentzel, *Zeitschr. für Physik*, 22, p. 199.
[2] Bohr, Kramers, and Slater, *Phil. Mag.* 47, p. 797.

lose its prescience? "The stationary state is the time during which the atom is radiating or absorbing; the transition from one state to another is not accompanied by radiation. The radiation emitted or absorbed during the stationary state includes all the frequencies connected with all the transitions that the atom could make. Then the atom is under no necessity of knowing what transition it is going to make ahead of time."[1]

These remodellings of the model, till it could finally turn itself inside out, pointed to the single trouble of a twofold element. The working dependence of the two, electron and wave, was well known in electromagnetic theory, and the theory looked for their better connexion to the minute dimensions in the atom, where the quanta cannot be overlooked. The forcing of the analogy was of crude on fine, in order to bring out the resisting factor already in the crude but concealed. It brought out that the working dependence, however modelled, was not enough. The value of the model was in continuing pliant to its original task of embodying the empirical but precise results of the serial cultures.

Finally, the energy equations began to find the model irksome, as they began to reach the cultures of themselves. Also the profusion of facts began to find it at fault, and the fault grew to be more than its failure to embody the source of the finer cultures that were coming. When the two foreign fields were put on at once, the model still predicted, and was now wrong. And at last it had to turn from the prospect which had made it so attractive. Its ambition had been to take up the atoms after hydrogen in their numerical order, and be the model of each, as each new electron was captured and bound.

[1] Slater, *Physical Review*, 25, p. 398.

T

§ 5. Without model or picture, however, the correspondence principle was reaching the data from dispersion, and also those from absorption. Could the translation from electromechanics be made not into model, nor any sort of picture, but from the classical form of mechanics to a new form. Having seen a way, Heisenberg brought back the radical broom. Why should the growing profusion look for its roots in a picture that could probably never be seen? Let the principle find the roots from the new translation. It found them, and began to find that they lie beyond the capacity of any picture, however perfect. That could seem a misfortune, but it did not come from sweeping the pictures away, but from a new origin for h, the quantum of action.

The translation, instead of now giving the changing position of the electron in the atom, stops at the energy changes there. They are equal to the radiation quantities that the serial lines require. The quantities, being each determined by two spectral terms, need each two connected numbers to specify it. And the series can take a form in which the translation has only to substitute a two-number constant, for the one-number constant, in each component. The result yields a table in place of a picture, a two-dimensional table of numbers (rows and columns), a matrix. There had for years been an algebra for the handling of such numbers, the operating rules being the same as for ordinary numbers, except that, owing to the difference of row and column, there is not one product from multiplying two matrices, e.g. p and q, but pq and qp. The previous correspondences for the levels of energy, and for the amplitudes, find themselves again in the new language. A syntax, or new mechanics, was developed by finding the forms and operations that should correspond with the classical kinematics and kinetics. The Hamiltonian forms, expressing the energy in terms of the co-ordinates and momentum, come in as they stand.

This gave the cue for the fundamental equation, where the unit of action makes the difference. Formerly h came in like a stranger to select the possible orbits; now it does better as a difference. In the picture h had been defined from 2π times the angular momentum, now it is from 2π times another quantity with action dimensions, which is written pq-qp. q remains the Cartesian co-ordinate, and p the momentum, of the classical form; in matrix form they give those two products, and the difference between the products is a numerical function of h. But h found a more definite, even a systematic place, when the new way was generalised, at several hands, into an independent quantum mechanics, where the positions of the electron are again determined, as well as the energies. It overtakes the difficulty which had always been ignored, though foreseen as a barrier, that the quantities to be cultivated and measured would become so fine that they must be altered by the means taken to identify and measure them.

§ 6. The departure to the matrix way had hardly begun to prove its power when the classical way responded by developing into wave-mechanics, which does the work of the impossible postulates without them. In a year or so, atomic mechanics was being compared with celestial,—a proper ending for the planetary theory, which thereupon departed.

Its loss may be regretted because its picture is replaced by a complexity, to which no perfect picture, nor model, can be adequate. But hardly for the failure of the analogy. The model had revived the comfortable way of uniting the world by universal analogy. That synthesis of nature, minds, and institutions, in large and in small, by the same laws, which was made in despair of knowing the real existence of anything, has no support from the ground that is reached in quantum mechanics. But the ground offers crucial conditions for our question of knowing as living, and against knowledge being a duplicate, or a model. Sensory knowledge is obviously not, as we saw from the hundred sensations of the sky (ii. 5). But theories may look models, and therefore copies of the surface. If the hydrogen model had continued to work, did it follow that the electron keeps careering six thousand millions of million times about the nucleus every second?

First, then, there is the old route, which now finds its way to wave-mechanics. This will show both how great the classical organisation is that matches itself with nature's, and how it is that abstract experiment on the body of knowledge can be as physical as concrete experiment on the body of nature. Secondly, there is the articulation of the two bodies with each other, if theories are organs related to understanding as eyes to seeing, and related to their objects as eyes to light. Thirdly, from quantum mechanics, there is the sense-barrier become systematic, there is the uniting with wave-mechanics, which means the unity of wave and particle, and there is the place of probability, which revises our notion of nature's responsibility for mental life.

XII

THE PRODUCTS OF THE FAILURE

§ 1. THE correspondence principle by its failure brought a farther effect than the broom for pictures, and the transcription into energy instead. The energy would not remain bilingual, one kind for particle, one kind for wave. Size came to count, but not as was expected. What but shifts were to be expected from an analogy that pressed large, tangible, and visible, into the intangible and invisible small of an atomic interior? But again it is the small that comes out, and instructs the large. The interior allows the two readings, but now it insists on their quarrelling; which the large could not do.

Optics and mechanics had long made an agreement as good as the facts had required; it had settled both their general and their special quarrel about light. The general quarrel whether light is wave or particle had been settled with an either-or, by defining means to distinguish the two; now the fine facts ask it to be both. But they also offer a way in the two new expressions for energy which were discovered, one for wave by the quantum, the other for particle by its great speed. Would they unite as well as equate? "The idea that with the motion of a material point there is always hidden the propagation of a wave would, if it reached a form entirely satisfactory, mean a synthesis of great rational beauty." Wave-mechanics entered on that ground, in a thesis of L. de Broglie (1925) which recovered an old synthesis, and saw a way of bringing the fine field into it.

The work of Schrödinger took the unity to greater fullness by merging the 'material point' in its wave-system, making the particle a wave-group. The cue came from the way in which the special quarrel had been settled: ray-optics to continue but to stand on wave-optics. After it had been seen that light consists of waves, wave-optics found it hard to do the work that had been done so visibly by ray or straight line. When it succeeded, it could let the geometrical ray work as before, and retire to the elements, the waves, which account for the ray, and for which the ray cannot account. Could that result for light pass now to all nature, and light become the universal element? Classical mechanics, which is particle - mechanics, would come to rest on a wave-mechanics. The classical form had served without correction, because the wave-lengths are so small compared with the apertures and lenses of the apparatus through which they had been cultivated. But the ground is lost when, as in hydrogen, the length of wave is comparable with the length of the normal orbit.

The experiment of mixing the expressions for energy lets the wave-length divided by h be equal to the momentum of the moving particle. When the particle is an electron, the quantities are all precisely known. The question then was to devise a concrete experiment like that for x-rays, using electrons instead, and the new difficulty was their poor penetrating power.

You may have seen how picturesque the results have been, for Prof. G. P. Thomson began his cultures in Aberdeen. A homogeneous beam of electrons was secured, and sent through the thinnest possible leaf of matter of known structure (gold, platinum, celluloid), at a range of high voltages. It reported on a plate set at a known distance behind the leaf. The report is a picture of interference rings, alternately dark and light, round the spot that receives the undeflected electrons. The radius of each ring depends on the wave-length, and the wave-length professes to be the quotient of h by the momentum of the electron. The pattern and the rule for its measurement are as for x-rays; but the electrons themselves must be there with the waves, for, when a magnetic field is imposed, it pulls aside the whole picture, including the spot. "The sizes of the patterns agree to 5 per cent with those predicted on the de Broglie theory of wave-mechanics, regarding the phenomenon as one of diffraction of the phase-waves associated with the electrons." The electron is not broken, but proves itself to follow a wave-length connected with it, and, in turn, to determine the wave-length by just its momentum. These products in phenomena have been multiplied in other laboratories from a great range of beam strength, and through many kinds of leaf. They join the results of earlier experiment by Davisson and others, earlier also than the theory, where the beam, after striking a metal surface at a known angle, makes an electrical record of the angles to which it is scattered for different voltages; and there are now exacter means of measurement, and a greater range. Both forms of the analysis join the x-ray field, whose results are to its hand; they add the field of harder rays, which only the rare gamma-rays had been representing; and they discover the far field to be as common as matter. They join and extend older studies on material surfaces, and on the electrical conductivity of metals.

§ 2. We have once more nature for itself absorbing nature for us, rejecting only our arrogance that the two are connected by a likeness. And still we have theory, itself unexpected, able to stake its life on unexpected cultures in phenomena. For here it professes to give the individual roots of the cultures. And yet it goes farther than ever into the formal region where, while our grasp of nature grows better than ever, it is more than ever obviously ours.

A notable instance of this introduced the new waves. If an electron has limits, its electrical reach has none. Not the space, therefore, that it occupies can define its oneness; it is an individual morsel of energy; half of the energy is not half an electron. The morsel combines two kinds of energy, the kind for particle and the kind for wave. In combining it should equate them, and, equating, unite them. The Bohr model, which equated, could not unite them. After all manipulation there of particle and wave, two marvels persisted: the particle gains or loses energy by waves or not at all, and the wave-lengths are prescribed by the momentum of the particle, its level in the atom. What if the marvels are prior to the atom, already in every moving electron? "The fundamental idea of the theory of the quanta is the impossibility of picturing an isolated quantity of energy without associating a definite frequency to it." The frequency must reach as far as the electron's influence, which is *tout entier*, instead of being in its interior; for what would the interior of a morsel of energy mean? There is therefore good ground for putting the two new expressions for energy together, and experimenting with them. One is mc^2, the amount of energy in any particle whose mass is m; the other is hn, the unit of wave energy. By way of experiment let the particle speed past a fixed observer, and consider the change in the values of the two variables, m and n, for the other two are constants. Neither m nor n alters for an observer speeding with the particle; and the rule is known for transforming the values that he finds into those that our external observer ought to find on his fixed axes. The transforming factor is a fraction whose denominator is the speed of light, and whose numerator is determined by the speed of the particle. The fraction is a multiplier to n, diminishing it, and a divisor to m, increasing it. But since hn and mc^2 remain equated, n has also to rise and fall directly with m. Therefore the fixed observer should have two frequencies passing before him "essentially different, a difficulty that intrigued me for a long time, till I was able to remove it by demonstrating a theorem of the harmony of their phases": the particle's waves are in phase with a wave advancing in the same direction with a velocity which is the inverse of theirs, always greater than that of light; the product of the two is always c^2. The solution brought the analogy between optics and mechanics to their identity as wave-mechanics. But the difficulty itself has an equal interest for our question. Why should an abstract experiment be able to force it on us, and require us to find in nature a speed greater than that of light?

Does it mean that, at the last, phenomena fail to keep theory in control? Are they handing over their authority to theory, and in a shape worse than at the beginning, where they let the theory of gas pressure go untrammelled into chaos? First they seem to fail by letting theory prescribe so unwelcome a speed. Next they seem to fail the new mechanics itself, because it has two interpretations, between which they would not decide. The safer of the two reads only probabilities; is it not a third failure of theirs that they make us content with them? Are not probabilities merely sub- stitutes for the actual causes, which can care nothing how they count? Add, as fourth seeming failure, the fact that the phenomena have become so fine that they are altered by being observed. And, more arresting than the four fears, there are the two unforeseen questions: If wave is to displace particle as final, of what stuff can its body be? And can we grasp it without particles to help?

The two questions, and the four seeming failures, reflect on the connexion between existence and our grasp. Physics has projected one closing place after another, and then found that phenomena push it farther. The four appearances of failure on the part of phenomena continue on that course, we shall find. The other two look upsetting enough to end the course itself, but they do not, nor even alter it. They lift the course as a whole to its farther placing; it had thought itself the end, in accordance with classical mechanics. The simplest cause of the farther placing is space-time. Let us include its effect before asking, from the super-light speed, whether phenomena surrender their control at the last.

§ 3. Answers to the two questions had been projected all the way down from surface to depth, and nature had allowed them until now. To learn at the last that the final particle may consist of waves, which do not consist of particles, goes against the whole habit of our thought; yet thought was free to somersault, and also to spring back, when it repented. But the other disappointment is harder to bear. The aether had been projected as the perfect answer to the surface question, What becomes of? Every deeper level had been answering with a more uniform stuff; and every stuff had supported a more universal form in answer to the other question, What are the laws? The laws of nature were the laws of a stuff, nature itself the nature of a stuff, and all change was the same stuff in other form. The outlook was to a final stuff, whose properties were mutually necessary, systematic. That is precisely the projection from wave-mechanics: the forms are no longer alien to the matter, and the matter submits without resisting.

It looks a peaceful ending to their ancient friction, and up-making. But the peace is more unpleasant than divorce would have been; their indifference to each other is complete; forms manage everything, and matter does nothing but submit. It is the settlement on which physics had long ago been glad to turn its back, and which it now meets again, having come in a circle. Nature is again form and matter, and matter has lost its two vague potentialities: it no longer has the power to resist, and it no longer owns the confusion that settles into higher and higher forms. By losing the two it has revenge for the old contempt of it. Forces, no longer coming from matter, might become insubstantial again, the very thing to be avoided; and evolution would revert to creation. To evade such a finish, matter as the aether was filled with secret power, an abyss beyond the power of phenomena. There was no suspicion of an alternative, but only fear of bodiless forms and forces. Nature had to be the nature of a stuff. The alternative lay in the opposite direction, and was unsuspected before the discovery of space-time. It is that nature will not set in any stuff, because none can be concrete enough.

That is the counter of space-time to the tradition about understanding that existence is too concrete for it to grasp. The tradition keeps a truth, and still gives warning. "The statement that what *really* happens is correctly described by describing a wave-motion does not necessarily mean exactly the same thing as: what *exists* is the wave-motion. In generalising to an *arbitrary* mechanical system we are led to describe what really happens in such a system by a wave-motion in the generalised space of its co-ordinates. Though such a space has quite a definite physical meaning, it cannot very well be said to 'exist'; hence a wave-motion in this space cannot be said to 'exist' in the ordinary sense of the word either. It is merely an adequate mathematical description of what happens."[1] The last words give us our question. Like maps, the systems of co-ordinates all more or less arbitrary, are means of studying real relations with freedom. The means are always one thing, nature another; it is the connexion that is important, the connexion between organ and nature. And it need not be a likeness:

Relations do not need to be copied; they are the same, and have the same properties, whether in nature, or in map, model, or theory. When they constitute the systems called pure theory, their structures have nothing unknown. Such are the systems that occupy logic, mathematics, and wave or other rational mechanics. A physical thing, and every other concrete physical system, is logical, mathematical, and mechanical. The grasp of theory on things, its 'physical interpretation', consists in finding it in them; any sort of mathematical function may find itself there, as does a piece of geometry.

Therefore a theory that knows itself needs no warning to keep its place. But there is one way in which it can criticise fact; it can discover how and why a thing or a process, torn from its actual setting, may take too little away with it, and yet seem complete. Nothing is more likely in fact; nothing would be more astonishing than that we did not lose in tearing. But we do not like to

[1] Schrödinger, *Four Lectures on Wave Mechanics*, p. 6.

believe it of the things we call concrete, and have always thought complete. Far from our grasp failing to reach their existence, because they are too concrete and particular, it has found in nature that they are not concrete and particular enough.

The wrench from tradition feels the greater for being due to space and time, which tear apart so smoothly from each other to suit our separate lives. Their mutual dependence came late to light, though it had always been indicated on the surface. The indication was overlooked, because phenomena were under suspicion, and because there was no suspicion that the times and the spaces, which we measure, are phenomena of their unity. Their unity is discovered, and calculated, from the differences in the time and space measurements made by moving observers of the same scene. It then prescribes the infinite variety of measurements, which nature makes equally good from as many moving points of view, whether they are occupied or not. The infinite variety of the times and spaces for the scene is the body of their one space-time, which is mathematical, and in our grasp. The space-time itself is not a space nor a time, nor a mixture of their substance; time and space are its factors, and it is nothing added to the two by mathematics.

Other factors that have been united were once about as confident as time and space of their mutual independence: aether and space, mass and energy, inertia and gravity, particle and wave. None of these unities takes a substance to hold its two factors together and make them aspects; there is just the embodied mathematics or mechanics.

Some men had always argued that nature must be more than the nature of a stuff; but they were eager for the greater power of our minds, and not for the greater

existence of nature. Their 'more than stuff' was regarded
by most as a remnant of the bisection of nature into
changing things and unchanging laws. The physical
fact lies beyond, and condemns that quarrel; it is the
fact that the concreteness of anything, in being a stuff
and substantial, is only phenomenon of its fuller, and
still particular existence. This concreter unity does not
wait for any grasp. And we grasp it mathematically
because it is already mathematical.

§ 4. When phenomena reach their barriers do they
hand over their control to the theory which they have
supported? They do not, but it is essential that the
theory continue to develop itself. And the necessity
may well seem a misfortune, as in our instance, where,
having found the wave that it wants, it must ask for a
second wave, which is faster the slower the other, and
always faster than light. "For a fast motor car the
waves are some 10^{14} faster than the car itself; for a
pedestrian the discrepancy is still greater" (Haas). To
ask us to throw waves forward at such a pace all the
time that we walk might well be the death of any theory.
Why should it go on to suicide, or even to risk its life,
after it has found what it set out to seek? May we not
lay the awkward burden on our grasp, on intellect, or
on sense, and let nature escape?

First, on intellect. The super-light speed carries no
energy; the disembodied phase-waves enter no new
region; they and their speeds are properties of the sine-
curve, which is already everywhere, if anywhere; why
not let them stay there, and be 'only a mathematical
conception'? That is the notion corresponding with 'only
phenomena'. But a mathematical structure is not partly
in and partly out of nature, in any important sense of
in and out. It never fails to distinguish between pre-

sumption and necessity; and here it finds that, if the one kind of wave is presumed to exist, the existence of the other is necessary. The theory cannot merely take the one that it likes. So, to find the other, it looked abroad. A wave bearing the same properties could explain the working of the Heaviside layer: the speed always greater than that of light, and greater the greater the wave-length; but that wave has body. And it is not abroad, but within, that the theory should look, if it is surprised by the result of its experiment. It has mixed mc^2 and hn, because they are equal quantities of energy; and it has found that nature must unite them more profoundly than by mixing.

The other bestowal of the trouble is with sense, or the observer. Now the search within succeeded. The discovery was that nature has a more fundamental connexion with the observer than had been suspected. If he were riding on the electron and its wave-system, he would get no hint of the unwelcome waves. There is no hint of them from axes on it, but only when it passes before axes fixed by our fixed observer. We had thought that the thing's own axes are final for its behaviour with respect to other things, and that the onlooker makes accretions. We were closing down nature too soon again. There are no accretions, and the estimates on and off the moving body are all equally good; for they are all inter-convertible through one law. In our instance the conversion needs only the relative motion of the two sets of axes, each of the two having its own time axis. No more is needed for the inverse and enormous velocity which the external observer should find. When the set of axes that is moving with the particle passes before him, it inclines itself to the set that he has chosen. The relative motion of the two sets records itself as the angle between the time-axis in each. The slower the motion, the smaller the angle. The smaller the angle, the greater the length of space-axis per unit of time that a wave-change requires when its reading on the moving set writes its equivalent on the fixed set of our observer.

Grudging to leave the old simplicity we try to stop half-way. The trouble, though sensible, being also formal, may not nature and phenomena discard it? The unwelcome velocity, the length of space-axis per unit of time, is due to a point of view; is it not an addition to the one course of nature proper? Only to the old nature proper, which is not concrete enough to be the real one; the one course of nature no longer exists.

But we persist. Allow that nature is responsible for the space-time results, may they not be absent from her body in the absence of her creatures, and be rather theirs than those of her very substance. No, they are not added by plus nor parasite. On the contrary, they are being used as a curb on the non-relative development of the theory, which we are to see, from its new start in the tiny volume of the hydrogen atom, where h becomes important. There, where particle-mechanics is too crude, and gives way to that for waves, the two velocities, that of wave-group and that of wave-phase, are related in the same inverse way, their product being c^2. The two developments are carried out alongside, and it is made a check on the interpretation of the non-relative one, when it fails to find a corresponding advance in the other.[1]

§ 5. The general answer to the question whether, at the last, phenomena lose control to theory is better introduced by a more ordinary instance. It came, like the other, at the first coming of wave-mechanics, and it

[1] L. de Broglie, *Wave Mechanics*, p. 187.

compelled a return for a more radical start. The waves associated with the electron could profess to account for one of Bohr's two impossible postulates, but not for the other one; they could select the stable orbits, or levels of energy, but they could not manage the leaps. The electron's momentum, in whatever orbit, determines that all the waves in its train have one length for that orbit; and, in order that the orbit be self-repeating or stable, the train must consist of a whole number of them. From so solid a ground it seemed at first that the leaps needed only "an electromagnetic theory fitly modified, which we do not yet possess". But more was needed; and first the planetary picture itself had to go. The neatness of this check at the first entrance of wave-mechanics lets us carry the general question farther:

If a theory has found phenomena that are crucial enough to remove all other theories, need it go farther, knowing the bounds of sense, and fearing to end in mere mathematics? It has no option. Phenomena withdraw their warrant from a theory that asks to be taken only in part; for, though the part has won from other claimants, the rightful claimant of part and whole may have still to appear. The situation is at the end as we have seen it all the way

The best instance is naturally at a farther end than wave-mechanics. The familiar law of gravitation had answered perfectly for two centuries and more; but it was the law of a force, and every change of the force had to be propagated with an infinite speed, which is a contradiction. No phenomena came to unseat the law, till after the rightful claimant appeared, and proved them to be crucial. The new law was able to require a new mechanics that sets nature on a more concrete, though a mathematical foundation. The need came in

U

sight with the failure of the perfect stream of events. It was mathematics that found in phenomena the power to reject the stream, and the power to tell absolute laws of nature from those that are good, but not final. And so it removed the fear that, when phenomena fail, the logic of the theories that they support may leave and lose nature in the weird speeds and other products of abstract analysis. The fear and the logic would be just those again that left nature, for so long, in the dust and chaos of the concrete analysis.

§ 6. While the body of nature divides in the end, as in the beginning, into phenomena and their system, the relation between the two has been developing into their unity. Their causal unity, as flower and root, has been opening out in accordance with the way of life, when life is mental, having objects for its causes. The surface objects have come to be represented by the systematic connexions, or functions, from which they can be predicted and cultivated. These, in representing, do not copy the surface. It was thought that they must be abstract; but abstractness has fallen instead even on the three final substances, as they seemed: matter or aether, time, and space.

The same error is involved when it is objected that physics does not deal with all phenomena, nor with any precisely as they are felt. For it is usually inferred that part must be mental, or that physics fails by having to select. On the contrary, physics can never be responsible for any phenomena but those that it predicts, the rest having small interest, though more for other studies. But, of course, the main source of doubt is the presumption that phenomena are an addition to nature.

§ 7. When the confusions are removed, and it is clear

that there is no question of lifting the bounds of sense, all fears about phenomena leave them, and settle on the conflict of theories between which phenomena fail to decide. This failure has always been a stimulus, and the stronger as the conflict looks extreme. A striking example will appear in the two interpretations of the main function in wave-mechanics. But the situation could hardly be better displayed than in the history of the planetary atom. Near the end a desperate issue could look possible, which is useful in order to distinguish the actual revolution. It was the prospect of "scientific bolshevism", or discontinuity in nature, if the whole-number data from the atom persisted in defying the elaborate classical system, which thinks finite numbers crude. "We have been taught that an integration of the infinitesimal elements of a continuum may be approximately replaced by a summation of finite terms, but that the former method is exact and absolute, while the second gives but an approximation. Are we now going to be obliged to reverse this decision, and to recognise that the branch of mathematics, which will come nearest to meeting the needs of science, will be the theory of numbers, rather than a theory of extension, and that measuring must be replaced by counting? . . . Whether the idea of *motion* of an electron from one level to another has any meaning is somewhat doubtful. As far as we can see, it disappears from one level and appears at another. . . . Should we not say, perhaps, that the distance between the first and the third levels is 2, and that the difference between the first and the seventh levels is 6?"[1] The ground of this despair was the very hope of the Greeks; they thought that nature could only be rational through the natural numbers in it. They found other numbers in it as well, but hoped that, like

[1] G. N. Lewis, *Valence and the Structure of Atoms*, p. 163.

phenomena, they were not quite real. Since then the opening of nature has been also the developing of the different kinds of number by which we take hold. Which kinds are only hold and ours, and which kinds are in real nature, was long thought a good question. The answers that were given remain in their names. We shall see how all are rational, and constitute our instrument for reaching the formal depths of nature. But, their power having been discovered, did it not look as if the material deepening were about to come to an end, and the power of number about to go on unencumbered? Hitherto its power depended on the reduction of change to motion, but now the spectrum, while growing more calculable and cultivable, was protesting against the reduction, and insisting that number was final. If that had continued, number would have been avenged by continuing to be real, after substances had come to nothing in the aether.

The chance of that gulf was removed by wave-mechanics. Space-time, too, when distinguished from space and time, looks naked number, a property of real nature, which on that account cannot be in motion. But the space-time number does not ask to be supported by a farther substance in real nature. It needs only the motions, or times and spaces, and the masses, which we had mistaken for independent. The number is exhausted in calculating their unity.

We are suspicious of unity superseding substance, fearing it our grasp, and knowing that nature should be the same, grasped or not. There is also the fear that, with the loss of substance, we lose the source of novelty and life; we had rather have an aether full of secrets. We are to look at that fear when we reach the present end of the material development. But our fear in approaching the end is because it looks a ghost, as if the body of nature were after all only the body of knowledge. The body of knowledge is only our means of grasping the real body; every life answers in that way the challenge that the feat is impossible; but, on reflection, we began early to suspect that we leave our mark on what we grasp. Looking at our means, we let in the conflicting isms, which all knew that real nature, or Nature, must be solid or substantial. And what could be solid but a stuff? That supported the fear of our means making a mark, and brought the remorse, which became familiar, at the recurrent cleansing of the body of physics. The cleansings were mainly from the stuff's effects, but, a stuff being beyond question, the defilement appeared to come from our constitution. After our senses were at last freed, the blame fell on pride and ambition, original sins because always recurring. Pride was easily deflated by putting the body of knowledge against the body of nature; but ambition was more difficult, for nature would persist in encouraging the way of life, as at the start. It has proved as catholic to theories, and their mathematical analyses, at different levels, as to the ways of sense in different creatures. The analogy between eyes and theories prevents the notion that theories copy the structures of nature in order to grasp them; but we are now to go farther:

Theories have their own structure; they know it precisely, and, if they do not also know their power, it is because they do not yet know nature. But, like every good analogy, the one from senses to theories leads to their better unity through their difference. There is a certain flexibility in our organs of sense, in eyes and ears as well as fingers, and it comes into no conflict with the rigidity of nature, for they are nature's. Their flexibility is slight compared with that of theories and their structures. The contrast between the flexibility of theory and the rigidity of nature produces the next fear, or challenge, forcing our problem to go farther into our articulation with nature.

How complex the flexible organ can be comes out in the new advance to wave-mechanics; for the classical route found the way from itself, and completed its own revolution. It proceeded without more concrete experiment, though in the old manner, pioneering by analogy. And so it also comes out how physical conditions are explored as directly by abstract experiment on the body of knowledge, as by concrete experiment on the body of nature.

XIII

RIGID AND FLEXIBLE

§ 1. THE new advance made the 'energy-morsel', the electron, stationary and moving, consist of waves. Its mass or energy was now concentrated as the wave-group without need of point or particle. We are slow to dismiss the particle, but from neither mental reason for making it final. The two reasons have had ages to grow into causes, if age bound minds to their beliefs. As early as the origin of common sense in brains, phenomena were united into things; and our earliest notion of thing or particle gave it a unity like our mental one. Though both reasons are older than man, neither stands in the way when we contemplate the new plunge. We merely dislike its unpromising look.

For, though the very life of electron and proton is electrical, the wave-group does not promise to maintain it, nor to explain the absence of other lives than those two. Seeing, however, that point-mechanics, which electrical theory had been taking for universal, must fail in the end, "it is not only not dangerous, but even desirable, for a time at least, to lay an exaggerated stress on its counterpart" (Schrödinger). And, given the new simultaneous waves, the plunge itself is old, being that which Newton contemplated for optics, and refused. Like ordinary waves of light, the new waves, because they too are so tiny, give birth by interference to the paths that had been taken for self-born and straight. They go behind the first law of motion to derive it.

Only the other day that would have looked a rock against the plunge. The question was current, even when Ward lectured here, whether the first law was not a law of thought, as universal as cause, of which inertia was the obverse. And, if inertial straight lines rest on wave-lines, which need straight lines to describe them, is there not a question of priority, like that of egg and fowl? The two questions will come up when we arrive at the grasp of geometry, and thence at inertia become flexible, and one with gravitation in the new first law of motion. They both belong to the mechanics of general relativity. But the way to wave-mechanics needs less. The particle and its line, in order to lose finality, and follow light, need only the flexibility that space-time imposes.

It imposes the super-light velocity as the ratio of energy to momentum, now mc^2 to mv. The ratio was known to wave-optics before the new readings of energy; it was used in describing the normal trajectory from one surface of constant phase to the next one. What if the succession of these enveloping surfaces is fixed, and by h? For, if the usual phase-angle description of vibration is to apply, the argument of sine or cosine should reduce from quantity to number. And, if the quantity is action, which is energy multiplied by time, the reduction needs only that the dividing constant be the elemental quantum of action. That gave the cue for converting particle-mechanics to wave-mechanics, and now without the original help of the two observers.

If wave-mechanics works, all nature has a unit of action, and it is h. And all is in action, or comes into action. But for that, the addition of time to energy might seem only a refining of the abstract machinery for generating wave-surfaces; on the contrary, the addition is that all else, including energy, is abstract for being out of action. The law of least action, which gave like foundations to optics and mechanics, now gives them the same one, and develops it still on the ground of Hamilton's law of varying action, "the one law being, as it were, the last step in the ascending scale of induction respecting linear paths of light, while the other law may usefully be made the first in the descending or deductive way. . . . Embracing every known combination of media, and every straight, or bent, or curved line, ordinary or extraordinary, along which light (whatever light may be) extends its influence successively in space and time, the law of least action is that this linear path of light, from one point to another, is always found to be such that, if it be compared with the other infinitely various lines, by which the same two points might be connected, a certain integral or sum, called often Action, and depending by fixed rules on the length, and shape, and position of the path, and on the media which are traversed by it, is less than all the similar integrals for the other neighbouring lines, or at least possesses, with respect to them, a certain *stationary* property." The same holds for the path of a particle, with this difference: the particle's path-element is multiplied by the particle's velocity, whereas the ray's path-element is multiplied by the ray's velocity, in whatever medium, divided by c. The two paths, from being similar, are taken to their unity by the super-light velocity. Their 'least' theorems, now coming from the original law of least or quickest time, provide a simple picture: they are "consequences from the very simple principle that elementary wave-motions only produce an appreciable effect where they reinforce each other, or agree in phase, which is the case only when neighbouring paths are all traversed in equal times" (Biggs). The element into which our minds at last emerge, after penetrating matter, would be as limpid as that.

§ 2. Far too limpid for our liking; for, dissolving all things but itself, how does the limpid aether keep them from confusion, and precipitate the familiar world again? Yet neither the ending is a wonder, nor that we like it so little. When we seek simple and simpler in order to explain, the more simple grows always more universal in both matter and law. Its direction is just the reverse from that of didactic simplicity. Not foreseeing this, we revolt when the end approaches, and the core of mystery disappears, as the last particle empties itself in a uniform stuff. But the 'exaggerated stress' takes the royal road, where insistence on a system, by defining the resistance to it, is able to break through the analogies. The insistence had behind it the elaborate weight of the classical body of knowledge, which had now to transfer its whole to the foundation that it had found for light alone. It possessed three analogies that were ready to light the way, one kinematical, one dynamical, and one physical. We have had the first: the bases of ray-optics and mechanics. These bases being analogous, might not the known cause of the final failure of the first be the unknown cause of the final failure of the second?

But how was a particle to unburden its mass on a merely geometrical (kinematical) description? There was an analogy offering for this too, had the quest been promising. The shapes of the waves, and their propagation, would still be described by points and their motions. The new fundamental wave equation uses the classical one, which equates the motion of a point to the propagation of a system of waves, and gives the velocity at every point of the space that they fill. But, while points remain available, point-masses do not; and they had made all the difference. The real difference in wave-shapes and their propagation had all been given to the difference of their matter. Now the particle-start of the mechanical properties of a wave would have to follow from the wave-start of the mechanical properties of a particle. The horse that pulls the cart would have to come into the cart, and be one with it.

To deepen to such a unity would have been attractive enough, had it not been by capsizing. And so two pointers, though familiar, remained apart. One to deepen was pointing from the new discovery that mass reduces to energy. One to invert was pointing from the new discovery that nature prescribes the units of energy, and that they are waves. When the venture was faced, the second analogy came in sight: least action offers an energy-form so analogous to the phase-form for a train of waves that it would let energy be one with phase. There needed only the welcome condition, as I mentioned, that the energy-form take for constant $h/2\pi$, so that the translation of it should give the phase a number-form. The energy-form, Hamilton's principal function, can be seen to translate itself directly at the simplest,[1] as well as to retain the generality of the highway, of which I shall speak later. The number-form, by quantising the energy to accord with the periodic factor in the propagation, furnished the new entrance for the stationary postulate. It converted the principle of Wilson and Sommerfeld into a consequence, or theorem. Both had taken it directly from the radiation data, and imposed it on the generalised co-ordinates, "giving an entirely new type of view of

---

[1] W. Wilson, *Theoretical Physics*, i. § 9. 4.

natural phenomena. The phase-space, the manifold of all conceivable states, is crossed mesh-like by the graph curves of the stationary orbits", the size of the mesh being determined by h, of which all distances, then, are whole multiples.[1]

§ 3. The new source of the stationary postulate would be able to carry the leaps with it, if another analogy offering would also break into identity. This third one had been obvious, unlike the other two; for the elastic response of gas particles, and the ordered response out of atoms, had always recalled a resonance. Now that all is wave, should not the analogy become identity, the whole behaviour identical with the stationary undulations of a violin string? If electrons are each a coalescing of waves, they are nodes, and their leaps are the loops; nodes do not have to leap, they have only to occur.

But where do they occur, and how do their places come to be connected by simple arithmetic? The analogy could not say; it had to break into a deeper ground; and the formal means were ready, now that the obstruction stood clear. Boundary conditions are indispensable, as fixed ends are for the vibrating lengths of a violin string; and they appeared to be lacking. The check arose from the matter, from the form, and from the form being now unable to leave any mystery with the matter. From the matter it was because electron and atom have now no boundary; from the form, it was because the form for superposed waves, being a partial differential equation, rather multiplies than restricts their possible compoundings; and from both it was because, the vibrating material being now of one kind, form cannot leave to matter even difference of timbre. The classical stream, though now of waves, would still

[1] Sommerfeld, *loc. cit.* ch. iv. § 1, and (4th Ed.) ch. ii. § 3.

seem to seek outside for a source that would lock the flow of energy in every atom, in each according to its kind.

But the analogy broke through the triple check into a deeper, though entirely formal level, where there is no counting nor weighing. The analogues had to seek for their source, and they found it by generalising. When a notion is generalised, as here the notion of boundary conditions to include those of a boundless sphere, nothing specific is excluded for being specific; all is held by the single common notion that boundaries determine events occurring within them. And then analogy can try farther: When the notion to be generalised is a law or equation, the specific forms may force themselves into the general one. A familiar equation describing the propagation of a wave, and containing a definite phase-form, can force itself into the equation for the new wave-function. The phase-form keeps the total and the potential energies apart, each multiplied by the same complex of constants. When the equation for our vibrating string is forced into the new form, the potential constituent is equal to zero; and there is a corresponding translation for vibrating systems of increasing complexity.[1] One experiment thereupon was to cultivate the general equation in the ample field of spherical harmonics, subjecting it to the Restriction that the function remain one-valued, finite, and continuous, through the whole generalised space.

The Restriction turned out unexpectedly able to do all for the hydrogen atom that the two impossible postulates of the planetary theory had unexpectedly done. The planetary hydrogen atom could then be robbed, and had to be, to test the experiment on the body of nature. The expression for the potential energy of the planetary

[1] L. de Broglie, *Wave Mechanics*, ch. 17.

electron was taken, viz. the product of the equal charges on proton and electron divided by the length of the radius. This quantity is usually marked as negative, because energy is added as the length increases, and therefore as zero when the radius is infinite, which happens when the atom is ionised. The radial form of the stolen quantity suggests the conversion of the general equation to polar co-ordinates, whose three variables let the equation break up into three independent equations in spherical harmonics. When the Restriction is made in these equations, and they are added, the possible values of the total energy give the welcome result. They are found to form a continuous series prolonging a discontinuous one. The total energy, when greater than zero, is found to take any value, but, when negative, to take only those values or levels connected by whole numbers, which Bohr had found. The story of the success of the planetary theory in a picturable space was now repeated in its original order [1] by the harmonic analysis in a generalised space: from circle to ellipse, thence to the number and variety of ellipses at each level, to the corrections for the electron's changing mass, and the motion of the nucleus, to the magnetic quantum number, and to the perturbations by electric and magnetic fields.

The strength of the planetary theory was in managing and predicting the phenomena from itself; that is the strength of the new one too. The old way was good without, as well as within the atom, except for the two postulates; but the new holds everywhere without qualification, for it is no more qualified, nor assisted, by the Restriction than a calculating machine by the problems that are inserted. The new progressed, like the old, by way of its own unity, or internal demands.

[1] Bloch, *L'ancienne et la nouvelle théorie des quanta*, ch. 16.

One demand was for half-quantum numbers; the old had had no place for them, but the phenomena had begun to require them. Another was from the appearance of conflict between the bounds of electron and atom and the infinite bounds employed by the Restriction. The analysis answers that the amplitude of the vibrations falls exponentially, and becomes negligible soon after the old measured bounds.

§ 4. The other successful theory of the hydrogen atom, which came in two forms at the same time as wave-mechanics, escaped expressly from the weight that the classical theory had to carry. "The only object of theoretical physics is to calculate results that can be compared with experiment"; there is no restriction to the kinds of mathematical construction; on the contrary, the main work is in the mathematics of transformations; and there analogies from the surface are more than likely to mislead, as would that from the violin string which could lead to wave-mechanics.[1] "It is not surprising that our language should be incapable of describing the processes occurring within the atoms, for it was invented to describe the experiences of daily life, and these consist only of processes involving exceedingly large numbers of atoms. . . . Words can only describe things of which we can form mental pictures. Fortunately, mathematics is not subject to this limitation, and it has been possible to invent a mathematical scheme—the quantum theory—which seems entirely adequate for the treatment of atomic processes."[2]

The theory carries in a new direction that farther placing of our lives in nature which began with the

---

[1] Dirac, *The Principles of Quantum Mechanics*, ch. i.
[2] Heisenberg, *The Physical Principles of the Quantum Theory*, p. 11.

discovery of nature through space-time relativity. This relativity removed one sacrifice that nature proper had seemed to demand. It left the classical theory good for our individual lives, and condemned it only for suggesting that our differences in viewing events must be shorn to find the same events for all. The quantum theory goes farther; it enters our individual lives to rescue them from the classical theory, which, if it were final, would remove probability from the foundations of nature. And our lives rest on probability. The junction of the rival routes therefore means a great deal. We shall reach it better, if we stay with the classical and conservative system to look at the junction between any formal system and the system of nature. The classical one is conservative, because it holds itself responsible for the knowledge at all levels. That is very useful for our problem of the deposit, and essential for understanding that knowing is living. But there is no difference in the relation between formal and physical system. Quantum and relativity structures copy nothing from the common-sensible world, and are free to define and use their own mathematical operations. In this they complete an independence that is already throughout the classical theory, and goes back to every formal structure that learns its power. Think now of the classical body of knowledge, organised through the law of least action, matching itself against the organism of nature:

The law is the highway on which the dynamical avenues rest that penetrate the different levels. They are one by carrying through, and elaborating in their levels, the functions and equations that have come in to constitute it. And it does not wait; surveys of uncharted country are made from it, and methods of invasion are projected. Survey and method are still space-words, and, like highway and royal road, they give only the rigid character of the advance. Its flexible character is as fundamental. Because flexible, though logical, it may seem only the invader's, and the invaded rigid only, or logical. And so, first from a distance, and then from close up, the formal complexity of the body of knowledge has more often been contrasted, than united, with the complexity of nature.

At the first and farthest approach the formal body could look mental, because all forms are conceptions, and go into words. Seen closer, when the conceptions become relations and quantities in algebraic language, it detaches itself equally from mind and from nature, and becomes a self-contained instrument made by the one, and true of the other. The quantities that it first handled for mechanics were space, time, mass, and force. The relations among them that it handled "require neither geometrical nor mechancial constructions, but only algebraical operations in accordance with regular and uniform procedure; those who love Analysis will see with pleasure that Mechanics has become a branch of it" (Lagrange). Its freedom to complicate and exercise itself on forms of its own making has made it, in both aim and intuition, the art which its lovers compare with music and poetry. All the compositions are at the prosaic service of mechanics, and, in notable advances, have anticipated its needs. The freedom and the luxuriance have given the impression, even to those who have been closest, that the endless complexity of form in theoretical experiments is artificial, and not so physical as the endless complexity of change. But the instrument, when detached, holds together. It does not translate into nature as prose and applied, and stay outside as pure and poetry.

The history of the instrument had to bear the same

x

sort of grudge from stage to stage as the material story
from level to level. A stage would take itself for final in
reason and in nature, and resent advance beyond it for
being outside its rules, and sometimes against them.
Each advance was a generalising of number, though
in a sort of its own; it gave and gives fuller value to the
earlier stages, and induces farther cultivation of nature.
These cultures of phenomena, from being mainly
causal, are now merely predicted; statistical mechanics
predicts phenomena from laws that do not need their
roots. And classical mechanics, which requires and
seeks their roots, prepares phenomena to suit its plough.
Both work the surface, bringing the surface laws into
functional form, which is also the pure empirical frame
for the laws of common sense, freeing them from the
imported agencies of our early explanations. Common
sense does not carry the analyses far, though infinitely
farther than we think from finding them as easy and
inevitable as animals do.

§ 5. But the farther analysis needs, with its new aim,
a new intuition, art or no art. If the new way of grasping makes old objects look new, the new are as purely
nature's as those born in our dove-cot. "Altering the
Platonic myth a little, we can compare the algebrist to
a man who, owning a dove-cot well-stocked, multiplies
his pigeons, and uses them up at his convenience,
whereas the analyst is a man whose dove-cot is not yet
occupied; he has to go hunting to catch the birds that
have to fill it." At first he handles them in the old way,
and fails to make them at home. But "to-day we no
longer regard an ellipse as really composed of an infinite number of infinitely small parts, called points.
No, an ellipse is a whole which refuses to be compounded
of parts; it is a sort of Leibnizian monad. This monad

is big with the properties of the ellipse; I mean that the notion ellipse contains them even when they have not been explicitly formulated, which they could not be, since their number is infinite. The task of analysis is to dissect the offered whole, in order to get the elements that give the best description of the curve's expression and behaviour." [1] With this abstract formal unity we begin to appreciate the concrete formal unity which is nature's. And, returning to the whole classical body, we can already throw on the shoulders of the ellipse two usual though opposite charges:

The 'offered whole', is it really offered? Not as part of the surface; but the properties of an ellipse do not wait till it be drawn, defined, or subjected to any human dealing. The other is the charge that nature is too subtle for man. The drawings and other measures by which he hunts to seize the area of an ellipse may be never so fine, it eludes them. That is because he is handling it, as he does nature, first in the ways that he knows, and not yet in the more general ways that it offers.

It was with a view to two farther challenges that I quoted from two makers of the classical way to wave-mechanics. In spaces that do not 'exist', if Schrödinger's adventures were hard, and the results unforeseen, are they not as in the making of poetry? And Hamilton's deduction after induction may seem the soft adventure in consistency that follows every gathering from nature. There the higher the class or law from which deduction proceeds, the less it could prescribe; the law of least action would have had to be satisfied if all the other laws consisted with it. But, like phenomena, the law goes farther, and asks them all to prove themselves through it. And then it goes farther than phenomena: it asks them all to make it their ground. The ground

[1] P. Boutroux, *L'Analyse mathématique*, ii. pp. 263, 266.

becomes their common logical body, their offered whole, a whole that has to be won, but that is offered, not imposed.

§ 6. The common ground is developed by an analysis growing always more general. That is the source of the spaces; they are not added but selected, as also are all other generalised co-ordinates. They are points of view from which quantities are defined and connected, though no longer measured. Their power is not at all created by our action; if they look too arbitrary to impose on nature, and be called nature's, recall the ellipse and add its appearances to our eyes. Geometry makes their number infinite, and makes the ellipse take them all. When nature too takes them, for eyes are nature's, it is not at all because eyes create them. If even we defend the artifice, we expose our mistake; we had as well defend eyes and light. There is a sense in which the equator and the lines of latitude do not exist, but we let the distances between them exist; and, in general, we do not grudge nature the quantities, but only the frame which makes them what they are. Light and dark exist only for eyes; as there was no dark before them, so neither had nature the quantities before the lines which define them.

The single difference between the material and the formal organs of knowing is, however, significant. Eye and light, being products of nature, take no share in accounting for events that preceded their own advent; but nature puts no such restriction on co-ordinates and quantities.

The distinction between matter and form is as fundamental as between cause which does everything, and law which does nothing. The surface of nature is as formal as material, and in that character, too, it is de-

veloped by analysis and cultivation, and not by continuing because phenomena fail. The formal progress
of the sensible into a common-sensible world needs no
words, and ends without them; already motion has
analysed itself into space and time, change into cause
and effect, quantity and order have analysed into number. It is the developments of number and the devices
for employing it that have appeared to impose on
nature and depart from reason. They can defy objection by their success and their consistency; but defiance is half-defence, and therefore mistaken. The
objections from 'physical reality', and from the ex-
uberance of mathematics, are the same as once were
made against our eyes; we have exuberant visions when
they are shut, and we give a hundred shapes, never one,
to the same thing when they are open. It is not that
defiance has succeeded, but that the old view of nature
proper has dissolved into a fuller.

The discovery was due to the formal organ, which
reason had condemned. We are later to examine the
organ, not to defend it but because reason has to find
itself to be intelligible as well as nature. A more intimate connexion between minds and nature will then
be seen than by likening formal and material organ.
But the same physical articulation of both kinds remains essential. Let us run over the situation as it
expands from the ellipse to include all kinds of space,
and then all the work done in them.

The forms of the common-sensible world grow more
formal when words take them up. They continue to
discard irrelevant matter, and then they find themselves too simple and too separate. Space found itself
both. One form of space looked final, though both eye
and geometry were offering others. The dynamics of
general relativity displaced it, requiring them all, but

they were already an offered whole in the equation for the line-element of whatever space. Not one kind of space, but the equation, secures to them their differences when they are united. For curved surfaces do not in general reduce to plane, nor therefore do the frames that are placed in them to measure their distances and directions. But the equation is able to tell their kinds from the measurements. Like the ellipse, in being one for them all, it prescribes their possible varieties, and the properties of each.

Next there are the artificial spaces, consisting of generalised co-ordinates. They are questioned for bringing in too much, but they answer by reflecting on the simpler and earlier forms. These at first are just selected, being abstracted from the surface and smoothed out. They have developed with their duty. A point and a length, from needing small means to fix them, have later to reach a fixing as fundamental as the laws that they support. The abstracted length has to be generalised: it has to be so released from points of view that it can regain the differences, which they give it, by reaching the one quantity which unites them. This uniting quantity is precisely like the ellipse, and like the line-element equation; but it took longer to discover, being not of space but of space-time.

When we pass from line to point, there may seem less left to generalise, but in fact the undertaking is the greater. The point has to generalise itself to keep itself fixed within the motions of all sorts of material conditions, and fixed by means that must be offered by the conditions. The means that offer in the common-sense world become rectangular and polar axes. By them the position and motion of any material point in a system are analysed into mutually independent factors of the system. These factors give the number of its co-ordinates, and of its degrees of freedom to move. The simple treatment is to measure the co-ordinates into particular quantities of length and angle. When they cannot be measured, they are still quantities that are independent of each other, and can stand for the point-particle, after it is lost among others. Though lost among them, it may have its motion further analysed. In rigid systems of particles this is done by adding the co-ordinates, or degrees of freedom, that fix the motion of the system itself. But, when the system offers no such advantage, means of analysing remain: the unknown x, y, z co-ordinates of each particle's motion, can be expressed as functions of another set of independent quantities, which are known to determine the motion. These generalised co-ordinates do not substitute, they analyse; they analyse the problem into the number of equations that have to be solved. The point, which began as a sensible dot, is generalised by being released from its appearance to find its power. Its development is material and formal. The material fixing is by finer and finer pointers in the apparatus. In its formal development the point is fixed by the intersection of three surfaces, on each of which it is free to move.

By such reflection from later to earlier we see the obverse aspect of the offered whole, and lose the appearance of contradiction. The ellipse, while following the monad in refusing to be compounded of its parts, has no properties that are not demonstrable: they are analysable into parts or elements which have no secret of their own. It is otherwise with material elements and their compounds. The contrast holds when the forms are nearly crude, the ellipse only section of a cone, as well as when they are developing generality.

But the likeness, though not so evident, is as important for us as the contrast. Formal and material elements alike develop through their wholes. The material elements develop as each level discovers itself, and asks for deeper. The very whole that is offered on the surface is the same that in the end finds all its elements electromagnetic. Material analysis reaches these elements by penetrating, and dissolving, all others into them. Formal analysis does the like. It starts by collecting and uniting the points of view offered on the surface, and it develops them into the kinematical apparatus for reading the course of nature everywhere. Because the apparatus becomes very artificial, our early notion of nature protests, and betrays our persistence: we had rather assign to nature the work done, and to ourselves the points of view and the abstract instrument. All forms of relativity restore the points of view to nature, and the instrument proceeds to take up and incorporate all the work done. It incorporates the work in two kinds of dynamical system. One kind proceeds by way of the concrete structures through which the work is done. It makes use of the connexions between the particles that secure both the stability of a structure, and the transmission of disturbances through it.

§ 7. The other kind of system ignores the kinds of structure, rests the work done, by whatever means, on energy, and makes energy the offered whole. This kind, which we are now to consider, has the same character of an offered whole. Its power appears in the increasing variety of the applications of thermodynamics, which, at first merely an adjunct, securing maxima and minima for the efficiency of engines, now applies everywhere through physics and chemistry. One of the two laws on which it essentially rests, the

conservation of energy, means more than that the
quantity is constant in amount. It refers to actual
systems, and says that any gain or loss of energy by a
system is through its boundaries, and that the immediate environment suffers an equal loss or gain. That
is the ground which was developed in the highway of
least action. The second law, entropy, or the degradation of energy, rests on probability, a ground equally
fundamental, as will be found. The whole is an instrument for exploring the offered whole at the several levels,
as a servant, not a substitute.

It was generalised into the system called energetic,
on a theory hostile to handling work by means of unknown structures, including the atom, which might not
exist. Energetic surrendered the hope of reducing energy
forms to one. That had the advantage of making it look
for system within energy itself. It found every form
of energy to be a product of two factors, through one
of which they can be equated, as well as by the total.
Every change exposes the two factors. The constant
one throughout the change is the capacity or extensity
of the energy. The other, its intensity, determines
every course to an equilibrium; all the potentials are
instances of it: electric, thermodynamic, chemical,
gravitational. In the abstract instrument the intensity
is the partial derivative of the energy with respect to
its extensity. Instead of seeking to reduce the number
of the forms of energy, the theory accepts all that show
the two factors. In ordinary kinetic energy, the extensity is the momentum, and the intensity is the
velocity; in elastic energy, the extensity is the compression or expansion, and the intensity is the tension;
in the mechanical energy of volume, the extensity is
the pressure. The theory can derive the proper-name
principles as theorems, from that of Archimedes down to

that of d'Alembert. And the multiplication of energies is not in itself a defect; it says how directly the instrument can grasp phenomena by dividing them into fields, and reaching their laws as partial differential equations.

That ground was already becoming fundamental for the other kind of dynamical system, which, from being a rival, may be said to have absorbed it; and the directness of its application to phenomena remains for the whole work of micro-physics. The language from the founders of quantum dynamics, with which I began, was that used by the founders of energetic, and has only to be qualified by the discovery of relativity, or an absolute for relations. "For *general* theoretical physics there exist neither atoms nor energy, nor any notion of the kind, but just established experiences. The best thing in energetic I therefore take to be this that, in far higher measure than the old theories, it is capable of fitting itself to experiences immediately. . . . There is no absolute; only relations are adequate to our knowledge. It may be a comforting dream that our question can find rest in atoms, but it remains a dream. And it would be no less a dream to see in energy an absolute, and not rather the most forcible expression for the time being of the quantitative relations among natural phenomena" (Helm). The dream, which was Ostwald's, could be separated as outlook, and leave the working explanation, as he said, with as little to fear from later as a proposition on the similarity of triangles. A recent exposition calls energetic the common ossature of all the sciences.[1] Bones, too, live, and the difference is that eye, hand, and skeleton are outright gifts, while theoretical organs have to be created by exploring offered

---

[1] Helm, *Die Energetik*, p. 362; W. Ostwald, *Die Energie*, p. 127; Michaud, *Énergétique générale*, p. 2.

wholes to find the systems in them. The wholes, in then giving us grasp, are rigid because logical, and flexible because ours.

§ 8. The relation of theory to nature lifts phenomena to a higher power than they were given by the radical broom. The old cleansing gave them power to expel all idle factors from physics; the new one gives them power to expel factors that mislead. Why should the classical presumptions have persisted without question, till matrix mechanics discovered itself by discarding them in despair, and wave-mechanics discovered itself by proving them impossible? Because of our old arrogance in humility; we had been so sure of what reason ought to say, and of what nature ought to be, against our grossness. What they have said and done about it could not have been foretold, and the error was active and therefore useful. But so much the better reason for lifting phenomena to a higher power of expelling. Their first power comes easily from their being sensory objects and products; the higher power comes with difficulty from their constituting a world which offers the whole. The earlier power expels the factors that fail to become quantities; the later expels the quantities that fail to become systematic.

The expulsions are from the instrument, and the instrument is invented; nature is discovered. A thing so obvious would not have given trouble had not the analysis of the surface left nothing there, not even its elements, to be copied into the whole. In the common-sense world invention and discovery harmonise without being defined; it is unnecessary to define them; but, when they became theory and fact, their confusion required the new broom. Concepts and theories are inventions, but some are successful; they are discoveries.

That saves the contrast between successful theory and fact; for success is not created by the best invention; theory never dictates. Why then does everyone still find it useful to say that theory must keep apart from fact, as map does, or schedule, thermometer, equation, or other expression? It is confusion at their junction that gives trouble. The junction is called their application, or interpretation; and may seem to need a link or a likeness.

Map and schedule have to be read, but the reader is no link; he puts himself out of the junction when he joins instrument and nature. And a link, though better than a half-mental joint, would be a third thing, and only double the trouble. The link and the joint both appear when, after dividing theory into part pure, part applied, the applied part is made a buffer. It is made to take up the mathematical power of the pure part, while preventing the weirder operations from crossing into nature. To remove one-half of the trouble we have merely to take the broom at its first cleansing; it sweeps everything away but phenomena and instrumental concepts. Phenomena and concepts need neither link nor buffer between them, because concepts begin on the surface with phenomena, where they need none. The surface begins to offer the ellipse and the rest, as it begins to offer arithmetic.

The graver half of the trouble is due to using likeness to join map, thermometer, equation, theory, to the things that they grasp. A map responds, and to make a model is often the intention of the others, but they are not models. Likeness probably presumes that knowing is by duplicating, though not so crudely as before, where a light was put behind the eyes to know the light in front. To see the actual junction we have to see the greater object of which the two are factors, and in which they are articulated. The successful map, equation, or, in general, theory is part of the total object before us, which here is entirely physical. As eye neither creates nor dictates to light, nor to anything that it brings to light, so theory need not ask that its structure be copied by the part of nature which it grasps for us. Nature is rescued from successful theory as light is rescued from the eye.

The error of taking light, or other sensory object, for stimulus would be repeated by making stimuli of law and ellipse. But the inverse is the commoner error in dealing with them: it is that successful theory, instead of copying them from nature, imposes them. The error can look like truth, unless we see the continuity from eyes to theories, and thence to the theatre from which we see the whole play of nature. There has always been a fear lest the theatre restrict the play; and there has always been a conviction that the play cannot be that of absolute nature. The error, the fear, and the conviction would all become true by the very means that have made them false. For the new foundation of the theatre from relativity makes the play of nature fit the audience.

That is the greatest of our articulations within nature, and far enough from the simple one of eye and light, hand and tool. It is the articulation of our individual, the classical, system with the universal physical one. The joint occupies the place of the old final gulf. Our immediate question is the other junction in § 4, where the classical system, having brought itself to wave-mechanics, unites with its statistical rival, and finds nature to be responsible for our individual lives, in a sense that none had expected. We are now to reach both of those junctions by way of the principle of action, the more fundamental whole than energy.

XIV

CLOSE OF THE MATERIAL DEVELOPMENT

§ 1. THE principle of general relativity was dissolving particles in a tensor flux before wave-mechanics was thought of; and it has to question the finality of every theatre but its own. Finding no outlook from its own to the atomicity of matter, it could foresee "in the stationary variation of action, an indication of a way of approaching this difficult problem"; and yet action could be stationary only in empty space, "in fact only when it does not exist, and not always then". In calling the way deductive, Hamilton meant not merely logical, but 'descending' from fact. The kind of fact is that of the offered wholes. If we next include action among them, and the calculus of variations, we meet the strength of whatever challenge nature makes to abstract experiment being on itself. "From its first introduction action has always been looked upon as something whose *raison d'être* is to be varied, and, moreover, *varied in such a way as to defy the laws of nature!* When a writer begins to talk about action, he is probably going to consider impossible conditions of the world. That does not mean that he is talking nonsense; he brings out the important features of the possible conditions by comparing them with impossible conditions." It is answer enough that nature makes the difference.

Action has been found fundamental for the relativity structure as for the classical one. Eddington, whom I am quoting, thinks that the new one cannot contain the classical one except as one alternative among possible others. That depends on how to separate them, which is a question for the formal development; but the living fact is first. "The world which we have to build from the crude material is the world of perception, and the process of building must depend on the nature of the percipient. . . . The building process of the mathematical theory must keep step with that process by which the mind of the percipient endows with vivid qualities certain selected structural properties of the world. This creative action of the mind follows closely the mathematical process of Hamiltonian differentiation of an invariant. . . . When we consider how an invariant depends on the variables used to describe the world, we attach more importance to changes which result in creation than to changes which involve transfer from elsewhere. . . . It is a feature of our attitude towards nature that we pay great regard to that which is permanent. The Hamiltonian derivative has a creative quality, and thus stands out in our minds as an active agent working in the passive field of space-time." [1]

We can follow this into the familiar living articulations by expanding to them three remarks that Klein made, in his *History*,[2] on the living value of the action-function, which Hamilton's modesty had rather caused to be overlooked on the Continent, as in England also before Thomson and Tait:

The first remark is that so abstract a principle as least action gave the laws for constructing optical instruments, keeping track of the complexities in the course of light through different media. It completed

---

[1] Eddington, *Mathematical Theory of Relativity*, §§ 60-64, 103.
[2] *Entwicklung der Mathematik*, i. 197 ff.

the reciprocity law, which makes eye and object inter-changeable, as if parts of one instrument. There, and this is what concerns knowing as living, sense-organ and object are like parts of one limb. It is the distal part, the object, that is the more pliant and in our power. There is the same useful arrangement in all our organs. But, if that were all, the analogy between object and the peripheral part of a limb, would hide the advance, the new articulation, that started from the coming of consciousness. The articulation of eye and object, or hand and tool, is no other than the advance of nature itself to having objects at all. The one instru-ment, eye-and-object, is about to concern our living question in another way. The improvements, through theory and skill towards finer and finer particles and events, have come in sight of their limit. But, instead of bringing merely a barrier, the limit has brought one of the grounds on which quantum mechanics has reversed the view of our life in nature.

The second remark is again on the power of the mathematical instrument. To meet the error of using purpose in explaining nature, due to the early reading of least action as least effort, "there came the other fundamental error that the mathematical science of nature, especially analytical mechanics, has only to ex-plain nature. Not *Naturerklären* but *Naturbeherrschen* is its proper task. The principle of varying action does not answer what nature intends in optical courses, but it does answer the instrument-maker's very proper question how they can be set artificially to get the best possible instrument. Theoretical science is converted into deed." All is converted that means to be converted, and not by finding its like, nor its double, but by finding its own self in company that proves it to be nature's. The identity is fundamental, and, owing to the irrelvant sensible elements, it is again rather hidden in its lower living forms: as in pointing, in grasping, so also in the instances of our ellipse.

Thirdly, "the Hamiltonian system of differential equations realises the ideal of the *Energetiker*, because it makes the total energy of a system supreme, and is able to derive the motion fully from it". Conservation of the energy had long been known to be unable to do that for itself, except by the introduction of time, that is to say, of action. This went against the unquestioned picture of the course of nature that the course is always at a present instant, and the instant one throughout the world. Energy enters that picture, but action, whose energy at an instant is derived from a period, has to stand out; for the picture prevents a period from ever being in existence but for an observer. Did not action, therefore, put a mental taint on nature? Hamilton had shown a way of moving a system from one configuration to another without using action; it was enough to use the mean value of the difference of their kinetic and potential energies at the beginning and ending instants of the course. Might not that remove the taint? There came increasing enmity within physics between energy and action. It was on the same ground as the outside quarrel in philosophy, where, however, time's need of an observer was the desire, not the defect. Both quarrels ended abruptly with the discovery of space-time. Action belongs to universal nature, which needs observers nowhere, while providing for them all.

But a question remains. As conservation does nothing to account for the dissipation of energy, so least action lets all processes be reversible, while nature appears to let none. Dissipation is derived from probability. There is now, however, nature's unit of action. Quantum mechanics takes it into the explanation from

Y

probability, and makes an answer which involves nature in a final responsibility for mental life, though not, as had been thought, by producing it. The answer is the present close of the material development of our knowledge of nature.

§ 2. The final sense-barrier provides an instance. The electron's position and momentum in an atom have to be inferred from their joint record in the spectrum. But the means of exciting the atom to make the record makes them rivals. Position is found most exactly if the atom is excited by radiation of high frequency, or electrons of high speed, but in that same degree the electron's momentum is disturbed; and the disturbance is discontinuous, and the discontinuity great the greater the disturbance. Conversely, the electron's momentum comes out best if the exploring means are not also searching for its position. The more searching the means of observing the atom's interior, the more it is altered. That looks our failure, but again from a presumption that closes nature too soon. The seeming failure proves a gain. If we bring into the account the means of taking the record, as well as the means of exciting the atom, the joint inexactness is of the order of h. The final barrier to the fineness of the cultures is as exact as that. And it is nature's, not now because of our senses, which are hers, but because of her means that stretch beyond them, each defined with such precision. But there is a greater gain: h unites two fundamental factors which had hitherto been only aspects.

So long as our senses were to blame, we thought that nature was good enough to allow us a margin of error, and even to force it on creatures for their good; are we now to think that she allows a margin of error to herself? The margin is her fact; it is we who call her in error from an error of our own: we have been asking nature to perfect our world instead of to complete it. The revelation is a confession again. The notion of momentum at a place works perfectly for small and smaller places, till we thought that nature must carry momentum to a point, and fail if she does not. When we are arrested at the barrier, it seems the human stopping-place, whence nature, leaving us, proceeds herself to the point of simplicity. Not seeing that we are the source of the point, we are unwilling to release her. We are more willing when, from the momentum at a place, we go to the energy at a time, which is the more usual analysis, and coupling, of the factors of action. We are more willing, on account of time, to stop short of reaching a point, because the energy of radiation goes entirely with the frequency, and, though we were willing to say energy at an instant, there is no sense in frequency at an instant.

But we should hardly ask at all to be reconciled after seeing the coupling of time and space themselves, which releases us from our presumption that the course of nature needs a single time-stream. Man had been narrowing nature to the perfection of his individual worlds, though they had then to sacrifice their individualities, if they would unite in one world. The action coupling, through the quantum, creates a parallel situation, and a parallel advantage.

§ 3. They have not been so clear, because the couple is not so abstract as space-time or motion, but also from two confusions about our means of knowing. How the two occur may be seen at the first appearing, to Heisenberg and to Bohr, of the view which they have developed into general acceptance for the outlook of physics on nature. Our means of observation, both the living and the instrumental means, brought themselves into notice in a way that had not troubled the classical system:

Whereas we explain phenomena due to complex conditions from phenomena due to simple, "there can be no explanation of an atom in that way, seeing its expressions are simpler than any. Phenomena are joint effects of a great number of atoms; we have therefore to be more modest in our demands, and content ourselves with ideas that are formal, in the sense that they offer no such pictures as we are wont to expect from the ideas with which scientific theories work." [1] Among the atoms of the joint cause are those of our sense-organs. Remember the notion that the intervention of their structure is a pity, and that the object has to be extricated. It came from dipping our bodies a second time into nature, forgetting that they are there already. The living immersion has only to be analysed; there is nothing to criticise. But the error persists, if it looks a paradox that atomic interiors are altered by the light that searches, and by the light that reports them.

The power of the error is familiar in other observations. The more you watch your anger, or your skill, the more they disappear. The living advantage there did not prevent us from deploring: Was not consciousness proving itself sometimes unreliable? We were so set on making it a running copy. And what worse could happen to knowledge than that observing should alter the objects observed? Nothing worse, but observing never does make a difference. The means make it all, and the object includes them, and lets their share be analysed out, as it comes to fuller knowledge of itself.

Another familiar mental advantage comes nearer to what is new. The more closely we observe, the more we

[1] Bohr, *Bau der Atome*, p. 59

select; we give advantage to one object at the cost of others, which would otherwise have been felt, or felt better. The usual means are sense-organs, as when we turn our heads to listen; and the objects won and lost may very well be complementary, as aspects of a cube are, when we close either eye. A one-eyed man finds their mutual dependence when he moves his point of view. He knows that he cannot have more than one view at once, but that the cube offers them all at once. Though he cannot even picture our solid view, which has two of his at once, he can learn the necessities in ours as well as if he had it; and we have to make our view one-eyed in order to analyse it. That is an important character of the new fact.

But not all. The two factors that the general equation (both classical and quantum) requires, the position and the momentum of the electron at one time, are given together; the means of exciting and reporting them give the pair differently, and correctly; the new fact is the law of their mutual dependence. It can be seen by no solid combination of images, but it can by the eye of understanding, which is much more exact and exacting.

The fact prevents the classical theory from being final, and removes the nightmare, as Huxley called it, that "the present state of the universe is the effect of its antecedent state, and the cause of the state that is to follow" (Laplace). The hope was revived of an opening for free will, and in the very structure of nature at last. But no one wants causeless events; the hope is rather to exclude them from the chances of life.

Resting on the chances, on probability, seems resting on ignorance. That would be the other confusion, and its place of entering can be seen again from the first approach: "Wherever in the classical theory there are relations between exactly measurable quantities, like momentum and energy, there are correspondingly exact relations in the quantum theory; but there is an error in the classical way of formulating the causal relation, viz. 'if we know the present exactly we can reckon the future'; and the error is not in the consequence, but in the assumption." [1] But the nightmare might persist, and employ the new 'principle of uncertainty', to establish its old reason. Having always assigned our sense of freedom to never knowing the full cause, it could now prove our ignorance inevitable. But that has proved its own undoing. For why should theory bear a weight that cannot be demonstrated? Matrix mechanics dropped it, and, proceeding without it, found nature to bind herself in a different way, and one that prevents the nightmare from returning:

§ 4. Surrender of the assumption meant surrender of the classical theory, and imposed the duty of still deriving its truth. It was no longer enough to derive it for large conditions; nothing can be more minute than wave-mechanics, and it is classical. The need to take the matrix way seeming a misfortune, wave-mechanics was the more welcome, and coming with so full a hand, it could look a superseding rival. But the two refused to conflict at the places where they met, and soon Schrödinger introduced the reason. Each of the variables of the general dynamical equation,—momentum, energy, position,—converts into an operator, and their connexions let them form an operator calculus, through which the wave-equation and the harmonic analysis can be transformed. The calculus yields a rule through which the series of values found for the total energy takes a two-term coefficient for each of them. These yield a matrix to correspond with Heisenberg's, having

---

[1] Heisenberg, *Zeitschrift für Physik*, 43, p. 197.

the same arithmetic, the same type of law, and the same fundamental set of equations. But there is no superseding; wave is no more final than particle against matrix mechanics. On the contrary, there has come one more defeat of an unquestioned expectation. The notion that either wave or particle, not both, must be final has found itself wrong and misleading.

It is one more instance of the royal road through phenomena to a deeper level. Their resistance was well defined by the exaggerated stress, which dispensed with the particle. The exaggeration found itself to be due to the end that was expected. There is no exaggeration if the stress is diverted to the statistical end. And that needs no more than to stay at home, for configuration spaces, to which wave-mechanics found itself confined, are the home of statistical mechanics. There the fruits of the stress can be tested immediately, and only they can do no injustice to the fineness of the phenomena, which is also their uncertainty, or duality. There, too, continuity, as well as quanta, can be final.

The conflict between those two ends became precise when ψ, the new wave-function, was brought farther into the electromagnetic system. A cue was offered by adding the other surface demand. The demand of the radiation frequencies having been met, each as a difference, there were still the radiation intensities. These, for waves of light, have to depend on the squares of the amplitudes. The two demands on the source, the frequency difference and the square of the amplitude, appear together in an equation, which a mathematical handling derives from the ordinary use of the imaginary in describing the propagation of waves: when ψ is multiplied by the corresponding conjugate quantity, the imaginaries cancel out, and the equation to the product reaches a form containing the two, the amplitude squared and the frequency difference. Up to that the stressing holds good, and nothing is altered by finding that the product may take two entirely different readings. The product is a density; it might be the density of something 'real': of mass, for instance, or energy, or electricity. That was the alternative taken at first. Multiplied by the unit charge, it is the classical electric density of radiation from a system of charged particles, the varying of the density with the time being the source of the radiation. The other alternative, the statistical end, reads the product as a density of probabilities.

It may seem the inferior reading of the two, and preferable only from the other's internal troubles. For the individual or real reading, besides having to borrow the point-charge in order to pass from artificial to actual space, is held in a final grip of the impossible postulates. Though the leap from level to level is overcome by being a loop, its prescience persists in the two levels having to be present at the same time, like two nodes. There is no such need for the statistical reading into waves of probability. The density in the equation can mean the relative number of hydrogen atoms whose electron is in some required condition per unit volume of the gas. The reading holds the facts without prejudging the fuller unity of particle and wave, and without prescribing that it be reached within a four-term co-ordinate system. The ending is the more challenging for us that the surface gives the last word of the material development to probability, and allows it to complete the greatest of the cycles that return to complete the statistical theory of gases with which we began.

§ 5. It also completes the surprises to the quarrel

between genuine and human in the known laws of nature. When that ancient quarrel was arrested and given shape in Mach's *Science of Mechanics*, it was seen to stand on a presumption about nature, and its removal to stand on a presumption about reason. Both are natural presumptions, that have proved themselves in error:

The presumption about nature made it rigid, inviolable, and therefore genuine, against the vacillations that we appear to find. No one doubted that the genuine real was reached in Newton's laws of motion. Their realm could be advanced by analysis without fear of admitting a rival. But there were two weaknesses in their claim to rule. They could not claim that the realm is all-inclusive, but only that all else must consist with it. And then worse: they could not derive, but only hire, the physical principles that were advancing the realm into unknown country. The principles became rivals with one another for a seat beside the genuine laws; and the principle of least action went the length of claiming the laws and their realm for its own. When dignities were abolished by the radical sweep, which made service to sense the measure of honour, the genuine real became human. That is one of Mach's two theses: the nature that we know is the system of phenomena. But, while genuine, the system did not profess to be nature except for man. His other thesis is that the laws of motion, and the principles, have been abstracted from experience, and perfected for their purpose by being idealised. That should have been all to the good, but looked all to the bad from the natural, if also arrogant, presumption that reason knows the claims of nature proper against any that can be deposited from experience. Really reason never but projects from a world already in its view. We have seen all the way how, in seeking deeper connexions for the sensible world, the projects or analogies have succeeded by defeating themselves, till nothing remains copied. Now, looking from depth to surface, there is the converse and three-fold surprise:

It is that the depth accepts three surface characters which had never been projected, because they seemed unworthy of real nature. Conscious creatures have to know, and use or avoid, qualities and powers of things that have no place in the depths, where yet all takes place. Were not the surface causes therefore spurious, and the lives that have to use them parasitical? The unflattering answer, after being rejected all the way by the material advance, was finally reversed by the principle of general relativity, where the absolute laws of nature make the surfaces fundamental, not the depths. The other two surprises are also the reversals of an answer on the very ground on which it was made. One concerns probability, the other flexibility:

Probability is the guide of life, but is it not our poor substitute for nature's necessities? So we thought, though, if we knew the necessities, nature would still insist on our using the deplorable guide. When the theory of gas pressure began to extract rational from empirical necessities, was it not resorting to an average, and abandoning the real pursuit, because the particles were out of reach? Not quite that even then, and now not at all. When the average made each particle open, and become for us less and less abstract, the statistical theory neither departed, as a substitute should have done, nor persisted because we are helpless. The openings to deeper levels, or fuller equations, were all measured from an average, or equilibrium, that was expected. And the gas equation, advancing itself with every advance into the particle, has now become active in astrophysical surveying. The statistical way has made of itself a highway serving the classical one, which it resembles in being both rigid, as nature and number require, and flexible for the surveys and methods. The interrelation of the two highways has an outstanding interest at our close of the material development. And it supports the third reversal.

§ 6. The third reversal is that the flexibility which we find in nature is entirely nature's, and exists at all depths, as much as at the surface, where all sorts of creature know and use it. It is, if possible, the most important of the surprises to reason, partly on its own account, partly because it provides a principle for them all. It was mainly on account of the flexibility that nature as we know it seemed unreal, or mistaken. The flexibility is through connexions, and they have to be discovered by analysis. Till that was clear the projection of deeper levels was through likeness. The principle in all the surprises is that when an analysis comes to likening instead of determining, it is at a dead end; abstract experiment has failed, and asks for a better analysis in order to advance to better connexions, in other words, to generalise.

At the surface, where everything is practical, rigid and flexible are working easily together: nature is rigid for itself, and flexible for our grasp, yielding to our physical means. It is the way that physics has followed up, disregarding the appearance of contradiction, and making no effort to remove it. The effort was made by speculation in several ways. The worst way was to remove the line between rigid and flexible, thing and idea, thing and grasp. The other ways drew the line of rigid round nature proper, letting the rest of nature be mental or tainted. But, as at the surface, nature has throughout no mental quality, nor therefore mental aspect. The line between nature for itself and nature for us is within nature; it is not between knowing and the thing known, doing and the thing done, feeling and brain, mind and nature. Between these the relation is like that between life and its body. But the line between nature for itself and nature for us is within nature, and as if between dead and living; for we do not describe the dead as though they had never been alive. The line used to be drawn round nature proper, in order to exclude the rest of existence as mental; it was therefore taken to be the line between mind and nature, and to mark whatever the joint between them. It became harder and harder to draw, and so its proper drawing looked the problem. But every drawing had to put the joint not at the line, but across it among the rubbish; the line could not let the invading surveys, and abstract experiments, be free and flexible, without making them mental.

To see them not to be mental we had only to turn to the living analysis that every thought makes for itself. When in doubt, it never compares itself with its object, you remember. Not that it cannot, but that its doubts are always about the objects in its hand and the objects that it wants. Comparing object with object it secures both from all taint of itself. It has both in its grasp when, for instance, one is a conception and the other a physical process. In comparing them it rarely seeks a likeness, even when one of them is an abstract model. It looks on any likeness as incidental to the power of the flexible one to analyse and determine the rigid behaviour of the other. That is equally the aim when both objects are conceptions. And one of them can be the known, the other the unknown system of nature.

Therefore the simplest situation and its question can

be taken for typical; it is when the two objects are both of them things. Here is a question in rigid dynamics, answered by Newton's principle of similitude: "A model is made of a machine, and is found to work satisfactorily; what are the conditions that a machine made according to the model should work as satisfactorily?" (Routh). The principle requires a different identity of relations in the two from the set that a copyist would take; the velocity in working the model has to be made proportional to the square root of its linear dimensions. The principle is itself a theorem from the principle of virtual velocities, from which also the equations of motion may be derived. Equation, theorem, principle, every rise beyond the model in generality, loses nothing that is in the model. They can take its place in experiment, not it their place. Their grasp on the practical machinery is more powerful because, experimenting in the body of knowledge, they make room for the real factors to show their power.

There is also the abstracting, the releasing of the real factors from irrelevance, the negative aspect; it imposes the duty of not losing connexion in view of the return to the surface. The return consists in cultivating phenomena from roots that the theory must profess; the return is as physical as the way from model to engine. From the question of making a model we can pass at once to this one: "What are the conditions necessary that two systems of particles, which are initially geometrically similar, should also be mechanically similar?" The distance between the two questions was far for human analysis and its theoretical instruments; it took them many centuries to arrive; but for nature the two questions are identical. That holds throughout, and with it this: no artifice in the means makes the thing discovered artificial. The abstract and artificial char-

acter of the second question is incidental to the generality of its object, which takes up countless models, and
offers to take their place. It is only incidental, as in all
analyses, that the lines which we draw appear to be
discarding crudities. Generality has to be discovered,
and so have the analyses that it needs. If the way was
far between those two simple questions, how much
farther for the highway, the common dynamical system, which has to unite all the levels, including the
surface, by crossing them together. The analyses of the
surface that it needs are of data that have still to be
cultivated; but so had they in the typical case, where
the analyses were of engines that had still to be created.

There are two issues from these comparisons that
carry the surprises from the material to the formal development. It being always possible to separate nature
from our grasp, and then to separate object and the
organ, given or created, by which we grasp it, we can
see the physical articulations between organ and object, which make them one limb. But we do not like
to call the distal part ours, nor even to think theories
to be hands groping with their fingers. The other
issue gathers, and gives, more courage to believe,
we shall find. In our early notion of deep levels the
surface threw light on them, and they reflected it; but,
from the highway, it is seen to break up instead, and
its factors to reach their reason or necessity. The way
down is continuous, and the continuity is formal, not
only flower to root. When the view from relativity
arrived, it might well have looked unable to take over
the view from the classical highway. But it did, finding
merely that the surface could break still farther. Space-
time relativity found that the empty surface connexion
between space and time is only individual; general
relativity found that real nature takes over what used

to be deprecated as merely individual. The material development has carried every level to the electromagnetic one; the formal development has carried their several systems to the one which crosses and keeps them all. From it the sensible world is seen to be just nature at the narrowest, or least analysed. All the time it was the whole that was being determined. That has its bearing on our other worlds, as well as that the good adventures of the early stages were being excluded from the surveys for farther advance.

XV

TRANSITION

§ 1. THE three questions that begin as challenges to the mental surface, as if we were living in error, contrast the feat of mind with our poor notion of it. For, of course, to live it is not to grasp it; though we think so at first, as we did that nature consists of phenomena. The whole situation for mind is no other than it used to be for nature. Reason used to produce the conviction that we are living in error about the physical surface: where could phenomena be but where they were born? The answer there answers for the mental surface too, provided there is neither doubling nor idealism. Neither is known in practice. Though clearly isms, and hopeless against each other, the two persisted as the only alternatives, because the mental feat looked impossible, and the way was not clear even for nature. To double was to immerse our bodies a second time into nature, and a single immersion would be into a Nature whose objects could never be known; the mental feat looked as impossible as that. The new way of ideas, or known objects, did no more than free the only way that had ever succeeded; it was new merely against the presumption that the eye of reason knows more than it meets.

If, looking at the far end of the way, we ask how far it promises to go, one first thinks of time, and may have read the words with which Jeans ends his *Cosmology*: "Mankind is at the very beginning of its existence;

on the astronomical time-scale it has lived only for a few brief moments, and has only just begun to notice the Cosmos outside itself. It is perhaps hardly likely to interpret its surroundings aright in the first few moments when its eyes are open." But neither infancy, nor length of years, offers hope to one final sense of loss. Nor does the number of insuperable difficulties. We have reached the elements of the energy and the structure of which all matter consists, dead and living; and we can return to the things of common sense, for we took the pedestrian route in order to see it good at every distance. The deeper we have gone, the wider the world, the greater the number of junctions, and, in the end, the roads have covered the whole country of matter. The roads are not the country; they have been taken only through the fertile valleys, and the narrow if well-defined passes between. Every science can see difficulties without limit in its province, and every superficial province opens into every deeper, and uses the deeper where it can, so that the task is infinite, even where it is possible. Adding insuperable to infinite, can we say that nature is unintelligible from its difficulties? Not from being incalculable, like the sand or the rain drops. If we blame our equipment, it is as we blame the shortness and every limit of our life; the limit is itself intelligible, due to nothing unknown. Add intricacy to numbers and fineness, and again blame falls better if we charge our equipment, and see, for instance, how soon mutual change can slip from our grasp, as in the three-body problem. Our limit is intelligible still, as intelligible as the sand slipping from our hand. It does not matter whether the long future will make the solving of such difficulties possible and worth while. Possibly the best of them will reach a moral ground, one well trodden on the soil of Aberdeen.

z

They have been counted even a virtue in the kinder land of France, where the opening of the atom promised "a better future and a golden age, . . . though an ending that will sadden some who were still hoping that science would one day give the key to all the enigmas of the universe. The world would be *mortel d'ennui*, if everything in it were known and foreseen, and the joy of discovery lost with the tantalising labour of research" (Boutaric). Fortunately our question is not whether nature has a moral excuse, but only whether it is all intelligible, inter-legible, the very thing that we make object and comprehend. But a hope that did come into our question has disappeared with regret. It began to disappear when the substance of a thing was degraded from being bearer and agent of its properties to being one of them. We had been giving a substance to everything that had found nothing of which to be a quality, one to space, one to time, one to consciousness, one to mind, one to nature. When nature was not content to be the nature of a stuff, we felt the drag; but it had been possible to cling to stuff by dividing the system into pure and applied, and calling the pure part only ours. The applied part grew fuller all the way to greater depth, which was also the way to the vast expansions in time and space. The earth became merely a corner in the world laboratory; events could be cultivated to identify their roots a hundred million years ago; and there was the self-evolution of organic life. But one hope faded, and finally disappeared. With all the increasing fullness, the approach to depth and generality has found the stuff to grow simpler, out of which all was expected to come, and into which all was being analysed without remainder. How can the system of phenomena be nature, and nature be just the system of phenomena, if the opening of the atoms finds them to

consist of nothing but the two electrical elements and
light?

It has deprived atoms of their old office as the source
of our ignorance. While they were closed, they could
hold a secret energy on which it was possible to draw
for the novelties that appear with their compounding.
New properties begin with diatomic molecules, and increase with structure up to the living cell that carries
the factors of heredity. This recourse to secret energy
could still be made in the best theoretical forecast up
to the date of the discovery of the nucleus: "As regards
laws of general physical interactions, the nucleus of the
atom may be left out of our discussions; but in the
problems of biology great tracts of invariable correlations have to be dealt with, which seem hopelessly more
complex than any known or humanly possible physical
scheme. To make room for these we have to remember
that the atomic nucleus has remained entirely undefined
and beyond our problem; so that what may occur, say,
when two molecules come into close relations, is outside physical science—not, however, altogether outside,
for we know that, when the vital *nexus* in any portion
of matter is dissolved, the atoms will remain, in their
number, and their atmospheres, and all inorganic relations, as they were before vitality supervened" (Lar-
mor). But the elements of the nucleus have offered
nothing, and all chemical compounding remains peripheral. Carbon, hydrogen, and oxygen qualify themselves for life by the number and variety of their com-
binations, and by nothing peculiar to their cores. The
atom, like the living cell, remains an individual system,
whose powers are revealed by interaction with its environment, especially with the similar systems with
which it is compounded. You recollect how Driesch,
in his lectures here on the organism, thought the powers

of a growing cell impossible to any physico-chemical machine. His reasons were unconvincing while the machine was full of secrets; but it consists of atoms, and they have lost their mystery, so far as their mystery was indefinable; it is easier than ever to look at the powers of their compounds, and call the elements incapable. Suppose the known atomic structure to continue to complete our knowledge of its working, then not only is the alphabet of matter complete, the ninety-two letters themselves are reduced to their common elements. Everything, living and lifeless, analyses into these without remainder? A book analyses into its letters; but that is not enough. Is it also the fact that once there were only the common elements, that they became letters, and that the letters arranged themselves in syllables, became a book, and produced its readers as well?

§ 2. Having lost the atom as the secret source of unexpected powers, may we not move the secret deeper, and pool all nature in the aether? Most of the atom consists of it, all but the two structural elements, and they are presumably centres of strain in and of it. If the aether does all the work of nature, does it not deserve the paean better than phenomena? "Looking below the surface of things we find the semi-fabulous quintessence to be unobtrusively doing all the world's work. It embodies the energies of motion; is, perhaps, in a very real sense, the true *primum mobile*; the potencies of matter are rooted in it; the substance of matter is latent in it; universal intercourse is maintained by means of the aether; cosmic influences can be exerted only through its aid; unfelt it is the source of solidity; unseen it is the vehicle of light; itself non-phenomenal, it is the indispensable originator of phenomena. A contradiction in terms, it points the perennial moral that what eludes the senses is likely to be more permanently and intensely actual than what strikes them." [1] It would be a poor ending for the course of knowledge, and a poor beginning for the course of evolution. But there are two facts about the aether as an ending, and a question about it as a beginning, that make it useful.

One fact is that all the properties of the aether, except its room, depend on matter, and that no force has been found to come from it, and no energy to go into it, and become intrinsic energy of the aether, and lost to matter. The other fact is that the demands made by matter on the aether are specific, like a hotel bill; a charge may be too great, it may even be too small, but the items are known; and they and their amounts all define themselves in a methodical way. The situation for electromagnetic theory and its aether is now at the end, as it was when the kinetic theory of gases and its particles were at the end. There is no difference in the situation for those who expect the world of the aether, and for those who think little of it. But first there is the question; for, unless it is settled, the different views of the aether may be views of different things:

Nearly every description of it is in negatives. It must have volume, the very volume of space; that is the only positive property that everyone gives to it, whether as substance, or in exercise. It includes all that there is in open or empty space, the void, which is actual space as against the abstract spaces of the geometries. The absence of matter serves to point out the aether, and the absence of the properties of matter serves to define it. The negatives are usually summarised by saying that the aether is not molecular. Plato chose a negative that

---

[1] A. M. Clerke, *Modern Cosmogonies*, p. 197.

exactly fits the notion; Aristotle says that he spoke of space as 'unembodied matter'. That coincides with the character which Einstein gives the aether: "According to the general theory of relativity, space is endowed with physical qualities; in this sense, therefore, there exists an aether, . . . but, unlike ponderable media, it does not consist of parts which can be tracked through time".[1] The rest of the notion of the aether is repeating the history of the notion of 'matter' (ix. 2). From being the meanest thing in nature, because without limits, unintelligible, nothing in particular, all potential, matter could become, by way of those very grounds, the substance and potency of them all. But it still occupied space on the high view, as on the low one. Now it is the turn of the aether to be the substance which is the source of all, and always does everything. If its powers are not spread out, except by a 'contradiction in terms', there need be nothing in dispute but the use of the word.

But is there any beginning, was there ever a time, at which the world could be spread out in space? Would any one think so, if reason did not appear to compel him to put it somewhere? The compulsion is from the metaphor that space and time are fields in which nature runs its course. They compel nature to indulge in infinite secrets behind every event that makes itself known. Every time and every space would have an infinite number of parts, all filled with invisible event. In that way the mind can be given infinite ignorance. The known events of the aether are simpler than those of matter, and its elements are all alike; but the metaphor of the two fields induces us to say that the simple sameness must be only apparent.

Secrets of the kind are easy to distinguish from those

---

[1] *Sidelights on Relativity*, p. 23.

that are real. If we knew them, they not only would not alter the knowledge that we have, they would not make it better. They are infinite fields asking to be filled, not offering to fill gaps in our knowledge. The real secrets of the aether, on the other hand, fill real gaps. The hope of filling them lies in finding fuller units, not in reaching smaller and smaller times and spaces. Natural units are unities. Like the quantum of action, and the hydrogen atom, they are more useful for knowledge than if they were simple. Therefore simplicity should not be used in proof of our ignorance. These two beliefs in a simpler and simpler stuff, and a shorter and shorter event, lying always beyond us, are no support for any mystery of the aether; they have to be supported by it. Space, if we mean by the word only room, extension, volume, is an abstraction without existence except as already a property of what is extended. Actual space is not abstract; when empty it is empty of the matters which roll through it, but it is, or has, a material infinitely vaster, which does not roll. This is the use of the word space by those who reject an aether. The advantage is that it denies existence to a field without a filling. That is better than to argue that aether fills all space, and therefore cannot be molecular. But it is also better to have a word that distinguishes the physical from the geometrical properties.

The physical properties of space are the functions that the aether performs for matter. They are found first as qualities and powers of perceptible matter. When analysed they are as many energies crossing empty space, and completely measurable: light, heat, gravity, electric and magnetic attraction and repulsion. They all follow the inverse-square law, depending only on the distance, undisturbed on their journey by any variety in the aether that is said to bear them; they meet no source of aberration in it, and they excite nothing new. The factors other than the distance are also known; gravity depends only on mass, and the rest unite themselves in the electromagnetic system.

The structural elements of that system are connected by lines through the aether, Faraday's lines of force. The electric lines are primary, straight lines that radiate in all directions from the electrical elements. This the electrostatic condition has inertia, which has to be overcome to set the elements in motion; each elementary charge has therefore inertial mass. When they move as an electric current, or when a charged body moves, two new conditions appear. The lines that would point in the direction of the motion fall back till they are across it; the current has been likened in shape to a caterpillar. And the magnetic field appears; it consists of loop-lines of force curving round the moving body at right angles to the electric lines, and also to the course; no other source of magnetism is known. Each electric and each magnetic line is called a line of force, because it tends to contract lengthwise, and exercises a sidewise pressure on its immediate neighbours, repelling them. The two fields consist of their lines, or tubes, of force; together they occupy a volume of empty space. They fill it, as J. J. Thomson says, "like a stack of hay or straw"; and his discovery of the electron did not alter the picture. Every electrical element is the centre of such a load of lines, and one load has no existence but for another one towards which its lines extend. It is constant for all speeds, while its mass increases with the speed, though nearly constant up to a tenth of the speed of light. When a speed alters, the self-induction of the system asserts itself as inertia; the lines of the two fields take time to reach their new equilibrium. In the process we have the source of all radiation. Pulses of energy pass to the aether, which carries them, large and small, at one speed.

§ 3. Here, it has been thought, the aether must betray the stuff that it is, and the strength of the stuff; and here the theories of the aether mainly settle. They rely on analogy: they say what matter would require to have and be, if it had to do the work, and then they transfer this power and structure to the aether.

Another physical function has also been assigned to the aether by those who think it a stuff. The hope that all mass will prove to be electromagnetic has been realised for the mass of the electron both where it is constant, and at the high speeds of beta-rays where it increases at the rate predicted by the theory, as well as by space-time. The whole inertia of the electron is that of its charge; its mass is the mass of the charge; the load is its own waggon. The great mass of the proton is a puzzle; but the positive charge never appears on a less mass, nor on any other mass, than that of the hydrogen nucleus. If proton or electron is called a strain, a knot, or a twist in the aether, the strain is always a whole one; there is only one or other of the two elements.

That is fundamental for the question of evolution; it means that the answer has not to wait for the farther analyses which will account for the equal charge on electron and proton, the difference in the two masses, the reason for their attraction, and the effect of their collision. When the aether is given the function of one day giving the answer, it has to be added as fundamental that proton, electron, and photon carry on all that is doing, and that the aether retains no remainder to interfere with their work. The normal atom is neutral, bearing an equal number of both loads. Their number, arrangement, and self-maintaining activity have suggested its likeness to a living cell. But also, when it breaks up, the freed elements are not free, but carry the lines with them. The lines do not vary with the aether, through which they reach, but only with the positions and the motions of other charges.

And, in small or large, the structure is a structure of energy without remainder. The indication came again from the electron, whose mass and energy are one. It holds of radiation, where there is no particle but itself, and has been carried by space-time relativity to all mass and all energy. When mass increases with speed, it is the energy of the motion that is added. The energy called the mass of a body is mainly concealed; but, when it receives or loses energy of whatever kind, its mass increases or diminishes by that amount, for the two can be expressed in the same units, and have a natural unit, the unit of energy.

These discoveries, whereby the material analysis continues at the end to yield unities, have been thought consistent with the notion of the aether as a stuff. "By transmitting waves at a finite and measurable speed the ether has given itself away, and has let in all the possibilities of calculation and numerical statement." The electron is made to offer a more direct means of calculation than was possible for the aether-models of last century. Its mass having been measured, and its radius therefore inferred, its density is known and gives that of the aether, which ought to be incompressible; the electron would be a torsion like a knot. The density being known, the elasticity of the aether follows from the speed of light. Kelvin's kinetic theory of it gives the intrinsic structure of the energy. Far from being at rest, the aether has to take "an internal squirming circulation, . . . a vortex motion of a kind far more finely grained than any waves of light or any atomic or even

electronic structure. . . . . In every cubic millimetre of
space we have a mass equivalent to what, if it were
matter, we should call a thousand tons, circulating
internally with a velocity comparable to the velocity of
light, containing an amount of energy . . . equal to the
energy of a million-horse-power station working con-
tinuously for forty million years." The same aether
has to support gravitation. "The force with which the
moon is held in its orbit would be great enough to tear
asunder a steel rod four hundred miles thick, with a
tenacity of thirty tons per square inch. . . . Maxwell
calculates that the gravitational stress near the earth,
which we suppose to exist in the invisible medium, is
3000 times greater than what the strongest steel could
stand. . . . The intrinsic energy of constitution of the
ether is incredibly and portentously great."[1]

If matter had to do the work. The properties of
the aether are given it by analogy. The analogy should
complete itself to define its imperfections; but here it is
doing the reverse, turning its imperfections into perfec-
tions of the aether. That the aether is not granular like
matter and electricity, that there is no friction in and
between its vortices, nor between it and matter, that
its transverse waves do not bring longitudinal ones, and
that, though all is in such orderly commotion, there are
in the end no particles to move, these negative perfec-
tions of the aether are at the same time imperfections
in the argument. Other selections for the bridging of
empty space have been made, even to the opposite one,
which I shall mention because we like it. It was expressly preferred by an eminent engineer, and not
by way of a curiosity but through twenty years of
research on "the sub-mechanics of the universe".[2] He

[1] Lodge, *The Ether of Space*, chs. vii., viii.
[2] Osborne Reynolds, *Rede Lecture*, 1902.

packs infinite space with spherical grains extremely minute, completely inelastic, all close enough to keep always the same neighbours; and, across each, when they collide, the displacement of momentum and energy is instantaneous. The difference between matter and aether is a difference in their piling; in empty space "there is one and only one purely mechanical system capable of accounting for all the physical evidence, as we know it, in the universe". Except where there is matter, "this is the structure of the universe: grains in normal piling, of which the size, mean path, relative velocity, and mean pressure are defined, and extend to infinity. Could anything be more simple?" Simplicity is a virtue of all the models, for all they do is to embody a dynamical system in a material unknown, but perfect for the purpose. The perfect bridge has one peculiar merit: its material satisfies our appetite for a rigid indestructible particle, however small, as the final carrier. Here the motion of light is given all the way a solid stepping-stone, which, because it is minute enough, has no need to be elastic; its diameter is the seven hundred thousand-millionth part of the wave-length of violet light, and its mean path is the four hundred thousand-millionth part of that diameter. If the causeway is rejected, that kind of particle must go too, and energy carry on without it.

The models are all simple both by their structure and by their monotony; for they make the aether repeat the minute design of the model throughout an infinite volume. Such a thing makes us ask our minds why a stuff-like aether can remain attractive to them. And it is not only the extravagances that are suicidal. "The real death-blow to the materialistic conception of the aether was given when attempts were made to explain matter as some state of the aether. For, if matter is some vortex-motion or beknottedness in aether, the aether cannot be matter. . . . If physics evolves a theory of matter which explains some property, it stultifies itself when it postulates that the same property exists unexplained in the primitive basis of matter."[1] Whatever fills the void must make no more difference than space makes, in securing that action through it is from point to point. We shall ask whether the void has to provide a bearer for the action. But no answer can encourage the hope that the void is also the mother and the nurse of matter, life, and mind. Indeed, the universal mesh and models of the bearer would be in the way.

§ 4. What is the ground of a desire so persistent that it requires the void, which originates nothing, to originate everything, and that blames our equipment without ground at all? "The fact that our senses reveal molecular matter, but not the aether, is explained by the organisation of our body, which itself consists of molecular matter."[2] Another ground, but no better, blames the absence of a sense. Lord Kelvin thought it likely that a strong magnetic field, though it looks and feels like empty space, would give sensation of itself, if made strong enough. He thought the sensation would be new, and therefore the experiment worth trying. If the energy did become an adequate stimulus, it would use an old route, and reach an old terminus; and the consequent feeling could not well be new. But suppose it new, and its object a quality of something, the quality would not be like the stimulus. Would it be a sensation of the aether? And why are we said to have none? Perhaps no more is meant than that aethereal stimuli are quite unlike the light and heat which they give. But

---

[1] Eddington, *Space, Time, and Gravitation*, p. 39.
[2] Wiechert, *Der Äther im Weltbild der Physik*, p. 44.

that is true of every stimulus; in whatever sense aether gives no sensation of itself, matter gives none. A stimulus, though it never gives a sensation of itself, may send another stimulus to another organ, and so become object. Aethereal stimuli do not do that, nor, as it happens, do most material stimuli. Therefore fault cannot lie with our organs; it would not matter if they were made of aether. The blame has to lie with the waves themselves that they are stimuli, and send none. We have to complain not that nature is hiding something, but that nothing is there. And, if nature did have the new sense to give us, what addition should we have to our knowledge of the aether? We should merely be like men born blind receiving sight. Empty or open space, space without matter, would have one more sensible filling, but only another.

What, then, is the persistent source of an impulse that can take such poor sheltering? There are two sources: the one that Tyndall called an 'intellectual necessity', the other that gave Maxwell an 'intellectual satisfaction':

The aether came into the inheritance of that universal "promise and potency of all terrestrial life" which Tyndall gave to matter by an 'intellectual necessity'. There is less objection to the heir, because the aether is without the structure which matter has; the only restriction is that its potency must have volume. But in what does the potency consist? The best claim to an answer would lie with the kinetic theories, but none does claim, because the potency of every aether model is that of matter pruned and perfected; if material or electrical structures are states of the aether, the aether stuff itself is without them. But, when physics refused, there was another way of answering, and, because it was taken by so many, it remains to search ourselves. If all that exists in nature has always occupied space,

and real nature consists of the aether, may not phenomena report it like product or like shadow? How little
is reported may be seen from the answers that could
satisfy men so devoted to knowledge as Haeckel and
Spencer were. And they selected the only two alternatives:

"The views of the most eminent physicists, who have
made a special study of the ether, are extremely diver-
gent; they frequently contradict each other on the most
important points. One is, therefore, free to choose
among the contradictory hypotheses according to one's
knowledge and judgment." Instead of a kinetic theory,
Haeckel chooses "a pyknotic theory by which the ether
passes into the gaseous state under certain conditions
by progressive condensation, just as a gas may be converted into a fluid, and ultimately into a solid, by
lowering its temperature". And, because phenomena
have a mental character, the elements of mind must
also be all through space: "both ponderable matter and
ether are endowed with sensation and will, though
naturally of the lowest grade; they experience an inclination for condensation, a dislike of strain; they strive
after the one, and struggle against the other".[1]

The alternative is to rely on laws. It is more attractive, because it follows the familiar habit of giving laws
an independence that lets them outlive their instances.
A law found in one province can then run in another,
if there is nothing to prevent it; should not one part of
the universe behave and be ruled like another? Spencer
thought that the part which we know should give a fair
indication of the whole, distorted merely by our make
of sense and intellect. The synthetic philosophy brought
together the laws common to every field, physical,
mental, and social, on the ground that there must be

[1] Haeckel, *The Riddle of the Universe*, ch. xii.

one persistent Force in them all. The work of the Force over a long period having the character of an evolution, there were laws of evolution, and of dissolution too. They were everywhere, and they were not in addition to the laws of the means, but in consequence. Nature could be seen to come from chaos by means of laws: two laws of matter, two of motion, and three more corollaries from the 'persistence of Force'.

The schemes of aether-structure, and these two alternatives for evolution, have it in common to throw the later structures and energies of space that we know into others there that we do not know. It is done either by means of the persistent laws of a persistent Force, which is always everything, or by making the primitive aether contain duplicates of the matters that come out of it, whether in a very superior form, where the secret models are perfect, or else in a very inferior form where the pyknotic impulse is held in check. They all have it also consciously in common that they are dealing with an unfortunate situation: phenomena had to be circumvented. That makes it the easier to declare our minds free, and then to set them the final and really searching question. "Let us suppose that a physical picture of the universe were found fulfilling all our demands, and therefore representing completely and accurately all the empirical laws of nature, it could not be proved at all that the picture represents real nature. But there is another side of this, and one seldom observed. For, in just the same sense, there is no refuting the far bolder assertion that the image does represent real nature in all points with absolute fidelity. The first step in refuting it would require us to say something certain about real nature, and that is quite impossible, as every one knows."[1] The difference that would remain be-

[1] Planck, *Phil. Mag.* 28, p. 69.

tween the two worlds is that the known one is in our
heads and an image, while the real one is outside, or
somewhere equally out of reach, when we try to compare
them. The two rest on nothing but that the feat of
consciousness is impossible, or that the known one is
knowledge.

Putting unknown worlds out of the question, we have
Tyndall's intellectual necessity where he meant it to
be, viz.: within the system of phenomena. He meant
that the present comes out of the past, and by transformations of a matter. Both meanings close the system
too soon, for space-time takes nature out of the stream,
it deprives the protean matter of unchanging space,
and space needs physical properties in order to change.
To see the transition as a shift of the same grasp that
began on the surface, let us leave the intellectual
necessity for Maxwell's 'intellectual satisfaction' with
the aether: "The vast interplanetary and interstellar
regions will no longer be regarded as waste places in
the universe, which the Creator has not seen fit to
fill with the symbols of the manifold order of His
kingdom".[1]

Now the wastes look vaster still; they put our corner
out of sight, and compel the opposite view to our living
one. Set the volume of all the stars against the boundless volume of the void, and matter and phenomena,
instead of the flowering of nature, become a rare froth
on an ocean, of which they must reveal very little.
Atoms themselves are mainly void. But they are full
of radiation, the great wastes are fuller than was
thought, and the aether-ocean has yielded without
resistance first to space-time, and then to the new law of
gravitation. The two yieldings came from two discoveries regarding mass, and, on that account, they do

---

[1] *Scientific Papers*, ii. p. 322.

more than mark the final yielding of substance to system. In both discoveries the contrast and the coincidence of the material explanation with the new formal one open our closer articulation with nature.

§ 5. The first of the two discoveries ends the traditional way of answering the question, what becomes of things when they disappear. The question seeks a stuff that can take one phase or form after another, and remain the same. Should not the laws of nature be laws of it? There are also laws for the changing, for all is regular, but should they not come to the substance in the end? That outlook at the start gave the only solid satisfaction. But the substance kept receding. The laws of the surface, taken below, were becoming equations, and the equations were finding constant and equivalent quantities, but the quantities were not quantities of a substance. They were of compounds, all but one. This was mass, or the 'quantity of matter' in a body. Hitherto it had proved itself only a dead-weight coefficient. What more it would prove to be was answered by the conflicting forecasts of atomism and energetism, themselves the outcome of the two common-sense analyses of a thing (ix. 2, 3), where they do not quarrel. Their quarrel ended, in a way that neither expected, by the discovery that all mass is energy, and that all energy has mass.

That mass consists of energy was found from the measurement of electrons moving at great speeds. Each proves that its mass, which is the same for all at rest,

increases with its motion by the law $M = \dfrac{m}{\left(1 - \dfrac{v^2}{c^2}\right)^{\frac{1}{2}}}$,

M being the mass in motion, m the rest-mass, and v the velocity. The law carries to matter in bulk, and to every

distinction of mass, and had fortunately kept out of sight. The honour fell to the electron because its velocity can be so great, and leave the charge unaffected. At a speed as great as a third of the speed of light m has increased only by about an eighteenth, at two-thirds by about a third, at about four-fifths it is doubled, and the law says that if the electron could reach the full speed of light in empty space, as it very nearly can, its mass would be infinite, which is impossible. The tax that a mass levies on its motion is by so steep a gradient, after the slow rise that had concealed it.

When part of the electron's motion is lost for any reason, it suffers a corresponding loss of mass. The rebate is made as an amount of radiant energy by a law $m = \dfrac{E}{c^2}$. It is the law of the mass or inertia of energy. Presuming the law to be general we can substitute the total energy E for the total moving mass M in the other equation, which then reads, on expansion as a series $E = mc^2 + \frac{1}{2}mv^2 + \ldots$ The first term on the right is the quantity of internal energy, the second the familiar quantity of kinetic energy, and the later terms are for quantities too small to have made themselves felt. The contrast is between the enormous amount of internal energy and the amount of the rest. The physical writers vie with one another to impress it. A gram concentrates an energy as great as that released by burning three million kilograms of coal (Langevin), or by lifting thirty million tons to the top of the Eiffel Tower (Becquerel). If an artillery shell speeding a kilometre a second would add a grain to itself, it must already have a rest-mass of 180,000 tons (Birkhoff); and the energy that a man puts into a long lifetime of heavy manual labour weighs only a 60,000th part of an ounce (Jeans). Such figures account for the lateness of the discovery that, in proportion as a body is absorbing or emitting heat, or other energy, it is adding to its mass, or pouring itself away. For fine events the figures become important, as for the pressure of light, the structure of atoms, and the smallest residues of atomic weights for which radiation may be responsible. In totals these too can be as impressive as they are important. Let us return with them to the filling of the aether, and thence to the notion of a thing:

Day and night the sun pours itself by radiation into the void, losing every minute about two hundred and fifty million tons. What becomes of all that energy when, leaving the sun, it occupies in the minute a sphere whose radius is eleven million miles? In any region of the sphere the energy of the radiant waves is very small, it has a mass that is c^2 times smaller, and it has weight, like any other body, in proportion to its mass. Besides these three properties, the radiation has momentum, for the law of action and reaction will not wait for matter to be met and take the pressure; and, slight as it is, the quantity has been proved. Add volume, density, and action to the waves, and what better equipment in properties has an ordinary thing when out of sight? And we do not think that an ordinary thing needs a bearer to carry it through space.

Besides rescuing radiation from the need of an aether to support, convey, and give it one speed, the analysis, as usual, reverses the order: When as yet there was no thought of wave-mechanics, it could be said: "Atoms and electrons are not ultimate invariable elements, which forces attack from without, pushing them hither and thither; they are each continuous, and minute changes of a fluid character go on in their smallest parts. Not the field requires a material character in order to exist; it is matter, on the contrary, that is offspring of the field."[1] Farther evolution continues to be left to the offspring: "Matter and the electromagnetic field are identical. Like matter the energy of the field is something apart, not tied to a medium independent of it, the ether of classical physics."[2]

Besides converting substance into system, and separating the material system from the aether, which has neither mass nor energy, the junction of the material with the space-time analysis has a farther effect. It is one that, carried to general relativity, promises to complete the data from which we take the problem of our articulation with nature. The material and the space-time explanations that connect mass and energy look as if two explanations of one fact. Their coincidence becomes a challenge.

It points to a more intimate relation between the play of nature and the theatre from which we see it. Newton's laws of motion had seemed the permanent foundation of mechanics and physics. An elaborate theatre had been raised on them, from which the course of nature had been seen more and more perfectly. The play of forces could not conflict with it. But it had prescribed its own failure, believing that space and time must prescribe it, and in their double capacity as phenomena and as real. As phenomena the two prescribed the difficulty of being measured apart, and as real they prescribed the impossibility of being measured at all. It was just an evil if the distances to be measured are moving, twice an evil if we are moving as well, and not with them. Though the intrinsic speed, and the absolute lengths of yard and second could not be reached, there was no doubt of their existence: the majestic march of nature down the corridors of time,

[1] Weyl, *Space-Time-Matter*, p. 203.
[2] Kopff, *The Mathematical Theory of Relativity*, p. 113.

or else a chaotic tumbling of its waters through the bridge. That was the picture.

Yet there is no such thing to reach; the majestic march, or other picture, was of our prescribing; we had once more been completing nature from our point of view without first asking how it is nature's. There was no suspicion that space and time depend on each other. Suppose that an observer on a plane flying fast at a uniform speed parallel to a straight stretch of road is using instruments that enable him to measure its length exactly, and to note the instant that he is above its beginning and its end. Let another do the like on the same course at a different but still uniform speed. When they compare their estimates of the length of the road, they discover, if they have been exceedingly exact, that they differ by an amount which they cannot adjust. The cause appears when they measure the length and the speed of each other's plane as they pass; for each finds that the other is using too long a yard, and too long a second. To settle the dispute, if they use a chain on the road, they find a third estimate which agrees with neither, nor helps the two to agree. The old inference was that the men are right from their points of view, and that the chain gives the degree of their failure. In general it was that, while all the phenomena may be in nature, the bulk of them have to be converted into those that are independent of the motions of their observers. When they would not convert, they could still be signs of the one best course, and refuse correction from it. That was not all: the one best course had itself a corresponding defect and virtue. For, placed against nature's one, it failed: it could not give the absolute flow, the one length of yard, and the one length of second, and yet it could refuse to be corrected.

But the two observers are in better agreement than

they know, and than any chain can tell. Instead of appealing to it, let them go to arithmetic. Each has only to square his estimate of the length of the road, square the distance that light travelled in the time that he took, and subtract. They find that the difference for both is the same. The square root of the difference gives a line which no chain can measure, but it is nature's, for the rule is universal. The line has been named the world-line, the interval, the separation; and its points are called point-events; but the discovery is new to names. It is no longer enough to say that all observers can be correct from their points of view, and that no one can correct them, because the real time and the real space cannot be separated and known. They do not exist; the invariant exists, the space-time line; and it is nowhere but in the endless variety of estimates, whether they can be made or whether they cannot. It unites them and makes each of them necessary.

If the real invariant for the road can admit so many true estimates, imagine the endless actual number from the free air that birds are always making, and proving or disproving. But from every point of view? From every point of motion, view or not; and all is in motion. There is, therefore, a far fuller prospect from this coherence of space and time than from their cohesion or cementing, as if they lay on each other.

The course of nature had been running in three courses of time: the surface one, which rested on the one sought by physics, which rested on an absolute flow. This third one is replaced by space-time; on it the other two are still supported, because it accounts for them. The old absolute flow did not account for them, but copy them, seeking not to complete but to perfect them. The new one is like the old second, in being now the one sought by physics. And it takes up and makes necessary all the times of the surface. That should reconcile us regarding time.

The hope for space had been to break through the relativity of motion to a fixed frame and a constant observer. Neither star nor aether would provide such a frame; but now it is found that nature does offer one which is universal. Astronomy had sought a frame as wide as possible. How wide has become a possible physical question. But that is a consequence; the advance is not to the vastness of the frame, but to its being everywhere, and in the smallest regions. It is where physics aims at finding it for all change.

The mechanical system, the theatre from which physics looks on nature, has reached the frame by carrying farther the abstraction of space, till nothing spatial is left but the ordered continuity which it has in common with time. Time enters on identical terms by substituting for a second, which is its unit, the distance that light travels in a second. Their continuum consists of point-events, each determined by four co-ordinates; the square of the interval between any two is determined by the squares of the four co-ordinates, as in a four-dimensional geometry.

The change from the old theatre is already fundamental. The seats have been advanced from fixed to moving. They lose by that the simple views of the classical theatre, whose austere lines between mass and motion, mass and energy, force and inertia, are its essentials of order. The last line, that between force and inertia, remained, for the seats were restricted to uniform rectilinear motion in Euclidian space-time. Their freedom to take up forces came later, when the law of inertia was generalised, and became the law of gravitation. It is there, in the articulation of theatre and nature, that our articulation with nature can best be

seen. But, without that for the present, we see that real
nature holds phenomena in the way that space-time
holds the spaces and times which are its phenomena. It
is neither sum nor substance of the nature that we know.
The notion of sum and the notion of substance had
steadily grown too meagre for the parts that were discovering themselves under the surface. Hitherto the
substantial and separate character of space and time
had saved them; they could ask what becomes of, and
hope to find the answer in an everlasting redistribution
of indestructible elements. It could be said, if all change
is motion, that the course of nature is a stream, a tide, a
course of events, all of it imaginable, though not by us.
But the real course is too full to be imagined by a power
however perfect. Like sum and like substance it is
concrete, but, unlike them, it is too concrete for a
picture, no matter how perfect. All the pictures, perceptible and imaginable, represent individual views.
Nature includes all, if they make themselves good, both
the endless variety of sensible worlds, which it requires
different creatures to know, and all that we grasp
correctly on the surface and in the depths. With that
we turn to the other discovery regarding mass which
brought the final yielding of substance to system.

§ 6. The classical theatre separates inertia from
acceleration, and makes inertia the straight-line stage
on which all forces play. Nature was known to do better,
staging itself on the field of a force; for gravitation does
not interfere with other forces, nor allow them to interfere. Its field covered the classical stage like a carpet,
because it has the same potential at each place, however occupied, and only differs for different places. The
carpet lay as smoothly on time and space as time lay on
space; and it could be stripped as easily. It lay so well

there was no opening by way of exception; but it was wearing. There had always been grounds against the force; now the law itself began to suffer from the stage beneath, and the play above, and from both independently. More fatal than either has been the discovery that, when space-time takes up gravitation, physics can match nature in freeing its laws from depending on external frames of reference: ·

The gravitation force had the defect, which troubled Newton no less than its early enemies, that no means of producing it, and none of carrying it between the attracting masses, had been found. Its effects, too, are everywhere changing in direction and intensity all the time, and in the same instant at every distance, or with a speed many million times that of light. The force is independent of the motion of the masses on which it depends, and it knows no obstacle. The facts could be extricated from these troubles by ignoring the force-notion, and using only the law and the field. But now the law fell on trouble; of the two factors, which had been independent, for determining the potential at a place, the fixed distance was lost. The carpet could lie on space, but only a magic carpet would fit space-time. Could mass, the other factor, from being like a rock, become flexible enough to save the law?

It can for observers. When a speed measures differently for observers in relative motion to one another, they find a compensating difference in the mass. And the difference is instantaneous, as the third law of motion requires. This complete flexibility holds for all kinds of mass, and not only for the ordinary inertial one. But do they too have weight, and their weights a numerical equality with their masses? No reason was known why they should.

But also none was known why the ordinary inertial

mass, defined by acceleration, should equal mass defined by gravitation. "The equality of these two masses, so differently defined, and recently confirmed by experiments of great accuracy, has no explanation from classical mechanics. Science in the long run is finally justified in assigning such a numerical equality only after the equality is reduced to an equality of the two concepts."[1] Mechanics had been careful of the striking difference between the two, inertial mass being independent of the place, while gravitational mass is local. But locally there is independence too: in the same region the attraction is the same for no matter what the matter. The place of itself prescribes the same course to everything there, and different places prescribe different courses. They are the actual or natural courses, and the straight line course of the first law of motion is not. It has the advantage of being the same everywhere, but all actual courses are accelerated; and to abstract a straight line course needs a frame, whereas nature uses none. There is gravitation everywhere in space, and so the next measure for the new theatre, after subjecting space and time to space-time, was to generalise the first law of motion by subjecting inertia to gravitation. Instead of lying like a carpet on space, gravitation became the changing texture of space-time. Just as the inertial lines of the old theatre were not drawn in space itself, nor found as grooves already there, but were taken from rigid bodies, so the new texture is of a field which without it is amorphous. Since it is abstracted from moving bodies, the texture can take with it a fabric as useful and picturesque as Eddington makes it.[2] There has to be added without conflict that "such expressions as crinkles and warps,

---

[1] Einstein, *The Meaning of Relativity*, p. 63.
[2] *Space, Time, and Gravitation*, p. 138.

which refer to sensuous impressions, are exceedingly inappropriate when taken to refer to such an abstract conception as a metric."[1] The fabric, being everywhere and of one sort, may be called the aether, and be given all the properties of space other than those of room. Gravitation comes first by making it metrical; it "charges the metrical field as electricity the electrical one" (Weyl).

There is the same relation of surface to depth or generality that we had from the space-time instance. If the path of a group of meteors were correctly measured from the sun, from the earth, and from one of themselves, the results would agree badly for the rate, worse for the direction, and not at all for the sense. On the old view they could all be only approximate, though never knowing how near. Our interest is with the dweller on the meteorite, who could prove his few beliefs by experiment, and yet his ignorance would be greatest. His narrowness of view is like our surface one. When he feels his vehicle at rest, and sees the sun rushing at him, the situation is ours; we do not feel uniform acceleration unless we resist it. Unless it is like the spin of the earth and never stops, it can seldom deceive us; and so the instances are striking: the double reading of experiments made in a moving lift, or on a rotating platform, or Einstein's instance of the chest housing a physicist and his instruments. Each instance offers two self-consistent, yet conflicting laws of the same course of events, one to a prisoner of the accelerating body, the other to an outside observer. When the prisoner, emerging, finds that the frame, on which he had recorded, was not at rest, when the earth-dweller discovers the spin of the earth, and goes to views that are more and more comprehensive, he no longer inclines to save himself by his

[1] E. W. Hobson, *The Ideal Aim of Physical Science*, p. 31.

ignorance; he takes his ignorance for error, and blames the smallness of the sphere which confined him. He does not insist and quarrel like the aeronauts, and so he misses the solution. There is no error; small sphere is like fragment, or superficial level; the error is in presuming the whole to be like it. The narrow views can save themselves, of course, by merely dropping the presumption, and adding 'to my mind' or other piece of equipment. They can always do better. Here they yield an 'equivalence-principle', which offers the prospect of uniting them all.

For, again, they are made one not by taking a longer view, but by finding the law or system which makes them necessary. In a small field of gravitation events have one description from a frame at rest, another from the frame in constant acceleration. At the simplest, let the frame be a lift that has been raised and is now fixed, and let the events be things falling in it, or outside; then cut the support. The gravitation field remains the same while the lift falls, and yet the things falling in it appear at rest and without weight. The equivalence of the two descriptions means the equivalence there of gravitation and acceleration.

That kind of fact was well known: why was the coincidence not pursued? A body remained with two kinds of mass, one depending on other bodies, the other absolute. When equated the two were left without a uniting concept; but, in the equation, they have only to be given numerical identity, and the uniting concept is seen to be the identity of the courses that define the two, one of them acceleration, the other gravitation. The answer is that eyes were turned the other way, till the discovery of space-time. Mach had used thought-experiments, like those of the lift, in disproving absolute motion. That controversy had arrived at the

definite, and also dead, end, which Ward adopted in
his lectures to mark the bounds of theory against the
course of nature. Since an absolute inertial system
could not be found, nor therefore absolute motion,
what reason was there but our convenience for taking
the sun for centre instead of the earth? None so far, and
it was also agreed that uniform translation in empty
space cannot be felt nor known. There remained uniform
rotation. Thought-experiments were made, in order to
say whether such motion could be felt. That prevented
the real question from being put. The experiment with
a revolving platform would have shown that the events
occurring on it, felt or unfelt, are as if subjected to a
field of gravitation. The force varies with the distance
from the centre, careless of the presence or absence of
obstacles, and of the constitution of bodies and their
behaviour. But the confusion about the importance of
being felt barred the way, because sensations had to
be in heads or in duplicate. The solutions were physical,
however; and Mach's insistence reached a point which
found its opposite. We may well make it our final instance of the route. But the start, I should add, is the
important thing; for only last night I heard Eddington,
constructive as he is, begin with the taste not being in
the apple, and go on to the complete separation of the
physical from the familiar world, which his chairman
(Bertrand Russell) carried much farther in the way of
Socrates, after which, in thanking both, Professor
Muirhead rescued beauty. It might have been Athens
come to Gower Street.

In Mach's time the conservative could say that, while
all points of view are good, they are not equally good,
and that absolute motion may be reserved for the best,
though it may never be found. The one conservative
ground had become that the radical's argument was

only kinematical, and unable to reach the mechanical question. If the spin of the earth be taken over by any circling of the heavens, the heavens would have to account for the earth's flattening at the poles, and for the surface of the water in Newton's revolving bucket. And Mach agreed that 'the entire universe' comes in. He thought that a solution might be found if the experiment were carried farther, for "no one is competent to say how the experiment would turn out if the sides of the vessel increased in thickness and mass, till they were ultimately several leagues thick".[1] A dead end indeed; its value is to bring out the truth by way of contrast. An experiment was made with an enormous fly-wheel by J. Friedländer, who added: "The proper grasp of the law of inertia will have been reached only when relative inertia and gravitation are reduced to a single law, for both are effects of masses on one another."[2] The single law, which came twenty years later from Einstein, does the reverse. Instead of making the inertia an effect like gravitation, the law makes gravitation a property like inertia, and both of them one property of actual space, or space-time. Mach's entire universe comes in, but through the theatre. Experiment, which might well look a thing impossible, had to be found and predicted; and the three well-known cultures were successful, one of them already made.

§ 7. That is arresting enough, and it says more than may appear, for the old theatre did, in a sense, also take the whole play. The new one, which builds on the natural courses, has to disturb the other straight lines, which were still sufficient for space-time: the ray of

---

[1] *Science of Mechanics*, p. 232 (tr. 1902).
[2] Reichenbach, *Philosophie der Raum-Zeit-Lehre*, p. 249.

light, the world-line, and the usual axis-frames. The ray, the model of straightness, not only bends to the motion of its observers, like everything visible, but, like everything physical, it bends a little in the neighbourhood of large masses, and by a crucial amount. The world-line between two events, instead of being the straight line of uniform motion, has to be any line for uniform acceleration. And, involving all, instead of a law proving that it is universal by holding for frames in merely uniform relative motion, it has to satisfy frames already united on a universal ground. The ground is developed from the 'intrinsic geometry' which Gauss introduced for describing a surface without leaving it. The surface is crossed by a series of lines, as near and parallel as need be, but never in contact; and they are numbered in arithmetical order. Between every two another family of nine lines can be inserted, and given a decimal ordering; then another nine between every two of these, and so on till every point on the surface can have its line. Cross-lines are drawn in the same way, woof to warp. Every point of a surface becomes uniquely determined by the two numbers given to its lines. These occupy the whole surface, and take up all its inequalities.

The problem of different observers becomes that they choose the direction of the lines, and find a different appearance for the same inequalities at rest, or due to motion. One use of the nets is to take this into the pure theory of space connexions, that deals with deformations and the equations of transformation among the co-ordinates. Observers then go out of the question, leaving all to nature and the nets.

This function of the nets begins to be practical through a second one: the use of their meshes for measuring. The side of a mesh may be as long as a surveyor's chain; long or short it can be divided by any convenient unit. When the like is done with the adjoining side of the mesh, every point within the mesh is determined by drawing parallels from it to the two sides; and the general equation of the square of the diagonal gives the distance. The equation holds better the shorter the distance, because, the shorter the portion of an arc, the nearer to straight. But in the net there is no defect of being only an approximation. The line-element is element of the straightest, which has an element because it is everywhere 'stationary': between any two points any other is longer.

If the surface is not flat, the lines of the net have a third duty. Curved surfaces, other than those of cylinder and cone, refuse to fit cartesian co-ordinates. Their radii being out of reach, the lines on them have to tell; the equations for the square of the shortest distances have to tell the gradient and its changes. The secret is told in the formulae for different classes of curve; and the region about a point can be explored for their presence.

Every surface is within a volume, and every point within a volume is fixed by adding a third infinite family of lines. The equation to the straightest line, from one point in the volume to another, is built as before, and keeps the same form with the addition of more terms. That ends the structure of the net for space, but it can add fresh dimensions indefinitely, each an infinite family of lines. A fourth one has found its practical use by representing time, whose unit can be represented by the spatial unit of the speed of light in empty space. The line-element then means the element of interval on the world-line of a moving point; and the equation continues to give the length in the same form with the addition of more terms; it does not matter that

2 B

the straightest line and its element are now stationary by being the longest. The equation for the line-element, the elemental invariant, gives the fundamental point of view on which the theatre builds, presuming that all motions are relative, all forces in space-time fields, their action continuous, and therefore expressible in differential equations.

The fields of force have to separate themselves, as before, in order to come in. Gravitation does this for itself by remaining the same for the same region however occupied; it is a specific invariant there for every set of measurements, however the axes are chosen. Our freedom to choose them, instead of being a defect, becomes the fruitful part of the situation. It provides the means that make a law absolute, independent of points of view; for the law has to equate the sets of measurement from them, just as in the instance of space-time.

We are to stop at the plan as a project for the present. The present outlook is that it is not likely to be abandoned on account of the shifts that will have to be made in taking over the old theatre. They will close the story of the charges against our created structures for being, and succeeding, against reason. There is a corresponding story from the theories, and theatres or institutions, by which we grasp the other worlds. That will let us take them together. But in one character we can take them now:

§ 8. They all come into the general charge of being 'only concepts'. While phenomena were losing their 'only', this one was growing heavier, till the very ground that Weyl took for their paean was that on which Eddington set nature as only human, and even only mental. "Where science has progressed the farthest, the mind has but regained from Nature that which the mind has put into nature. We have found a strange footprint on the shores of the unknown. We have devised profound theories, one after another, to account for its origin. At last we have succeeded in reconstructing the creature that made the footprint. And lo! it is our own." "I am almost inclined to attribute the whole responsibility for the laws of mechanics and gravitation to the mind, and deny the external world any share in them. It will probably be objected that this is going too far, . . . and that surely Nature deserves some credit for furnishing material with such convenient properties. I doubt it. So far as I can see, all that Nature was required to furnish is a four-dimensional aggregate of point-events; and, since these and their relations are undefined, and may be of any character whatever, it should in any case be possible to pick out a set of entities which would serve as point-events, however badly Nature had managed things in the external world. For the use of point-events mind alone is responsible."[1]

That may seem to increase the grudge against phenomena, and shift it to new shoulders. And it is better for them to take up the old man of idealism than again to double and evade him. We need be merely a little willing to analyse the rubbish-heap, and the burden falls. Thought slips to one side, that being its function in making object. Then the object has two parts that thought separates and connects: there are the existing things that it wants to grasp, and there is the organ for grasping them that it has created. It sees the power of the organ to be as non-mental, and out of its own power, as is the power of the other part. But the other part, nature, is human too. So much the better for the feat of con-

[1] *Space, Time, and Gravitation*, p. 201; *Mind*, 29, p. 155.

sciousness; and, for two reasons, so much the better for our world. The part that is nature, or human, ought to lose some of the horror from its vastness and its temperatures; and, nature is no longer a product of Nature.

With the departure of Nature the old ground of regret becomes a turning-place. We thought it a dead end that the causes of sensation refuse to tell why they cause any. Other regrets came with it: that we have to take nature as we find it, and that anything might be the cause of anything so far as reason can ever find. The truth and the error in them all are easy to separate, and then the error is seen to be the sole support of the regret. "Why grass is green, or why our blood is red, are mysteries which none have reached unto." They have yielded, since Donne's day, and will open farther, but never to tell why green is green, and red is red. If we see there at last an unyielding mystery, we betray the error and our failure to see the advantage. One day green and red will be taken back through the colour-blind retina to drabber or grey; but why grey? The error has forgotten what we are seeking. The quest is for connexions; there must be elements to connect; and the happy thing is that we can stop anywhere. There is never anything to correct by farther analysis; it is because the sensory objects are objects, and have the sole right, as well as the duty, to vindicate their claims. The principle of general relativity provides, and applies, a criterion of invariance for all laws that would be universal. Not only does nature for man and beast consist with the unity of nature, the final unity of nature proves itself in being for them. Our turning, then, is not from Nature, but from knowing nature to other forms of living it, and from nature to the other worlds of life.

To turn to them is not to leave one aspect of the world for its other aspects. That would once more subject the whole to a child's grasp of a thing. It is the junctions between the parts of the world that are important, and that make the internal unity of the physical part important. The relation of the unity of nature to the unity of our grasp will be seen to be more intimate than the relation of play to theatre, as indeed it always was from the theatre being a living organ, though created. But let us leave it there for the present, and end by recalling two fears which have always been with us, whose grounds it has reversed. One has been the fear of closing nature too soon, and grasping only abstractions; the other has been the fear lest nature, however concrete, may be deferring to our grasp or constitution.

The relativity grasp of gravitation continues that expansion in concreteness which we had with space-time, and carries it farther with equal precision. From finding that nature is positively boundless, not negatively infinite, the grasp has closed in to find the 'expanding universe', which the cultures from the extra-galactic nebulae appear to require for the speeds of recession. At the moment, the grasp is even offering to connect that hold of the farthest heavens with the mass-ratio of proton and electron, which rules the structure of the atom. However such projects will fare, they serve to release our minds by their free handling of space. For our minds need releasing, willing though we are that nature should take up space instead of lying in it. We grow more willing to release our minds from lying in it, now glowing, now fading in our heads.

Our unsettling by way of time is again greater than by way of space, and reverses the other fear. It was hard to think that time would be nothing if it were empty, harder to bring it into nature against nature flowing in it, harder still to think our individual times to be phenomena of space-time intervals, neither parts nor aspects of a universal flow. But it is when we see these times extending to our lives, and thence to the course of evolution, that we fully realise our release. From being a succession of emerging miracles, the course of evolution becomes phenomenon of the full or universal nature which we had formerly copied instead. Not that nature grows mental, or otherwise meta-physical, by containing its time instead of rolling there. Its expansion to greater concreteness makes us more willing to face the place of our minds, and to turn from their place and function with reference to nature to their place and function with reference to the rest of the world. It is the feat of consciousness, thought im-possible, that the expansion is the feat of nature. The evolution to mental life, and that alone, advances nature to a world of objects and their power. The coming of objects, and their becoming a sensible world, made them look a late appendage hanging to living frames, and mental lives look parasites. But, having seen that the sensible world offers the whole, and its history, we take up afresh the early saying about nature that a growing thing is known from what it grows to; it is nature, nature proper, which refuses to confine the body of our mental life to the 'province packed up in two yards of skinne'.

THE END

Printed in Great Britain by R. & R. CLARK, LIMITED, *Edinburgh.*

WORKS ON PHILOSOPHY

THE FAITH OF A MORALIST. Gifford Lectures, 1926–1928. By A. E. Taylor, D.Litt., Professor of Moral Philosophy, University of Edinburgh. Series I. The Theological Implications of Morality. Series II. Natural Theology and the Positive Religions. 8vo. 15s. net each series.

STUDIES IN PHILOSOPHY AND PSYCHOLOGY. By G. F. Stout, M.A., LL.D., Professor of Logic and Metaphysics, St. Andrews University. 8vo. 15s. net.

COSMIC PROBLEMS: An Essay on Speculative Philosophy. By John S. Mackenzie, Litt.D. 8vo. 6s. net.

WHITEHEAD'S PHILOSOPHY OF ORGANISM. By Dorothy M. Emmet, late Research Fellow of Somerville College, Oxford. Extra crown 8vo. 8s. 6d. net.

FACT: The Romance of Mind. By Henry Osborn Taylor, author of "The Mediæval Mind," etc. Extra crown 8vo. 7s. 6d. net.

THE GROWTH OF PLATO'S IDEAL THEORY. An Essay. By Sir J. G. Frazer, O.M. 8vo. 7s. 6d. net.

THE ZERMATT DIALOGUES. Constituting the Outlines of a Philosophy of Mysticism; mainly on Problems of Cosmic Import. By E. D. Fawcett, author of "The World as Imagination," etc. 8vo. 21s. net.

ESSAYS ON THE NATURAL ORIGIN OF THE MIND. By C. A. Strong, author of "The Origin of Consciousness: An Attempt to Conceive the Mind as a Product of Evolution." 8vo. 12s. net.

ADVENTURES IN PHILOSOPHY AND RELIGION. By James B. Pratt, Ph.D., author of "The Religious Consciousness." Crown 8vo. 10s. net.

MACMILLAN AND CO., LTD., LONDON

WORKS ON PHILOSOPHY

By PROF. H. WILDON CARR

The Philosophy of Change : A Study of the Fundamental Principle of the Philosophy of Bergson. 8vo. 7s. 6d. net.

The Philosophy of Benedetto Croce : The Problem of Art and History. 8vo. 7s. 6d. net.

The General Principle of Relativity in its Philosophical and Historical Aspect. Second Edition. Crown 8vo. 7s. 6d. net.

A Theory of Monads : Outlines of the Philosophy of the Principle of Relativity. 8vo. 8s. 6d. net.

The Scientific Approach to Philosophy : Selected Essays and Reviews. 8vo. 8s. 6d. net.

Changing Backgrounds in Religion and Ethics : A Metaphysical Meditation. Crown 8vo. 7s. 6d. net.

The Unique Status of Man. Crown 8vo. 7s. 6d. net.

By PROF. NORMAN KEMP SMITH

Kant's Critique of Pure Reason. Translated. 8vo. 25s. net.

A Commentary to Kant's "Critique of Pure Reason." Second Edition. 8vo. 25s. net.

Prolegomena to an Idealist Theory of Knowledge. 8vo. 10s. 6d. net.

By DR. BERNARD BOSANQUET

The Principle of Individuality and Value. Gifford Lectures for 1911. 8vo. 12s. 6d. net.

The Value and Destiny of the Individual. Gifford Lectures for 1912. 8vo. 12s. 6d. net.

The Meeting of Extremes in Contemporary Philosophy. Crown 8vo. 6s. net.

MACMILLAN AND CO., LTD., LONDON